Millennial North Korea

Millennial North Korea

FORBIDDEN MEDIA AND

LIVING CREATIVELY

WITH SURVEILLANCE

Suk-Young Kim

STANFORD UNIVERSITY PRESS
Stanford, California

Stanford University Press
Stanford, California

Printed and bound by CPI Group (UK) Ltd, Croydon, CR0 4YY

Library of Congress Cataloging-in-Publication Data
Names: Kim, Suk-Young, 1970- author.
Title: Millennial North Korea : forbidden media and living creatively with
    surveillance / Suk-Young Kim.
Description: Stanford, California : Stanford University Press, 2024. |
Includes bibliographical references and index.
Identifiers: LCCN 2024005257 (print) | LCCN 2024005258 (ebook) |
    ISBN 9781503614918 (cloth) | ISBN 9781503640870 (paperback) |
    ISBN 9781503640887 (ebook)
Subjects: LCSH: Mass media—Social aspects—Korea (North) |
    Cell phones—Social aspects—Korea (North) | Information
    technology—Social aspects—Korea (North) | Generation Y—Korea (North) |
    Electronic surveillance—Social aspects—Korea (North) | Mass media
    policy—Korea (North)
Classification: LCC HN730.6.Z9 K46 2024 (print) |
    LCC HN730.6.Z9 (ebook) | DDC 302.23095193—dc23/eng/20240313
LC record available at https://lccn.loc.gov/2024005257
LC ebook record available at https://lccn.loc.gov/2024005258

Cover design: Lindy Kasler
Cover art: *Success at Work* by Hong Geun Chan and Kang Yong Min, Koryo Studio
Typeset by Newgen in Adobe Jenson Pro 10.75/15

For Dongjoo and Dongjin,
my favorite millennials

Contents

Illustrations

Preface and Acknowledgments

The world is at a critical juncture, caught up in the rapid digital transformation forcibly brought about by the COVID-19 pandemic and the resurgence of major global conflicts on multiple fronts. The arrival of COVID-19 was a catalyst for change at an unprecedented scale, pushing the whole world to make a radical leap forward into a noncontact mode of communication. In North Korea, as early as March 2020, news reports surfaced of the use of virtual meetings by the Central Emergency Prevention Command (Bisang bang-yeok ji-hwi-bu) to confer with local branches.[1] Nothing in the contemporary world has been analogous to the lockdown situation—a moment that dove deeply into the unknown abyss of imperiled lives, livelihoods, and face-to-face human interactions. New algorithms of sociality and commerce have been created as a result, forcing the world to be ever more connected while lacking physical contact.

Barely out of the worst impacts of the pandemic, armed conflicts erupted in Ukraine, Russia, and the Middle East. On all military fronts, North Korea is cited as a possible supplier of weapons. Although North Korea is not a direct participant, its association with these wars certainly increases the risks for the nation, which is already enduring a perilous existence under heavy sanctions.

Writing a preface to a book titled *Millennial North Korea* at the dawn of 2024 is an exercise that is both hopeful and ominous. A sense of tribulation overtakes me as I contemplate how ordinary folks have been persevering through unending hardship. The depth of economic hardship they have experienced must have been compounded by ruptures in trade with China during the pandemic, and as the nation has already been under unfathomable duress, the current moment could destabilize social structures. But for many decades, has North Korea not already been living in the kind of extraordinary isolation that suddenly besieged the world in early 2020?

This book is a humble testament to the precarity of North Korean millennial lives, which are mostly marked by suffering and resilience. It is a pale outcome considering the rich array of resources, helping hands, and moral support it has received. In addition to the Association for Asian Studies travel grant and UCLA's faculty research grant, the Academy of Korean Studies grant (AKS-2015-LAB-2250002) generously supported my writing time and provided an opportunity to interact with the members of the research team; Youngmin Choe, Chris Hanscom, David Kang, and Akira Lippit have been helpful throughout the entire process. I am particularly grateful to Gloria Koo and Erma Acebo, who administered the grant with such ease and grace so that I could fully devote myself to research and writing.

My ongoing fascination with how societies shape-shift as a result of media technology was harnessed during the 2018 Technology in East Asian Performance Conference co-organized by the Yannai Initiative and the Center for Performance Studies at UCLA. The presentations I attended influenced the way I have come to think about technology in Asia. Satoko Shimazaki and Michael Emmerich, the conference co-organizers and longtime friends, should take full credit for this. The intellectual community at UCLA's School of Theater, Film, and Television has been instrumental for this project. My thanks go to Jeff Burke, Michelle Liu Carriger, Felipe Cervera, Shelleen Greene, Brian Kite, Sean Metzger, Sylvan Oswald, Marike Splint, Dominic Taylor, Jasmine Trice, and Amy Villarejo.

Over the years, the National Intelligence Council, the National Committee on North Korea, the Korea Institute for National Unification, the Citizens' Alliance for North Korean Human Rights, the University of Bologna, the University of Sheffield, Goethe-Universität, Yonsei University, Seoul

National University, George Washington University, Central Washington University, St. Olaf College, Rutgers University, Arizona State University, the University of California, San Diego, the University of Hawaii, the University of Maryland, the University of Michigan, and Harvard University kindly invited me to share portions of my research. Miseong Woo, Stephanie Montgomery, Andrew Yeo, Scott Snyder, Jisoo Kim, Emmanuel Kim, Young-a Park, Cheehyung Harrison Kim, Sookja Cho, William Hedberg, Ana Hedberg Olenina, Lucas Klein, Nicholas Williams, Antonio Fiori, Marco Milani, Chong-Eun Ahn, Volha Isakava, Michael Johnson, Weijie Song, Jae Hwan Lim, Tarryn Chun, Jyana Browne, Van Tran Nguyen, James Harding, Emily Wilcox, Se-Mi Oh, Rossella Ferrari, Gabor Sebo, Douglas Gabriel, Carter Eckart, Sunjoo Kim, and Alexander Zahlten have given me insightful feedback, enriching my limited perspective on the subject.

I am always in debt to Leslie Kriesel, my longtime editor, who has worked on most of my publications. Sophia Weltman's assistance with research and final manuscript preparation was crucial for completing this book. This is the second time I am publishing with the Stanford University Press. I thank its talented designers, publicity team, and Laura J. Vollmer, who gave a final editorial touch to the book. Dylan Kyung-lim White never lost faith in this project, for which I will always be grateful.

As an emerging scholar in my early twenties, I had the fortune of having Professor Seog Youngjoong as my mentor; she not only taught me the enduring joy of research but also showed me a way of life dedicated to creating something meaningful that will survive the test of time.

Colleagues and mentors across various fields—Heather Nathans, Catherine Cole, Elizabeth Son, Kimberly Jannarone, Sarah Bay-Cheng, Tim Tangherlini, Rey Chow, Carlos Rojas, Peggy Phelan, Andrea Goldman, Eng-Beng Lim, Elise Morrison, Tobie Meyer-Fong, Namhee Lee, Theodore Jun Yoo, Charles Kim, Choi Kyeong-Hee, Michael K. Bourdaghs, Ariel Fox, Melissa Van Wyk, Roald Maliangkay, Ruth Barraclough, Oh Youjeong, Yoo Hyunjoon, Joo Young-Ha, Kwon Bodeurae, Lee HeeJin, Yassi Jahanmir, Zachary Price, So-Rim Lee, Stephanie Choi, Kwon Hye Kyoung, Lee Wonseok, Shea Hwang, Edward Kang, Liana Chen, Katherine Lee, Laure Murat, Laurie Hart, James Person, Greg Brazinsky, Nick Bonner, and Lee Mukyung—provided me with enduring moral support.

But what would the long journey of writing a book be without friends? I enjoy lasting friendships with Karie and Clarice Dreyer, Leo Cabranes-Grant, Dan Jaffe, Diana Salvador, Ron and Susan Egan, Lily and Francesco Bullo, Rachel and Everett Lipman, Elaine Ho, Calvin Wright, Alexa and Basile Joubin, Lesya Kalynska, T. J. Collins, Elena Zotova, Leonid Trofimov, Carolyn Glassman, Josh Tanzer, Alex Burry, Bishnupriya Ghosh, and Bhaskar Sarkar, who enrich my mind and add layered perspectives to the work I do.

Needless to say, without family members' love, there would not be a rock on which the book could stand: Beverly, John, Tanya, Max, John Sr., Abby, Mee-Young, Young-Man, Young-Eun, Seonghee, Ho-yeon, Eun-jae, and my parents provide me with an unfaltering sense of embeddedness and continuity. Miles and Naima, my high-spirited children, light up every moment of my existence. The remarkably wise and inspiring Michael Berry shows me how to face the everyday challenges of being a parent-scholar. I have learned from you that there is a graceful way to accomplish these two most important missions in life. My two nieces, Dongjoo Yoo and Dongjin Yoo, collectively known as DJs in our family, present bright visions of the future. Seeing their kindness, beauty, and accomplishments makes me feel proud and hopeful.

The lived experiences of North Koreans themselves have been the true guiding light to glimpse millennial North Korea. Park Eunhee (Bak Eun-hui), Son Myung-hui, Jung Kwang-il, Na Min-hui, and others who did not want their names revealed told me their stories. Your generosity is what inspired life into this book. I am deeply in debt to Sandra Fahy, James Hoare, Joanna Hosaniak, Jisoon Lee, and Henry Song for helping me rekindle my connections to the North Korean resettler community. Kim Yonho's, Nat Kretchun's, and Jane Kim's reports on recent North Korean communication technology were foundational to provide much-needed context. Gang Jin-gyu, the force behind the news portal NKEconomy.com, is a true trailblazer, updating the world on a daily basis about North Korea's technological advancement. Thanks to your pioneering work, this book is able to address a few technological interventions made by twenty-first-century North Korea.

Due to the pandemic, it was difficult to travel to interview North Korean resettlers, as I had originally intended. For this reason, most of the primary sources gathered here emerged from preexisting online interviews produced by YouTube channels such as Baena TV and individual channels run by North Korean resettlers themselves. I thank these media outlets for accumulating so many invaluable testimonies. I am humbled by the enormous work they have put into creating living archives; these accounts would have disappeared into oblivion without their intervention.

Books are, in many ways, inevitable revelations of impossibilities—the impossibilities of knowing the past, the present, and the future. They blow in the winds of time like specks of dust floating in space to unknown destinations. From our limited vantage point at present, the pathways forward seem to lead to a hollow cavern at best, and looking back into this book from the future will inescapably reveal the limitations of my perspectives. But hopefully, this work will be remembered as a sincere attempt to present an attentive portrayal of the very confusing first two decades of our new millennium.

Notes on Language

1. For transliteration of Korean words, I consistently use the official Korean language Romanization system, also referred to as the Revised Romanization of Korean, released by South Korea's Ministry of Culture and Tourism in 2000. Exceptions are made for proper names well known in the English-speaking world by alternate Romanizations (e.g., Park Chung-hee rather than Bak Jeong-hui) and for authors who published their names in alternate Romanizations (e.g., Kim Suk-Young rather than Gim Suk-yeong). In the case of these exceptions, the official Romanization of Korean appears in a parenthetical after the first occurrence of the term.

2. For other East Asian names, surnames also precede given names according to the convention of the home country (e.g., Jeong Gwang-il, not Gwang-il Jeong).

3. For the combination of Anglicized given names and Korean surnames, the first and the second rules do not apply (e.g., Sunny Yoon rather than Yoon Sunny).

4. All translations not otherwise credited are my own.

5. When quoting others, I use the transliteration system originally chosen by the authors.

Into the New Millennium

"Turn your eyes toward the world while having your feet grounded in your homeland!"[1] Introduced in 2009 and prominently displayed in public squares, above factory entrances, and in school hallways nationwide, this slogan captures the aspirations and paradoxes of North Korea in the twenty-first century. In a country where smugglers of foreign media can still face public execution,[2] how do North Korean citizens gain knowledge of the world—especially millennials, who are more prone to adopt new technology and whose lives are most acutely affected by the changing media landscape? What kinds of forbidden foreign media do millennials watch, and why do they watch them despite the grave risk? How does the North Korean state control information, and how do people navigate through the tricky waters of state control and surveillance?

Millennial North Korea explores divergent ways the state and the people use media and technology with often-conflicting objectives in mind. From VCDs (video CDs) to cell phones, from smuggled South Korean TV dramas to North Korean state-produced YouTube channels, the past twenty years have seen a rapid change in how North Koreans produce and consume media in an increasingly discursive manner. Exploring this process demands tactful agility, engaging with the broader shifts in economic reforms and sociocultural changes that engulfed North Korea, the changing media landscape led by the government, the actual media content surreptitiously circulated among the people, and the consequential shift in people's value system as a result of consuming foreign media.

Coinciding with the irreversible process of marketization, the unstoppable spread of new media platforms and technology heralded unprecedented sociocultural shifts in North Korea. The millennial generation plays a crucial role in exposing the increasing tension between the state and the people, between the premillennial generation who lived under the state's centralized governance and millennials who have been relatively free from it,[3] and between thriving entrepreneurs and those left out of the growing market economy. Exploring the tensions between millennial North Korea and North Korean millennials leads to a more nuanced understanding of a fractured and fragmented society that has been largely perceived by the outside world as an unchanging, monolithic entity. Combining a close reading of North Korean publications and media to assess the state's media policy with interviews with North Korean millennial resettlers to understand their engagement with media technology, this book investigates the diversifying social strata that have come to characterize today's North Korea and the implications such changes bear for the world.

This research highlights a unique form of tech savviness brought about by media transformation in a country seldom associated with technological advancement. The book considers a broad network of media platforms but places a particular emphasis on cell phones since their rising use induced both bottom-up social changes and top-down government initiatives more viscerally than did other media platforms. Although known to be the world's most secluded society, North Korea has witnessed the rapid increase of new media technologies in the new millennium—most prominently, the introduction of a 3G cell phone network in 2008,[4] and the ensuing growth of cell phone use (see figure 0.1). In 2009, there were only seventy thousand cell phones in North Korea, 60 percent of which were owned by Pyongyang (Pyeongyang) residents in their twenties to fifties. That number has grown tremendously in just a decade: in 2019, there were six million registered users spread throughout one hundred cities and

FIGURE 0.1. Mobile telephone shop on Mirae Street, Pyongyang, May 2018.
Photo courtesy of Koryo Tours. Reprinted with permission.

towns. As of August 2022, North Korea is simultaneously developing 4G and 5G broadband-cellular-network technology for future service.[5] This expansion took place under the careful watch of the state, which has actively secured foreign investment and partnerships to catch up with the world standard in communication technology.

But the growing number of cell phones cannot be automatically interpreted as increased freedom for users. The North Korean state allows only intranet access for its people, officially blocking the free flow of information while using the network as a convenient means of surveillance. If the State Security Agency had to eavesdrop on citizens in person in the past, it can do the same work more effectively nowadays by tapping into cell phone conversations. When South Korean network-security specialist Gang Jingyu analyzed the software files on Arirang 151 (the smartphone model North Korea manufactured in 2017), he discovered a cell phone spy app embedded in the game app named *Gopseuli,* a North Korean copy of the popular virtual-kitten-companion app *Talking Ginger.* According to Gang, this spy app can monitor incoming and outgoing phone calls of any cell phone unit and send that information to an untraceable control center.[6] No wonder

North Korean cell phone users firmly believe their phones are constantly under surveillance.[7] Although most defectors could not explain the exact mechanism, the suspicion of government surveillance was so ubiquitous that most took measures to evade the state's unsanctioned access to their phones. For instance, a male user in his early thirties, who left North Korea in November 2010, notes in an interview with South Korean media scholar Kim Yonho [Gim Yeon-ho], "It's not easy to use a mobile phone. In order to make sure the mobile phone frequencies are not being tracked, I would fill up a wash basin with water and put the lid of a rice cooker over my head while I made a phone call. I don't know if it worked or not, but I was never caught for using a mobile phone. If you're caught, you have to pay a heavy fine, and could be expelled [from Pyongyang]."[8] On the other hand, there are other North Koreans, such as Gim Ha-na (female born in 1988 in Hyesan who left North Korea in 2014), who believe they have seen tangible proof of phone surveillance: "In preparation for crossing into China, I went to stay with my aunt in [the border city of] Hyesan. One day, I saw several black cars circling around my aunt's house. I panicked and told my aunt, who had just made a phone call to a broker in China. It is said that when you make a phone call across the border, the phone signal will be detected in thirty seconds [by the authorities]. In a minute, the authorities start recording the conversations."[9]

As these interviewees' paranoia attests, North Korean cell phone users are extremely careful in self-censoring their conversations, but fear does not stop them from using their phones. Even though cell phones in North Korea serve as a tool for state censorship, they have vitalized the marketplace outside the state's centrally planned economy by enabling merchants to compare prices in various markets throughout the country in real time. Bak Hyun-suk (female in her forties, born in Hyesan, who left North Korea in 2013), who supported her family by trading in a marketplace, emphasizes the significance of accessing information as the key element of success: "Nowadays, people can exchange information in real time by making phone calls."[10] The inseparable relationship between the exchange of economic information and cell phone communication is eloquently summed up by Kim Yonho: "Mobile telecommunications service is a double-edged sword for the North Korean government. It provides a tool to potentially support economic development, by allowing the state to control production, establish standards, and coordinate between the capital and more remote areas of the country in ways that were not previously possible. This could be an innovative way to increase productivity and efficiency for the dysfunctional planned economy."[11] While North Korea's marketization is hugely responsible for the proliferation of cell phones in ways that have reshaped the traditional top-down social network into a need-based, trust-based kinship (to be fully explored in chapter 2), it has also greased channels for corruption that strengthen North Korean cadres who collect bribes from prosperous merchants; these merchants pay in order to possess multiple cell phone units, which is illegal in North Korea.

But the most subversive use of technology is when cell phones are transformed into rebellious gadgets: USBs, secure digital (SD) cards, or multimedia cards (MMCs) loaded with forbidden foreign-media content can be connected to cell phones, allowing North Korean users to gain access. Being confined to using the intranet by no means limits users in North Korea as they find other creative means to communicate with the outside world. Media and technology have always been at the core of subtle shifts and power dynamics in a society that appears impenetrable and immovable from the outside world. To be more precise, what they watch and why they watch it using their electronic gadgets are of utmost importance for discovering subtle yet irreversible changes at a grassroots level.

Technology cuts both ways, introducing stronger measures of both state control and civilian freedom. Technology steers North Korea into subtle turns and changes, providing the people with a perspective on the world and the state with a highly effective means to surveil them and profit from the expanding market economy. But for the North Korean state, the escalating use of cell phones increases the risk of citizens being exposed to alternative perspectives that could threaten the legitimacy of its authoritarian regime.

The increasing tension between the technological need to be on par with the world and the ideological need to block the free flow of information shapes the incompatible faces of the Kim Jong Un (Gim Jeong-eun) era. To reach out internationally and resuscitate its devastated economy, the state has made unprecedented diplomatic moves to participate in the failed US–North Korea summit in 2018–19 and invest heavily in tourism all the while tightening its grip on the domestic population. Many North Korean resettlers say that it became much more difficult to cross the North Korea–China border under Kim Jong Un's regime as barbed-wire fences and closed-circuit televisions (CCTVs) have been installed under the new leader's watch. The regime intensified the War against Impure Recorded Materials (Bulsun rokhwamulgwaeui jeonjaeng), a campaign introduced in 2004 when the current leader's father, Kim Jong Il (Gim Jeong-il), established the so-called 109 Gruppa, an organization to censor foreign-drama content. Members of the Gruppa often enter schools to search students' bags and exercise a draconian degree of control by confiscating items and reporting owners of foreign media to the North Korean police. As one anonymous interviewee (female in her midthirties, born in Cheongjin, who left North Korea in 2019 and came to South Korea in 2020) attests, 109 Gruppa's crackdown was so severe that she did not dare play any South Korean content on her cell phone.[12]

On a broader plane, studying millennials, cell phone networks, and media consumption calls into question the convoluted relationship between technology and surveillance, intellectual property and a sense of ownership, and the ironic ways millennials achieve some degree of freedom under constant state supervision. Similar to how North Koreans can accumulate private property while not having any legal means to guard it,[13] North Korean citizens can use cell phones subversively to access outside information and think beyond state-approved ways while lacking measures to protect their freedom of thought. This predicament prompts people to use coded neologisms and bodily presentation to perform trust and gain access to secretive groups, in effect creating alternative social networks, which often provide business partnerships and other means of livelihood. As North Korea analysts Nat Kretchun and Jane Kim note, "Outside information and the activities North Koreans engage in to access it also are fostering the creation of horizontal connections between North Korean citizens. These horizontal bonds, facilitated by shared implication in prohibited behaviors, economic interactions, or simply curiosity about the outside world, and created outside the watch of the state, are a breeding ground for ideas that go beyond or run counter to the regime's espoused reality."[14] As a result, the vast majority of North Koreans today seem to exist in an ambivalent way between forced socialist collectives and spontaneously formed social networks. Millennials in particular learn to constantly negotiate and perform their allegiance to the state for political survival while forging social ties for economic survival and cultural diversification.[15]

Many scholars point to the existence of draconian surveillance in North Korea,[16] but few articulate how that surveillance has to be performed in a legible way for people to thwart it. While developing a watchful eye toward censors, young North Koreans learn from smuggled media how to stage coded fashions and use language subtle enough to gain the trust of like-minded peers. In other words, there has to be a degree of legible trustworthiness among the network of people who share the forbidden media. Most are "inducted" into consuming foreign cultural materials through their intimate—and carefully guarded—social networks. Such unique circumstances provide a possibility for considering North Korea not just as a passive—and illegal—smuggler of foreign media but also as a uniquely subversive yet proactive circulator of global-media content.

Millennial North Korea, North Korean Millennials

On a broader plane, this book is about the multilayered tension between North Korean millennials and the North Korean state in the new millennium. Like millennials in many other parts of the world, those in North Korea struggle to cope with technologically stimulated social shifts, though without access to the conventional social benefits. In general terms, "millennials" refer to the group of people born between 1981 and 1996 who have reached adulthood in the twenty-first century. Such generational classifications emerge primarily out of the US social and historical context, but even the millennials in the United States by no means represent a monolithic entity as their experiences vary widely according to gender, race, ethnicity, class, and cultural heritage.[17] Millennials in North Korea likewise are not a uniform group.

Similar to the conventions in the United States where approximately thirty years constitutes one generation marked by distinctive life experiences (such as the golden generation, lost generation, and baby boomers), in North Korea, there is a tradition of naming a generation after the representative state policy and their corresponding life experience during their twenties and thirties. North Koreans rely on the following categorization: the so-called partisan generation refers to those who were born in the 1900s to 1920s and were in their twenties and thirties during the Japanese colonial period; the so-called Chollima generation refers to those born in the 1930s and 1940s who came of age during North Korea's Chollima economic plan;[18] the so-called Arduous March generation refers to those born between the 1950s and 1970s who experienced extreme economic hardship in their twenties and thirties; and the so-called marketplace generation refers to those born after the 1980s whose livelihood depends on their marketplace participation.[19] Slight variations on this model exist. For instance, Ji Hye-yeon groups North Korean generations into categories identical to the aforementioned first and third generations but points out that the second generation was born between the 1930s and 1950s and the fourth generation, between the 1970s and 1990s. She adds a fifth generation to refer to those born after the 1990s.[20]

Although North Korean millennials are predominantly people in their thirties and forties, this book does not define millennials simply according to the facile generational classification. More significant than biological age is the fact that "millennial" is a constructed, claimed, and carefully performed identity. The definition used in this book primarily reflects an individual's receptiveness to changes and openness to the outside world. In the case of North Korea, this means that those born between the mid-1970s and mid-2000s who have claimed and performed inclinations toward accepting notable economic, sociocultural, and technological changes in the past two decades share a significant number of performative strategies with biological millennials and therefore should be seen as sharing cultural affinities.

The structural categorization by age groups should by no means be the only measure to determine who North Korean millennials are since even a single generation can share variable experiences. As performance and media scholar Abigail De Kosnik notes, "We are in the age of micro-generations. Huge differences [exist] between micro-generations. Different micro-generations have different commitments to different social media."[21] This is most true in North Korea. Although North Korea's conception of social media is distinctively understood as networks of trusted people who operate offline to share forbidden media secretly, their varying attitudes toward such networks are what make North Korean millennials an amalgamation of microgenerations.

In light of how North Korean millennials are a group of microgenerations whose overlaying characteristics emerge through their curation of ideological, cultural, and economic affiliations, the best known North Korean conjugation of "millennials" is the marketplace generation (*jangmadang saedae*)—mostly defined as those born in the late 1980s who experienced neither the central rationing system nor the strict centralized education system. This book uses a more fluid definition of the marketplace generation as those who support and participate in the marketplace economy. South Korean journalist O Ga-hyeon notes that the emergence of this new generation was marked by "positive notions about wealth, preference of individualism over collectivism, and flexible and open attitudes toward foreign cultures."[22] Reflecting these trends, a term more inclusive than "marketplace generation" is "N Generation," coined by the South Korean scholar Gim Gap-sik. This versatile term refers to North Koreans born after the mid-1970s;[23] N simultaneously signifies "new," "network," "new consumption," and "nuclear weapons" to collectively present the novel life experience of this generation. The N Generation is known for their audacity to depart from the previous modes of political devotion to the state, and it is not uncommon to hear an N Generation person say things like "He [Kim Jong Un] is not going to feed us, so let us take good care of ourselves."[24] The N Generation provides a productive starting point to think through the distinctive characteristics of the millennials whose life trajectories differ significantly from their predecessors'.

Extending the generational rubric further to the most recent times, the neologism *gangnam* generation emerged to refer to a more specific microgeneration of North Koreans. *Gangnam* here stands as an abbreviation for "liking South Korea beyond the river" (*gang-geonneo namhan-eul joa-handa*).[25] As the name suggests, the *gangnam* generation is marked by their passion for South Korean culture, but as Na Min-hui (female born in 1991 in Pyongyang who left North Korea in 2014 and came to South Korea in 2015) notes, "What makes the *gangnam* generation different from the previous generation, who also consumed South Korean culture, is their proactive emulation of the South Korean lifestyle."[26] An example is changing their names to "sophisticated-sounding 'Ji-ae' and 'Yu-mi,' styled after South Korean drama protagonists."[27] A microgeneration, the *gangnam* generation closely reflects the popular-culture-consumption patterns that have changed the lifestyles of predominantly young North Koreans.

All these distinctive ways to comprehend a new kind of North Koreans dispersed through microgenerations present attractive possibilities, but in order to accommodate these variegated segments of North Korean youth, I adhere to the comprehensive term "millennials." I use it to reference the generation in North Korea who face technologically driven social shifts in the new millennium; it has the flexibility to encompass the social-economic-military spectrum captured in various Ns and the proactive cultural practices of the *gangnam* generation. "Millennials" in this book will inevitably fall short of capturing the immense diversity of these microgenerations, but the term will be used as a shorthand to reference a group of North Koreans who are hybrid subjects of both a draconian state and a fast-changing digital culture.

The diversity of North Korean millennials rests with not only the terms used to describe them but also their gender, class, and regional differences and various performative strategies to anchor these identity-related vectors. The wide spectrum of their life experiences—from an impoverished teenager being sold into a forced marriage in China, to a top university student being privileged to study overseas on a full government scholarship—demonstrates the range of the millennial generation even in such a seemingly homogenous nation. Gender creates further divergent experiences since the millennial generation has seen an exponential increase in women's participation in the market economy (discussed in chapter 2). Oftentimes, various stories of North Korean youth seem as if they emerged from people who lived in different eras and in different countries.

In a racially homogenous country like North Korea, class background and economic status become huge factors in the diversity of life experiences. Millennials considered in this book hail from all walks of life. However, economically advanced citizens are more likely to use new technology. Kretchun and Kim note that "elites are important early adopters, who have the means to acquire and use advanced technologies."[28] In this regard, technology creates a gap between the "hereditary elite" and the "economic elite,"[29] further complicating the social stratification that results from North Korea's political caste system known as *seongbun* and *todae*.[30]

Lastly, in investigating the misalignment between North Korean millennials and North Korea in the new millennium, this book does not overlook the fact that Kim Jong Un himself is a millennial whose self-presentation in the public media differs from that of the previous generation of leaders. When he succeeded his father in 2011 as a young leader still in his twenties, the initial response from North Koreans was a sense of enthusiasm, even prompting many young women, such as Ryu Hui-jin (female born in 1991 in Pyongyang who left North Korea in 2012 and came to South Korea in 2015), to remark, "How great the young general looks!"[31] According to Gim Ha-na (female born in Hyesan in 1988 who left North Korea in 2014), "When Kim Jong Un appeared on TV, we were quite touched since he looked so much like his grandfather. The older generation especially felt as if his grandfather was born again as a young man."[32] At public engagements, the awe-inspiring new leader was accompanied by an equally young wife, Li Seol-ju, who held his arm. North Koreans previously had never seen leaders' spouses in public, not to mention physical intimacy between the leader and his spouse. To take the display of youthful leadership to another level, in 2023, Kim even showcased his preteen daughter in high-profile public engagements, showing unbridled fatherly affection and his status as a young patriarch of his family—another first in North Korean media coverage of national leaders.

Born in 1984, Kim Jong Un is portrayed by the official state media as a leader who deeply cares about young people and new technology. Digging deeper into official coverage of the new leader's vision for a strong nation, one quickly discovers that national strength is frequently predicated on the rhetoric of "fostering the youth" (cheong-nyeon), as Kim Jong Un's public speeches demonstrate: "Our country set a good example of solving the problems of youth. There are many countries that pay attention to youth, but no other country has placed young people at the core of the national and party strategic plans and foregrounded a strong nation of youth [cheong-nyeon gang-guk]."[33] Official North Korean propaganda produced an abundance of articles with titles such as "The Great Leader Paved the Everlasting Foundation for a Strong Nation of Youth" (Cheongnyeongangguk-ui mannyeong-iteuleul maryeonhayeo-jusin widaehan ryeongdoja), which sings boundless eulogies of how, under the leadership of Kim Jong Un, "the ideology of prioritizing youth culminated in the party's focus on emphasizing the importance of youth."[34] To further cement the image of the leader as a strong supporter of the youth, arts were actively deployed to the point that there is an entire collection of songs, *March Forward, Strong Nation of Young People*, dedicated to that purpose.[35] The collection even features a song titled "My Country Is a Strong Nation of Young People" (Nae joguk-eun cheong-nyeon-gang-guk):

> Ah, love the young people.
> Advancing even further the national project to prioritize
>   young people,
> Which had been adopted by previous leaders,
> The dear leader opened a period of prosperity
> Marked by his love for the next generation and for the future.
> Ah, even though the world changes a thousand times over,
> Even if the earth is one day destroyed,
> My brilliant country will soar up unharmed.
> It is a strong nation of youth paralleled by none.[36]

Putting aside the famed North Korean tradition of deifying the nation's leaders, there is something different about Kim Jong Un when compared to his predecessors. Stepping onto the international stage as the untested leader, he had to mark himself as qualitatively different from his father, Kim Jong Il, whose reign left mixed legacies of a painful deterioration of the North Korean people's quality of life and the state's emergence as a nuclear power. Also, having seen the world beyond North Korea in his youth, Kim shares the millennial generation's desire for technology adoption—to the point that he wanted to distinctively characterize his era by tech innovation. According to *Radio Free Asia* reports, "There was a rumor among the elite that the newly named successor Kim Jong Un would try to introduce a new cult around himself, partly supported by mobile telecommunications. Indeed, propaganda materials distributed to people in early 2011 claimed that the successor had been thoroughly conversant with the global trend of informatization since high school and that mobile telecommunications service had been realized, thanks to his bold initiatives."[37] Official North Korean propaganda also paints the new leader in a distinctive light—as focused on strengthening the nation through science and technology. In 2016, the North Korean magazine *Chollima* published an article, "Bolstering the Nation with Strength in Science, Technology, and Talented People" (Gwa-hak-gisul-gang-guk, injaegang-guk geonseol-ui naraereul pyeolcheojusiryeo), praising Kim Jong Un's leadership after he declared his plan to build the Center for Science and Technology. The article confirms how the centrality of Kim's leadership is embedded in his support of science and technology: "The workers reflected upon the significance of the multifunctional Center for Science and Technology and reminisced how previous leaders in the 1980s built the Great Hall of People's Learning [*Inmin-dae-hakseupdang*] and ignited the passion for learning among people. Just like them, the Dear Leader is addressing the needs of the twenty-first century by establishing a multifunctional and technologically advanced Center for Science and Technology in order to pave a way for our country to become a nation with strength in science, technology, and talented people. All marveled at his grand plan, inimitable skills, and deep wisdom."[38]

In fact, Kim Jong Un was not the only one who emerged as a visionary leader of youth; his sister and his wife have also surfaced as notable public figures in the new millennium. Li Seol-ju is the first in North Korean history to have appeared in public as a spouse of the North Korean leader, gracing the front pages of domestic and international media with her youthful looks and high fashion. She quickly became the icon of the new North Korean woman, often inspiring her followers to emulate her signature "party-leader" (*dang ganbu*) style exuding affluence and power. Whereas Li Seol-ju captivated the new generation of North Korean women with her feminine looks, Kim Yeo-jeong, as the leader's sister, started to wield considerable power in North Korean realpolitik. During the 2018 Pyeongchang Winter Olympics, she came to South Korea as the North Korean emissary to pave the way for peace talks. She also accompanied her brother to the historic—yet failed—2019 Hanoi summit between the United States and North Korea, assisting Kim Jong Un every step of the way. The retinue of female figures surrounding Kim Jong Un further includes a child literally born in the new millennium. Kim Ju-ae, allegedly born in 2012 or 2013, made her debut in the North Korean public and the world when she accompanied her father to a test launch for an intercontinental ballistic missile (ICBM) on November 18, 2022. A year later, the North Korean state designated the date as Missile Industry Day (Misail gong-eob-jeol) in order to commemorate the successful launch. But perhaps more significantly, the day was declared a special occasion to highlight Kim Ju-ae's public debut. Her public appearances continued into 2023, sealing the impression of this young person's role as the possible future leader of North Korea. When she was addressed as the "morning star of Korea" in the public media in late November 2023, many North Korea specialists saw it as a clear sign of Kim Ju-ae's strengthening political status since this is a special title traditionally dedicated to the leader's future successor.[39]

Kim Jong Un and prominent female figures of his retinue are ambivalent embodiments representing both the emergent energy of the new generation and the unchallenged authority of his family's sacred bloodline. In this regard, North Korea's paradox is increasing with the passage of time, and North Korean millennials—among them Kim Jong Un—must face and live with such inconsistencies most directly.

Why This Research Now?

The study of North Korea's recent media-technology development is a burgeoning field. Among the few existing studies, the vast majority are quantitative works driven by hard-data collection and analyses in the service of government agencies or think tanks. In rare cases where qualitative interpretation has been provided, it is for ideologically inflected projects on how proliferating technology, especially cell phones, affects US national security and international relations.[40] On the other hand, the study of North Korea's younger generation has been conducted by scholars such as Sunny Yoon but not to the fullest extent of tracing the correlation between the millennials' cultural inclinations and the digital transformation of the North Korean state over the past two decades.[41] Most crucially, there has been no full-length-book project that provides a close-up analysis of South Korean media content as a way to explain its transformative appeal in North Korea. This study dives deep into humanistic communication and interpretive narrative analysis based on the methodology of media and performance studies. It fully considers both the liberating and the oppressive roles of technology in today's North Korea, with data distilled from the North Korean state media and the North Korean millennial resettlers themselves.

My analysis also takes into account the complex diversification of today's North Korean experience, moving beyond Pyongyang-centric methods. Because North Korea has always been a highly centralized state where political and cultural power coalesce in Pyongyang, the capital city has seen a faster rise of technology than the rest of the country in the new millennium. According to a South Korean visitor, "Cell phones could be found practically in everyone's hands on the streets [of Pyongyang]" by November 2018.[42] Complicating this phenomenon is the fact that information flow within Pyongyang—the beacon of North Korean statehood—is more strictly controlled than outside the capital; An Hye-gyeong (female in her thirties, born in Cheongjin, who left North Korea in 2006) notes that Pyongyang residents are subject to a higher degree of surveillance when it comes to illegal consumption of foreign media.[43] While there is an undeniable gap in living standards and social infrastructure between Pyongyang and other places, the rapidly spreading communications technology has played a crucial role in revitalizing markets in provincial towns, especially those along the North Korea–China border, which serve as gateways for the influx of telecommunication technology and media content from foreign lands. Gim Hae-suk (female in her forties, born in South Pyeongan Province, who left North Korea in 2018 and came to South Korea in 2019) recollects how her husband wanted to move to the border area in order to start trading in the marketplace. She first refused to leave South Pyeongan Province since she wanted to be close to the capital city. But once she began crossing the border through Rajin-Sonbong Special Economic Zone, she started to see the reality beyond North Korea: "I was able to access more information through USB memory sticks that came from China. Pyongyang residents might have pride, but it's not the case that the capital city provides you with more things. Those with some resources might have a good time in Pyongyang, but the rest have to struggle."[44] Go Na-hae (female born in Dancheon, South Hamgyeong Province, who left North Korea in 2018 and came to South Korea in 2019) agrees: "Unless you have a good political background, have access to foreign countries, or are just simply rich, there is no reason to live in Pyongyang."[45] An anonymous interviewee (female in her twenties, born in Hyesan, who left North Korea in 2017) nails the point: "Hyesan is the best. Much better than Pyongyang. You won't starve there as you can work in trading [with China] and work as a broker."[46] The millennial reality in North Korea seems to have reconfigured the preexisting spatial hierarchy into a slightly more lateral playing field where border towns and other urban centers, such as Sinuiju, appear as attractive as the capital city. These are the fluid and fast-changing circumstances of today's North Korea that await deep interpretive analyses.

Notes on Interviews

The multidirectional flow of technology and information requires a broader consideration of various urban and provincial markets and social ties formed by the constant movement of people, information, and merchandise. There is nothing better than the voices of North Koreans themselves to explain how regional, generational, and gender diversity emerge through technology networks. Since conducting free, open research and interviews in North Korea is not possible at the moment, I instead turn to a group of North Koreans who ended up settling in South Korea. As of December 2022, an estimated 33,882 North Korean defectors from various walks of life have settled in South Korea. According to the 2023 *White Paper on Korean Unification* published by the South Korean Ministry of Unification, 72 percent of them are women. The reasons for their defection vary: 52.6 percent defected due to economic hardship, 17.2 percent due to family members' defection, 8.5 percent due to recommendation by other people, and 7.4 percent due to dissatisfaction with the North Korean regime. In terms of age, the vast majority are millennials because escaping North Korea involves the dangerous and grueling process of crossing many borders—a physical toll that not all generations can take. People in their thirties constitute 28.7 percent, and people in their twenties and thirties together make up a staggering 57.1 percent.[47] Therefore, the demographic makeup of the North Korean resettlers in South Korea is ideal for researching the millennial generation.[48]

A sizeable number of these North Korean defectors-cum-settlers in South Korea has created an active presence in cyberspace. Some join online communities while others appear on talk shows and variety shows to share their life stories on TV. Some become prominent YouTubers. Much useful information about the proliferation of new technology and the impact it has on their lives has been documented in these forums, and these accounts are considered with the defectors' particular background (gender, age, family, educational level, place of birth, and residence) in mind.[49]

In this regard, I also resort to a sizeable number of prerecorded interviews available in the public sphere, such as TV, online streaming, and social media. I am cognizant of the fact that on-camera interviews produced for these venues have notable limitations; the editing process can influence—and distort—the way the narratives are presented. Often, the stories become sensationalized to attract more viewers. Interviewees also have to curtail sensitive information and use predetermined scripts, and their full knowledge of their words' lasting nature and availability to a wide audience inevitably invites self-censorship. When interviewees are aware that recording is under way, it changes the dynamics of their storytelling.

For these reasons, I attempted to conduct as many in-person interviews as possible. To secure the safest possible environment and enable the resettlers' stories to emerge organically, the interviewees had a choice to speak with full anonymity; when they requested not to be identified, they are marked as "anonymous." The same principle applies to the identification of their place of birth, gender, age, and when they left North Korea. However, some interviewees clearly wished to be identified by their full names; in those cases, I have respected their intention and listed their personal information with their permission. This is why real names and "anonymous" are simultaneously used in the list of interviewees whom I personally interviewed. In total, I personally interviewed fourteen resettlers, five of them being male and seven of them female (the full list of primary interviews, together with forty-four interviewees cited from secondary sources, appears in the appendix). Although the sample number is not large by any standard, they represent a wide variety of millennial North Koreans. From political dissidents to economic migrants, from active seekers of better opportunities to unwilling border crossers who simply could not remain in North Korea, they constitute a diverse group in terms of gender, age, economic status, place of birth, schooling, career, profession, and when they left North Korea.

The interviews I personally conducted were not recorded in order to allow for free-flowing storytelling on the part of resettlers and deep listening on my end. I wanted each interview—usually lasting sixty to ninety minutes—to be as close to a natural conversation as possible. The use of recording devices may "produce very large amounts of data quite rapidly," and "the more intensive, micro-focused forms of analysis" might be useful for data-driven quantitative analysis,[50] yet the main aim of conducting interviews with North Korean resettlers is not to present as cohesive data as possible but to let the inconsistent and discursive experiences of North Korean millennials unravel. Akin to theater educator Kathleen Gallagher's use of "storytelling as a robust mode of research,"[51] I let their stories about their encounters with new technologies and forbidden media guide the unfolding of new knowledge. In a sense, these interviews can be a more concentrated way of investigating various modes of being and living, which extends the spectrum of knowledge and studies "what might be, not simply what is," as Gallagher contends.[52] Hearing out the dimensions of possibilities and imagination made up the most rewarding moments in interacting with these interviewees, who saw the confines of their daily realities in North Korea as inspirations for an alternative world.

Chapter Outline

The main narrative arc of this book hinges upon the inseparable relationship between North Korean millennials and new media, best represented by the growing use of cell phones, as both emerged as crucial forces carrying today's North Korea into the future. This is a story best told from a bifurcated perspective: a macroscopic overview of the transformation in media and technology and a microscopic analysis of actual media content. The two-part structure reflects this. Chapters 1 and 2 provide the context for understanding millennial North Korea: the historic, generational, and technological shifts that have swept the country in the past two decades. This story is best told against the theoretical backdrop of how digital transformation changes social networks—analogous to how blockchain technology unravels state authority—and how intellectual and creative properties can be conceived on the basis of the collective consumers rather than individual producers—a situation that uniquely defines millennial North Korea. With the broad context established by capturing the dynamics between the state and the people, chapters 3 and 4 introduce an incisive analysis of the forbidden media: what precise aspects of foreign-media content appeal to North Korean millennials and how they use those media to create new social ties and showcase unique interpretations of media ownership. While the first two chapters provide a panoramic view of the cultural and technological contexts, the last two chapters present a close-up view of media texts, which has not been previously presented in full detail.

Chapter 1, "The Millennium Comes to North Korea," lays out a comprehensive history of North Korea's recent top-down reforms in the media and technology sector and situates them against the backdrop of new political leadership and the expansion of the market economy. The introduction of internet protocol television (IPTV), high-definition television (HDTV), online commerce, and sleeker TV programming using drones and 3D graphics is discussed within the broader context of the rise of intranet and cell phone networks as an interactive medium to create an alternative social order and imaginary.

Chapter 2, "The Rise of North Korean Millennials," addresses the distinctive features of North Korean millennials as a particular kind of media user, especially in regard to how the proliferation of cell phone networks and the expansion of the market economy allow for the creation of an alternative social space as well as the rise of a uniquely North Korean platform. Examining these millennials' use of new media and technology to reach the outside world blocked by draconian state surveillance reveals that North Koreans are not just passive consumers of foreign media but subversively creative circulators of global media beyond their originally intended market.

After chapters 1 and 2 offer a bird's-eye view of North Korean millennials today while also providing a historical and theoretical arc of millennial North Korea, chapters 3 and 4 use those discoveries to dive deeply into specific media texts as a way to measure the heartbeat of the rapidly transforming society and culture. Chapter 3, "This Story Is Ours," provides a close textual analysis of a few representative South Korean TV dramas that gained traction among North Korean millennials, with a particular focus on how the latest cell phone technologies featured in the dramas play a pivotal role in shaping the narrative force. These examples are scrutinized vis-à-vis a broader context of how they might aid North Korean viewers' imagination in envisioning an alternative future. By engaging with how consumption of South Korean dramas has shifted over the years in North Korea, the chapter unpacks the particular appeal that South Korean dramas have had for viewers/listeners forging alternative modes of sociality.

Chapter 4, "Visions and Sounds to Change Lives," expands the analytic scope to encompass the consumption patterns of media content outside TV dramas, such as popular South Korean songs, films, and variety shows that enthrall North Koreans. By balancing a close textual reading with contextual consideration of what it means to live creatively in a place like North Korea, the chapter shows how these media forms complement South Korean dramas but also diverge from them with a fluid capacity to address a wider range of themes. Like chapter 3, this chapter pays close attention to how cell phones literally and symbolically stand for alternative ways of weaving social relations.

No matter how much the North Korean state hopes to reinforce authoritarian control, the tide has shifted—gradually but powerfully—to counter the North Korean state's empty rhetoric of its centrality on the world stage. In millennial North Korea, people have become much more aware of the circumstances beyond the border due to their increasing, albeit forbidden, consumption of foreign media. This is the reason a close textual reading of South Korean media that enjoy broad circulation in North Korea occupies half of the book. Although many scholars and journalists have previously provided passing comments on which South Korean media texts are popular in North Korea, few have provided detailed discussions of precisely why those texts speak powerfully to North Koreans. I believe the symptomatic characteristics of today's North Korea can only be gleaned from simultaneous consideration of the macroscopic and the microscopic.

Perhaps surprisingly to some, the story of North Korean millennials is not too different from that of other millennials around the world: they are hardly a monolithic group and struggle in all kinds of ways to make sense of the rapidly morphing world, sharing information with their selected communities at a pace faster than previous generations ever could. Just like millennials elsewhere, North Korean millennials are also the first generation to live in a world transformed in large part by cell phones. As a result, other generations surrounding them and microgenerations within the category of millennials are changing, and the book presents the broader intergenerational dynamics caught up in the longing for mobility, freedom, and change. Although heavy emphasis is placed on media and technology, this book is about the basic human desire to be recognized in and connected to the broader world.

ONE

The Millennium Comes to North Korea

A man in a black suit takes big strides in the air, which buoys his entire body effortlessly. He has his right hand freely resting on the roof of a running bus while his left hand holds a cell phone as he takes a selfie. Multiple spectators on the ground closely follow this gravity-defying performance with their cell phone cameras. Enchanted by the scene, both the performer and the onlookers record every moment.

As I watched this rather peculiar footage emerge from North Korea in early 2019,[1] I could not help but ask, Which presents a bigger surprise, the uncanny sight of a man floating in the air or the saturation of cell phones in North Korea? Although the spectacle was created as a promotional video clip for North Korea's national circus (*gyoye*) to dazzle the audience with their new magic show, the real surprise for outside viewers like me was the ubiquity of cell phones in this closely controlled society. Cell phones and North Korea might not seem to form a natural alliance since tech savviness is often strongly associated with the developed or heavily industrialized world. Moreover, there is also a close association between cell phones and an open society. The usual assumption is that "the cellphone is phenomenally democratic—and populist," as philosopher Janet McCracken notes.[2]

One could assume that tech innovation in Silicon Valley or mass production lines in Foxconn factory in Shenzhen, China, leaves places like North Korea untouched, but North Korea is doing its best to counter that notion with what it does best: top-down propaganda. One recent North Korean film points out how little attention has been paid to North Korea's self-perceived importance as a tech-savvy country on par with the rest of the world.

Story of Our Family (Urijip iyagi; 2016) is arguably the most representative film to emerge from North Korea in recent years. It features a telling example of how cell phones are used as crucial devices to enable social connections in both technological and ideological ways. By all measures, it is a typical North Korean propaganda film, with a heavy dose of political edification. The plot centers on a young female protagonist, Jeong-a, who looks after neighborhood orphans, whose parents died as workplace heroes. The orphans first resist Jeong-a's help, but they eventually come to realize her genuinely kind intentions. In the end, they all come together as one true family, and the film ends with the young neighbors dressed in traditional Korean garments laying flowers at the Revolutionary Martyrs' Cemetery. The North Korean regime perceived it to be an exemplary patriotic film, so much so that it was hand-selected by the North Korean government to be shown to the general public during the Bucheon International Fantastic Film Festival in 2018 in South Korea.

Kim Jong Un is referred to as "the true father" in the film, and in that regard, *Story of Our Family* follows in the footsteps of other classical North Korean films. But unlike the rest, it deploys cell phones to propel old ideology in the new era through crucial moments of plot development. The female protagonist receives an urgent phone call from her father notifying her of their elderly neighbor's stroke. This prompts her to go back home and save the life of that neighbor, which provides a moment of striking heroine's virtue. Cell phones' centrality does not stop there: in the documentary film about the making of the film, the actress Baek Seol-gi, who played the lead role, shows many text messages she received from fans, presenting her latest smartphone to the camera. Cell phones in these moments function as crucial devices to validate the political virtue of the heroine but also, and more importantly, as a central network through which citizens can form bonds; the phone could potentially replace the workplace political learning sessions (*saenghwal chonghwa*) and other forms of face-to-face collective gathering.

As is usually the case in North Korea, filmic illusion and social reality connect so seamlessly that it is hard to distinguish them. This episode from *Story of Our Family* does not just illustrate North Korea's wishful fantasy of building a networked society, it also presents the actual sweeping changes in science, media, and digital technology that have been transforming the country for nearly two decades. So what happened to North Korea around the turn of the millennium? How did cell phones and related technology come to serve as central media of social, economic, and political changes? The answers to these questions lie at the intersection of three trends of development: top-down state policy on information technology (IT) and digital communication, marketization as a middle ground where government policy and private initiative interface, and, finally, the documentation of accounts of everyday people who lived through those paramount changes.

Facing the Wind of Digital Transformation

The millennium in North Korea opened with grave challenges that, in their magnitude, made the worldwide *fin du millénaire* anxiety look like whimsical luxury. Still facing the hardship of the Arduous March—the famine during which millions starved to death[3]—the vast majority of North Koreans, including the citizens of Pyongyang, suffered from food shortages that threatened the minimum level of subsistence.[4] Li Wi-ryeok (male born in 1985 in Gimchaek who left North Korea in 2010), who survived this period as a child vagabond (*kkotjebi*), remembers people frequently saying, "Only wolves and foxes will survive the Arduous March."[5] Docile people who just waited for the government to help them were the first to starve. With the central rationing system officially coming to a halt in 2003, except for a few political elites still being cared for by the state or in positions of power to barter influence for food, the whole country coped with harsh living conditions, and many ordinary citizens, especially women, started trading in marketplaces to secure their family's next meal. There are countless stories by North Koreans who survived this difficult time period—too many to list in full detail here. Ordinary North Koreans' everyday lives were marked by conditions harking back to a preindustrialized era: breaking ice to wash clothes in the midwinter

river, collecting twigs and chopping down mountain trees to secure heating
fuel, and, in cities, climbing up forty flights of stairs to get to one's apartment
due to electricity shortages that halted elevators. Many young North Koreans were deeply affected by the hardship. Jo Ye-na (female born in 1993 in
Yanggang Province who left North Korea in 2012), for instance, had to bring
her infant sibling to her middle school because her mother had to travel for
days to buy products to be sold in markets to feed the family. In high school,
she constantly worked on farms and in marketplaces to support herself, including biking sixty miles a day to buy fish in the seaside village of Hwadae
to be sold in Gilju, where she lived.[6]

But the nation's destitution did not deter then leader Kim Jong Il from
pursuing his future-looking agenda. Despite the poverty of the vast majority
of its people, the North Korean government explored how to bring IT and
digital communication to the country. Kim Yonho sees Kim Jong Il's 2001
visit to China as a moment of awakening: "After visiting the Pudong Indus-
trial Complex in Shanghai, China, in January 2001, Kim Jong Il ordered the
Party to introduce mobile telecommunications service in Pyongyang by April
15, 2002, the 90th birthday of his late father Kim Il Sung. Following Kim's
instructions, the North Korean government suggested creating a nationwide
mobile telecommunications network in its 2001 long-term plan for developing the IT industry. The plan envisioned a network covering Pyongyang and
Rason [Rajin-Sonbong] by August 2002 and the entire nation by 2007."[7] This
ambitious initiative, however, did not commence suddenly with the arrival
of the new millennium but rather had a gestational stage in the previous
decade. In 1993, in a letter to the National Conference for Telecommunication Employees, Kim Jong Il "emphasized the importance of modern telecommunications not only as a primary instrument of ensuring timely vertical
communication for the central management of state affairs, but also as a way
to provide more self-reliant and creative living conditions for the general population."[8] Until this point, the use of mobile communications in North Korea
had been limited to the military and high-ranking Korean Workers' Party
officials. This was about to change as the directives from the top leader have
been of utmost importance for North Koreans from all walks of life, and this
particular directive certainly did not go unnoticed. A nationwide campaign
to digitize communication reverberated throughout North Korea soon after.

North Korean academia responded by introducing a curriculum based on science, technology, engineering, and mathematics into the educational system. Reading through North Korean academic journals published during the difficult times of the Arduous March presents a portrait of a country doing what it can to catch up with world standards in science and technology. For instance, a 1998 article in the North Korean journal *Jeonja jadonghwa* acknowledged that "the term 'information society' has long been in place, but today's information [*jeongbohwa*] is transforming beyond our recognition both quantitatively and qualitatively. Humankind has found itself in an unprecedented phase of civilization."[9] The journal's way of coping with the challenges was to run a regular column that included summaries of the latest foreign articles published in the field of automation. Various articles originally published in English, Russian, Chinese, and Japanese were regularly introduced in Korean translation throughout the 1990s.[10] The journal also advertised its free distribution system (*singan japji jigeup bokje bongsa*) for qualified applicants.

North Korea's desire to meet the needs of the changing world—as exemplified by *Electronic Automation*—was strongly echoed at all educational levels.[11] For instance, a junior high school computer textbook in 2002 clearly featured Kim Jong Il's directives: "The Great Leader Kim Jong Il said, 'If, in the past, illiterates were the ones incapable of reading, nowadays, illiteracy refers to those who do not know computer technology.'"[12] To illustrate how the directives from the highest leadership are put into practice, *Gyoyangwon* (a journal designed for pedagogues) reported that a kindergarten teacher named Gang Geum-sun from the city of Haeju used computers to teach children the names of different flowers and then had them plant those flowers in a garden on the computer screen (see figure 1.1).[13]

North Korean media also joined the campaign to educate the general public on the importance of digital-technology education in the new millennium. Their various outreach programs targeted people from all walks of life and across different media platforms: while oil paintings captured a dainty young woman lovingly gazing at her cell phone screen (figure 1.2) and a mother and a daughter taking selfies with a cell phone (figure 1.3), public posters did away with the highly tender and poetic strokes of paint brushes and sent edifying messages about cell phone etiquette loud and

FIGURE 1.1. Oil painting by Hong Geun Chan and Kang Yong Min, entitled *Team Members at the End of the Working Day Gather around a Young Man Who Appears to Have Achieved Success with His Work*. Photo courtesy of Koryo Tours. Reprinted with permission.

clear (figure 1.4). The official media productions were fully deployed, with some touting the virtues of advanced communication technology and others sending cautionary tales about its proper use in public. For instance, the public etiquette regarding cell phone usage was fully dramatized in a satirical comedy piece "So You Are Cheol-i's Dad!" by Korean Central Television (Joseon Jungnang Tellebijyon). Aired on June 3, 2012, this ten-minute skit starts with a wife urging her husband to join her visit to their son's doctor to thank her for having been kind to their son, Cheol-i. The scene then cuts to a bus, on which the father picks up his phone and starts talking in a loud voice, making other passengers frown. The father is so loud that he wakes up a nearby baby. Later that day, he and the baby's mother encounter each other again in a theater and bickering between them erupts since the father is once again speaking loudly on his cell phone in public. The scene finally cuts to the doctor's office, where the mother waits for her husband, but when he enters, he realizes that the doctor he came to thank is none other than the woman he argued with earlier in the day. Out of embarrassment, he hides in the office restroom before his wife spots him, only to be caught

FIGURE 1.2. A painting of a young woman with a cell phone on display at the Mansudae Arts Studio, Pyongyang, 2011. The title and the artist of the painting are unknown. Photo courtesy of James Hoare. Reprinted with permission.

4 월 　　주체1(1912). 4. 15.　　위대한 수령 김일성동지께서 탄생하시였다.

주체21(1932). 4. 25.　　위대한 수령 김일성동지께서 조선인민혁명군을 창건하시였다.
주체81(1992). 4. 13.　　위대한 수령 김일성동지께서 조선민주주의인민공화국 대원수칭호를 받으시였다.
주체82(1993). 4. 9.　　위대한 령도자 김정일동지께서 조선민주주의인민공화국 국방위원회 위원장으로 추대되시였다.
주체101(2012). 4. 11.　　경애하는 최고령도자 김정은동지께서 조선로동당 제1비서로 추대되시였다.
주체101(2012). 4. 13.　　경애하는 최고령도자 김정은동지께서 조선민주주의인민공화국 국방위원회 제1위원장으로 추대되시였다.
1892. 4. 21.　　우리 나라 녀성운동의 탁월한 지도자 강반석녀사께서 탄생하시였다.

일요일	월요일	화요일	수요일	목요일	금요일	토요일
28	29	30	31	1 2. 28.	2	3
4	5	6	7	8	9	10
11	12 3. 1.	13	14	15 대보름	16	17
18	19	20	21	22	23	24
25	26 3. 15.	27	28	29	30	1

청명 4. 4.　　곡우 4. 20.

FIGURE 1.3. A painting of a mother and daughter taking a selfie, which was featured in a 2021 calendar. The caption reads "First day at school." Artist unknown. Photo courtesy of Douglas Gabriel. Reprinted with permission.

FIGURE 1.4. In May 2023, Koryo Tours—a travel agency bringing Western tourists to North Korea—commissioned an anonymous North Korean artist to produce a poster about cell phone etiquette. The caption reads "Let's follow the public morals." Photo courtesy of Koryo Tours. Reprinted with permission.

in embarrassment when his wife calls him. Unwillingly, he comes out of the restroom and timidly apologizes to the doctor for having had bad cell phone etiquette. The takeaway lessons here is that cell phones are convenient, but when misused, they can be a source of public embarrassment.

The edifying narratives about new technology in North Korean public media has transcended the realm of the comic, at times, to become peculiar urban legends, ranging from the uncanny to the poetic. A 2002 article claims that "scientists in a certain country used a supercomputer loaded with new technology and successfully conversed with the dead."[14] The imaginative articulation of the computer's ability spilled into the literary realm as well. In a distinctive North Korean fashion, poetry was deployed as a medium to profess one's love for computers, as illustrated by the following poem, "Why Do I Love Computers?," published in *Cheongnyeon munhak* in 2001:

> Sitting by the window on campus,
> I continue to learn how to use a computer program.
> The more I use it, the closer I get.
> Why do I love computers?
>
> Oh, computer,
> I fell for you.
> Although not much time has passed since I started
>   going out with you,
> You are etched in my heart like a lover.
>
> I fell for you,
> Sitting before you,
> Which invites a touch that is both soft and calm
> and a meticulous skill to use it.
>
> Although I have yet to fall in love with a real girl,
> Computer, I confess to you,
> As a young man living in the information age,
> I love you with my burning heart.

How could I profess my love to you
Were it not for my ideas that make my eyes twinkle
And a passion that burns my soul?
How could I claim that you are in my heart
If I couldn't meet the demands of our time?

Computer, my love,
When I dedicate my entire heart to you,
You will show me the world of cutting-edge science.
Like a virgin who confesses love,
You will open the gates to your heart.

Now, I will conquer your fortress
And make my homeland glorious.
When I make the General [Kim Jong Il] rejoice,
You will know, even in silence,
How deep my love is for you.[15]

This North Korean poem could not have been a more truthful twenty-first-century echo of Soviet novels' boy-gets-tractor motif.[16] These students' passion translated into tangible results some twenty years later, with North Korean youth's success in international coding competitions: according to a 2022 announcement from Kim Chaek University, North Korean students have been quite successful in CodeChef, an India-based online coding competition, where they faced off against students from Japan's Tokyo University, Singapore's Nanyang Technological University, and Google employees from India and the United States.[17]

But excessive passion was accompanied by cautionary notes, which the North Korean media issued in abundance. Countless articles warning of the potential health hazards of misusing computers emerged in the spirit of educating the general public: while "eye fatigue, damage to the back muscle, weakening nerves, insomnia, and forgetfulness" could bog down those who used computers too long,[18] it was also "dangerous to drink water or eat in front of the computer" since "the interferences by electric waves may change the substance of water or food."[19] Warnings about the sanitary conditions were also issued: "Keyboards are dirtier than toilet seats since they contain 150 times more bacteria than the recommended level."[20]

Rather than simply alarming readers with these disturbing facts, the state media also provided a series of remedies for correcting such dangers. An article entitled "Why Should We Wash Our Face after Using the Computer?" recommends face washing to prevent skin disorders: "When we turn on the TV or a computer, much of their internal electronic flow clashes with the fluorescent plate, where static converges. The static pulls in all the dust in the air. According to experiments, the dust near the fluorescent plate contains large amounts of allergens and microbes. When people work on computers or watch TV for extended periods of time, allergens and microbes adhere to the skin and can cause skin disorders. This is why one should wash one's face thoroughly after using a computer or watching TV."[21] In a similar spirit of helping readers, an article in *Chollima* recommends drinking green tea in the morning and chrysanthemum tea in the afternoon to protect computer users' eyesight.[22]

Reading through the North Korean publications (mostly periodicals and textbooks) from the 2010s illustrates how North Korea saw computers as a versatile technology, applicable in literally all aspects of life: from foreign-language learning, piano tuning, and producing perfect sound effects for Korean musical rhythm to beer brewing and bread making, automation by computer programs provided a perfect technological solution for a wide array of human deficiencies.[23]

However, these official campaigns to promote computers should not be understood as a truthful reflection of North Korean realities during the 2000s. If anything, they illustrate the North Korean state's wish to fast-forward the country to a digitized society, but the actual accounts of North Koreans who lived during this time period tell of an uneven experience. Gim Ji-yeong (female in her early thirties, born in Hyesan, who left North Korea in 2012), for instance, notes: "During the Kim Jong Il era, computers were widely publicized, and Kim Il Sung University introduced a computer science department."[24] While Gim speaks for the privileged elites who saw the actual implementation of the directive, this was not the case for the majority of North Korean students. Son Myung-hui (female in her midthirties, born in Dancheon, Hamgyeong Province, who left North Korea first in 2007 and again in 2014) recalls that in the early 2000s under Kim Jong Il's regime, her junior high school attempted to teach basic computer skills, but as forty students were expected to share just two computers, "computer education" was in name only. But not knowing how to use computers did not present any difficulties in life since computer-keyboard typing was not widespread and virtually all official documents were handwritten.[25]

Ju Chan-yang (female born in 1991 in Cheongjin who left North Korea in 2010) likewise notes that "there was only one computer in the entire school, so all we could do was listen to the teacher say, 'This is the mouse since it looks like a mouse.'"[26] Jeong Yu-na (female born in 1988 in Hoeryeong who left North Korea in 2008) reflects upon a similar experience, noting that the directive could not be implemented in real life due to a lack of resources: "Every student had to contribute money for their school to buy computers, but the campaign was unsuccessful, and we, in the provinces, did not see any computers at all. Although schools had no computers, students were expected to take exams in typing on keyboards, so we had to buy fake wooden keyboards from the marketplace to practice for exams."[27] According to an anonymous interviewee (male in his early twenties who left North Korea in 2016), during his junior high school period, he was given a take-home assignment to make a computer program. Those who did not have a computer at home would have no way to complete such assignments, but the teacher would still get very upset and respond with corporal punishment to those who did not submit their work.[28]

While the leadership's initiative played out discursively at a grassroots level, new top-down measures were implemented between 2001 and 2003 to bring North Korea on par with the rest of the world. Kim Yonho notes, "In preparing for the introduction of mobile telecommunications, North Korea made a considerable investment in a fiber-optic network to connect all cities and counties throughout the nation in the 1990s, even during the 'Arduous March' period, in part with the help of UNDP [United Nations Development Programme] and investment by Loxley. By 2002, North Korea had established a backbone fiber-optic network for the entire nation, installed digital transmission equipment in all provinces, and completed the construction of infrastructure facilities for digital mobile communications."[29] Such changes enabled a limited number of North Koreans who could afford it—party elites, cadres, and those engaged in market activities—to purchase expensive cell phone units for the purpose of gathering information in real time. Before the widespread use of cell phones, traders would bring in goods from China and sell them at an incrementally higher price as they traveled farther from the border into inland towns. The advent of cell phones changed that business model as market prices could be checked in real time to even out price differences. Millennials of all backgrounds—from rich to poor, from high-achieving college students in Pyongyang to ordinary students in small towns—were affected in varying measure by the introduction of digital communication into North Korea.

Cell Phones as Economic Capital

The state directive to introduce mobile telecommunication had a twin policy: government-sponsored marketization. In 2002, measures were issued to ease control over market activity and thus improve the struggling economy. Known as the 7.1 Measures, these allowed provincial governments, enterprises, and factories limited autonomy to generate profit. The financially struggling North Korean regime no longer had the ability to support work units via central food rationing and other forms of subsidy, leaving every work unit in North Korea, including overseas embassies, to fend for itself financially. Previously branded as a capitalist pursuit, market activities started to encroach upon private households as a result. The country saw a rapid proliferation of marketplaces in the early 2000s.

As a crucial device to enable effective market activities, mobile-telecommunication infrastructure was often introduced in the form of a joint venture with a foreign country willing to take risks in an untested market. "Thai firm Loxley Pacific launched commercial mobile services in Pyongyang and the Rajin-Sonbong (now referred to as Rason) Special Economic Zone (SEZ) near the Chinese border. Northeast Asia Telephone and Telecommunications (NEAT&T), a joint venture between Loxley Pacific and [North] Korea Post and Telecommunications Corporation, provided 2G GSM service under a 30-year license. NEAT&T expanded its coverage to several major cities, including Nampo and Kaesong, provincial capitals, and major highways between Pyongyang and Hyangsan, Pyongyang and Kaesong, and

Wonsan and Hamheung, with the estimated number of subscribers reaching around 20,000 at the end of 2003."[30] North Korea expert Yi Yeong-jong notes that "there is a direct correlation between the growth rate of cell phone registration and the growth rate of marketplaces in North Korea."[31] Both create potential gain and danger for the state, but for the vast majority of North Koreans, they represent an irreversible course forward into the twenty-first century.

But expedited investment in the mobile network came to an abrupt halt, again in a top-down manner, when the North Korean regime started banning cell phones and confiscating devices from ordinary users in 2004. The ban came following a massive explosion at Ryongcheon Station in North Pyeongan Province in April 2004 that "allegedly targeted a train carrying Kim Jong Il and was triggered by a remote-controlled wireless handset."[32] Although Kim Jong Il emerged unharmed, the explosion was so powerful that a "nearby elementary school building was damaged" and over a thousand people died,[33] prompting the North Korean government to seek aid from the international community. An anonymous interviewee (female in her midthirties, born in Cheongjin, who left North Korea in 2019 and came to South Korea in 2020) recalls how she heard about this incident while living in North Korea. She came across official news reports that an accidental explosion had taken place in a cargo train transporting fertilizer. But the rumors were circulating about the attempts to kill Kim Jong Il, to which people responded, "How dare they claim the life of the Supreme Leader!'"[34] We can only imagine how deeply the incident shook up the North Korean leadership and incited paranoia when it realized the danger that the new digital technology could bring to the existing autocratic order. The four-year ban, which lasted until 2008, must have provided the regime time to think of ways to harness subversive usage and even to use cell phones to its advantage. Just like the government had to accept the irreversible trend of marketization and learn how to profit from it by levying taxes on profit-generating activities, it had to reflect upon how to benefit from the proliferating phone network. Its response was to turn it into a powerful form of surveillance, creating another harrowing example of digital authoritarianism.

After the 2004 Ryongcheon incident, cell phone usage was severely curbed, and a high bar was set for obtaining permits to use cell phones.

Gim Ju-seong (male born in 1963 in Japan who went to North Korea in 1979 and left the country in 2008) explains how laborious it was to obtain and use cell phones during this time:

> In order to apply for the permit to use a cell phone, one had to either be a party cadre or receive permission from the cadres. Outside the party, chances for a permit application were limited to those in leadership positions in an enterprise. If a permit was issued, they expected to purchase a handphone set at the staggering price of $1,000. Telephone towers were erected in Pyongyang and other major cities, so one could use cell phones in cities without major problems. But once moved away from the urban areas, cell phones became useless. Another major inconvenience was that SIM cards were sold with limited minutes, so as soon as the minutes were used up, users had to find ways to charge them in Pyongyang. They had to ask friends who had planned trips to Pyongyang, where their SIM cards could be recharged with more minutes. During the time SIM cards were taken away, one could not use cell phones.[35]

Despite the extensive level of bureaucracy and great inconvenience, cell phone service resumed for the general public in December 2008. That year, Kim Jong Il sent another order to "digitize" North Korea, very similar to the South Korean Digital Korea campaign.[36] But why would he have allowed the popular use of cell phones after having survived a nearly fatal attack triggered by one? I concur with Yi Yeong-jong, who sees the financial windfall from high registration fees as the main motivation for the dollar-strapped North Korean government. Yi notes, "It costs one hundred dollars to register used cell phones, whereas registering the latest smartphones can cost up to $1,000. Only US dollars are accepted for the registration fee, with one cell phone costing 300 USD on average. If you consider that there are 5.8 million registered cell phones [as of 2018], the registration fee would have generated approximately 1.7 billion US dollars for the North Korean regime"[37]—by no means a small amount for a struggling country facing prolonged international sanctions.

Once the North Korean regime decided to switch back to propagating cell phone networks throughout the country, it introduced a joint venture to handle infrastructure investment: "The 3G service was launched under the name of Koryolink by CHEO Technology, a joint venture between the

Egyptian telecommunication firm Orascom (75%) and Korea Post and Tele-communications Corporations (25%)."[38] According to Ellen Nakashima, Gerry Shih, and John Hudson, "Before 2008, North Korea struggled to find multinational companies willing to build a 3G network in such a risky business environment. That ended with the creation of the wireless provider Koryolink, which emerged from a discreet visit in 2006 by Kim's father, Kim Jong Il, to Huawei's headquarters in Shenzhen, China."[39] Alexandre Mansourov, an adjunct professor at Georgetown University's School of Foreign Service, claims that "this was the time that confirmed not only the top leadership's interest in dealing with Huawei but pretty much revealed a choice of Huawei as the primary supplier of technology."[40] The top-down initiative involved a multinational partnership that evidences North Korea's attempts to overcome limits imposed by international sanctions to build a digital eco-system that could bypass the usual business networks of the Western world.

With a better telecommunication infrastructure and services to handle a 3G network, phones themselves evolved in their design and function. In North Korea smartphones started to appear at the end of the 2000s and were given official names, such as *ji-neung-hyeong son-jeon-hwa-gi* (literally meaning "smart hand phone") or, in colloquial North Korean, *ta-chi-pon* (touch phone). The shift to smartphones represented a significant turn for the society since the video-processing feature created increasing demand for visual content that the North Korean official media could not supply. Kim Yonho notes, "While previous networks only provided voice service, the Koryolink network supports a variety of services. In the second quarter of 2009, Koryolink introduced free Short Message Service (SMS) for the first time. In the third quarter of 2010, it launched video calling service to high demand, especially from the youth segment."[41] There was such significant demand that "Orascom reported that video calling usage quadrupled in June 2011, after it was made available to the entire subscriber base, and that the usage was still accelerating since this move was conducted."[42] While video calling was a service officially provided by the state, North Korean cell phone users started using the video function in an unsanctioned manner to consume foreign visual media.

Expanding functions of cell phones inevitably changed the media platforms through which ordinary North Koreans consumed forbidden materials.

Up until 2010, "DVDs were the most popular form of outside media" since tablets were not introduced in mass quantity and cell phones were being primarily used for voice communication.[43] In Pyongyang, however, the introduction of USBs might have been earlier, as an anonymous interviewee (female in her thirties, born in Pyongyang, who left North Korea in 2008 and settled in South Korea in 2013) suggests: "Around 2007–8, when I was about to leave North Korea for China, I heard that USB drives were in wide circulation."[44]

Li Ung-gil's story presents the lived experience of this shift. Born in 1981 and raised in Cheongjin, he was first exposed to Korean dramas in 1998 when he visited his aunt's house in Yanji, China.[45] He soon started selling a large quantity of VCDs in Hoeryeong since he found it to be a quite profitable, albeit risky, business. He crossed the North Korea–China border over four hundred times, every time carrying a backpack that could accommodate 350 VCDs. Each VCD cost him "0.5 Chinese yuan [roughly 250 North Korean won around 2010] but sold for 500 North Korean won in the Hoeryeong marketplace."[46] But due to the diversifying functions of cell phones, the dominant gadget to consume foreign media shifted rapidly from VCD/DVDs to phones. According to an anonymous interviewee who formerly resided in Pyongyang (male in his late forties, born in Pyongyang, who left North Korea in 2010), "[The kind of media people can get has] definitely changed. With one USB stick, at least three people can watch [South] Korean movies. These days, when merchants from China send VCR/DVD players, they have an additional USB function."[47] O Cheong-seong (male born in Gaesong in the early 1990s who left North Korea in 2017), who crossed the demilitarized zone (DMZ) into South Korea on November 13, 2017, recollects, "In the army in my early twenties, I became first exposed to Korean movies. Watched *Dream High* on USB at a friend's house. USB drive was the main form."[48] At first, USBs were plugged into VCR/DVD players, but with the evolving cell phone models and functions, USB drives and SD cards could be connected to phones. The consumption rate of foreign media increased exponentially as a result.

Further testimony accounts for how the portability of USB and SD aided the further spread of foreign-media consumption. Go Na-hae (female born in Dancheon, South Hamgyeong Province, who left North Korea in 2018 and came to South Korea in 2019), for instance, told me that women could hide their USB drives in their bras.[49] The North Korean government responded by upping their game. Na Min-hui (female born in 1991 in Pyongyang who left North Korea in 2014 and came to South Korea in 2015) recollects, "In 2013, the North Korean authorities took cell phones away from Pyongyang residents. They disabled the T-card [SD card] reader and returned them to the owners. [As a result of this procedure,] red signals on your phone changed into green signals. After this, when a surveillance team asked to see your cell phone and it showed the green light, you were okay to go. If the signal was red, then your phone was confiscated. Newly issued cell phones do not have T-card readers."[50] This presents typical dynamics through which the level of surveillance and circumvention escalates, and each party gets smarter with their tactics.

In addition to video-call service, in January 2011, Koryolink offered multimedia messaging service (MMS) to its subscribers. Orascom reported that "the service was received positively by subscribers and continued to exhibit a healthy growth rate."[51] At this time, Koryolink "also provided voicemail, Wireless Application Protocol (WAP), and High Speed Packet Access (HSPA)."[52] These new features no doubt aided market activities, and the government implemented policies to expedite the symbiotic growth of cell phone services and marketization. In 2012, the North Korean government announced the 628 Measure, which consolidated the idea that the state would officially benefit from private profit generated from market activities by taxing 70 percent of the profit, leaving 30 percent to enterprises, factories, and farms. Whereas those with varying degrees of power (from high-ranking party members to petty police) could all profit from market activities by taking bribes from merchants, the 628 Measure was an official declaration that the North Korean state would profit openly from private-market activities. Two years later, in 2014, the state announced the 530 Measure, this time allowing limited freedom for enterprises to manage their business autonomously by ordering a self-supporting account system to be implemented.[53]

The government also kept developing better network services, cell phone gadgets, and other media technologies—not only to facilitate marketization but also to better manage and surveil phone users. North Korea's information and communication technology was developed by the Joseon Computer Center, which also had oversight over the development of operating systems and information security. The Pyongyang Information Center oversaw the development of embedded software and virtual-reality (VR) technology, while the Central Science and Technology Information and Communication Agency conducted surveillance and gathered information. The state took every measure to prevent unwanted spillage of information to ordinary citizens. Due to the increasing number of cell phone users, in addition to Koryolink, two additional service providers—Gangseong Net and Byeol[54]—were introduced, but a very clear system was implemented within these networks to segregate users into three groups: foreigners, common North Koreans, and North Koreans in leadership positions.[55] Yi Yeong-jong notes that this was to "prevent accidental cell phone communications between North Koreans and foreigners."[56] But such safety measures seem circumvented by savvy citizens with means to pay for their transgression. According to an anonymous interviewee (male in his early thirties, born in Pyongyang, who left North Korea in 2017 and soon arrived in South Korea): "I asked a college friend to install two operating systems [on my cell phone]: one, the North Korean official system and the other, a South Korean operating system."[57] Although the installment of a South Korean operating system does not necessarily translate into making phone calls to Korea, it serves as proof of how top-down measures to silo North Korean citizens away from foreign networks and operating systems are constantly met with challenges.

The internet as we know it (i.e., with access to the World Wide Web) is available only to foreign diplomatic missions, foreign companies, tourist hotels catering to foreigners, and some universities and research institutes. Known as Baekbo, its operation depends on two lines: the optical cable between Pyongyang and Dandung, operated by China Telecom, and the optical cable between Pyongyang and Vladivostok, managed by the Russian TransTelecom. For ordinary North Koreans, only the intranet is allowed. Known in North Korea as Gwangmyeong *mang* (Gwangmyeong network) or *gukga mang* (state network), it is heavily managed by the state. For instance, for North Koreans to use email via the intranet, they have to submit an application to their regional post office. If an account is granted, users are given email addresses and passwords by the state, which allows the state complete access to the email contents. Although the state promoted Gwangmyeong *mang* as "a convenient means to access information remotely,"[58] by creating many hurdles for the use of email and computers at large, it hoped to curb unauthorized computer activities, such as exchanging forbidden-media content.

Subverting the State Media

While keeping domestic computer users strictly at bay, the North Korean state started to mobilize YouTube channels on the internet for its image making, producing content intended to be shown to worldwide internet users. In 2018, the state started a YouTube channel, Echo of Truth, and uploaded content that features a positive outlook on daily life in Pyongyang, bringing viewers to department stores, amusement parks, and restaurants. In January 2020, the channel started to use English narration rather than subtitles, making its content more easily accessible to internet users worldwide. The channel became a unique mouthpiece to tout the country's successful containment of the COVID-19 outbreak. On April 12, 2020, the channel's English-speaking MC, Euna (figure 1.5), proclaimed: "We have become one of the very few COVID-free countries worldwide, people sure start to live an active life with more confidence and more vitality"

FIGURE 1.5. North Korean YouTube host Euna presents Pyongyang residents' vibrant lives and updates viewers on the country's success in combating COVID-19. Source: YouTube. Fair use.

FIGURE 1.6. Euna takes viewers inside a Pyongyang supermarket to show the thriving local economy. Source: YouTube. Fair use.

(see figure 1.6). She continued, "'So what's happening in DPRK this spring? How people are [*sic*] doing?,' one might wonder from outside."[59] A follow-up episode, "I Missed You, My School," uploaded on June 4, 2020, reported the reopening of schools after a six-month shutdown due to COVID, featuring mask-wearing children happy to be reunited with their friends.[60] Other episodes feature Pyongyang subway stations and the famous noodle shop Okryugwan. These footages will not be seen by the North Koreans themselves, whose lives are the main feature of the coverage, as the internet is virtually unknown in the country.

However, the channel had a short life span. In December 2020, YouTube's parent company, Google, deleted the Echo of Truth channel. When the channel came back with a similar name, Echo of Truth Returns, it too was shot down by Google. Euna, in response, provided a calm rebuttal: "The reason I started this work is to correct the delusive information regarding my homeland. I don't remember myself blaming anyone or spreading false news in my videos."[61] According to South Korean channel Seoul Broadcasting System's interview with Google, the YouTube parent company revealed that the channel is most likely run by the North Korean Propaganda Bureau, which is on the United Nations sanctions list.[62]

In a more devious instance of relying on YouTube to serve the state's interest, North Korea has reportedly been using the popular online platform for its espionage operations. According to South Korean news agency YTN,

North Korea had traditionally used radio to transmit coded messages to their spies, but August 2020 marked the first time they used YouTube for the purpose.[63] This, of course, is possible since North Korean agents can freely access YouTube when carrying out operations outside the country.

Although the North Korean state rigidly separates the internet and intranet, there are many instances where the state's wishful thinking was met by creative counterexamples. Before the use of cell phones started to grow in 2008, desktop and laptop computers provided North Koreans with a major means of entertainment. Not only were VCDs and DVDs with foreign media plugged into desktops and laptops, foreign video games also were widely enjoyed on computers during the first decade of the new millennium. After the North Korean government issued the 7.1 Measure in 2002, urging every work unit to be financially independent, Gim Ju-seong, who worked as a Korean-Japanese translator at the National Science Academy, opened a lucrative business using government computers. He ran a game room in his National Science Academy office, where old versions of Japanese video games, such as *Super Mario*, attracted nearby schoolkids en masse.

> Since the National Science Academy was regarded as an important government institution that treated sensitive information, there were armed units guarding the main entrance. In order to circumvent the main entrance, we drilled a hole in the side wall to allow entrance to our office. Back then, North Korea was importing many secondhand computers from mainland China, Taiwan, and Singapore, and computer science majors from Kim Chaek University and other technological universities were given the task of erasing programs in the hardware. Many students copied foreign films and video games [from the old computers], which soon started to circulate in North Korea. Our business was so popular that on a good day, the office earned $200–$300 [equivalent to 500,000–750,000 North Korean won]. We charged 200 North Korean won per game, which was expensive for North Korean kids when one kilogram of rice cost between 1,000 and 2,000 won. But charging one hundred won could potentially cause problems since the bill featured Kim Il Sung's face. As game-room business boomed, many students skipped school, and teachers who struggled to keep students at school started to petition the party to ban game rooms. Eventually all game rooms in North Korea were shut down as a result.[64]

Closely resonating with Gim's story is that of Choe Seong-guk (male born in the early 1980s in Pyongyang who came to South Korea in 2010), who worked as an animator in North Korea. He made illegal sales of the South Korean films and TV dramas he found in the imported secondhand computers from China, for which he was expelled from Pyongyang.[65] These episodes illustrate the ironic encounter of three factors—official government policy to digitize the nation, people's twisted use of that policy, and the profit-generating market activity that sprang from it—most palpably capturing the convoluted realities of millennial North Korea under technological transformation.

To a limited extent, television sets likewise played the double role of official government mouthpiece and medium for consuming subversive materials. Most TV sets widely used in North Korea are CRT TV, and with frequent power outages, they do not capture signals immediately even if the power is back. It was "during those three to five minutes when CRT TVs were getting ready to capture North Korean TV signals, South Korean TV programs were captured on North Korean TV if viewers were close to the inter-Korean border region."[66] North Korean cities adjacent to the Chinese border were able to receive signals from the Yanbian-based Chinese TV stations, which broadcast South Korean TV dramas. Li Seon-ju (female in her late twenties, born in Hoeryeong, who left North Korea in 2004), for example, recalls how residents of her hometown of Hoeryeong were able to watch the 2003 South Korean drama *Stairway to Heaven* (Cheonguk-ui gyedan) on their TV set without purchasing the version recorded on a USB drive.[67]

Even some of the seaside towns on the east coast were able to regularly receive South Korean broadcast signals. According to an anonymous interviewee (male in his early thirties, neither from Pyongyang nor from a border region, who left North Korea in 2014), when he lived in a high school dormitory in 2006, he was able to receive a signal from the KBS Gangreung station.

There was one TV in the communal room at our dormitory. Since I was an upperclassman, I was able to move that TV into my room, which I shared with three other roommates. Students usually go home on the weekends, but one weekend, I remained in the dorm and watched TV. Suddenly, I saw a brand new channel I had never seen before. They spoke in a different Korean accent that I was not able to understand. But the signal was so bad that when the pictures appeared onscreen, the sound was mute, and then when the sound came through, the picture would go out. When my roommates returned home, I told them about it, but they were reluctant to watch it out of fear. Eventually, they ended up joining me out of curiosity, and we collaborated in moving the antenna around until we were able to capture a good signal. We watched so many programs—dramas, commercials, news, and weather forecasts—that opened our eyes up to a new world.[68]

Similar accounts are provided by an anonymous interviewee (female in her midthirties, born in Yanggang Province, who left North Korea in 2018 and came to South Korea in 2019): "I lived quite close to Changbai [Korean Autonomous County in China], so we could catch broadcasting signals in our hometown. This is how I got to watch bits of Korean dramas like *Stairway to Heaven*, *Boys over Flowers* (Kkotboda namja), and *Lovers in Paris* (Pari-ui yeonin). They were so interesting, and I tried so hard to write down the lyrics of the songs they played in these shows."[69] No matter how astringent the government prohibition, it cannot stop the terrestrial air signals that cross one of the most heavily guarded borders.

While a closer analysis of the implications of watching these South Korean programs will be provided in the following chapters, these stories illustrate how media receptacles in North Korea could play a subversive role regardless of how strictly the state wishes to impose control.

Returning to the official side of the story, along with the developing wireless intranet, televisions also went through makeovers in the new millennium. In 2016, North Korea developed an IPTV named Manbang, which became available in Pyongyang and Sinuiju. Although limited to these urban areas, Manbang made it possible for viewers to select from thirty-one TV programs and watch reruns of popular content. Prior to Manbang, there were only five broadcasting channels available between 3 p.m. and 11 p.m. in North Korea.

I have yet to encounter instances where Manbang IPTV has been able to decentralize the state's ideological indoctrination carried out on a unidirectional broadcasting model. In the meantime, what seems to be an irreversible move forward is the state's attempts to make its official media more attractive for viewers by appealing to young and modern sensibilities. In 2015, Korean Central Television (Joseon Joongang TV) attempted to launch an HDTV system and introduced young anchors garbed in dapper outfits to present a newer image of North Korean broadcasting. The latest North Korean news from Korean Central Television features new technologies such as drones and 3D charts as major tools in a visual makeover. Despite the efforts, there is a shortage of programs suitable for HDTV format due to the lack of funding. "That's why they convert old documentary films and show them on HDTV for the most part," notes Yi Yeong-jong.[70] One can understand North Korean media users' thirst for new software to fit the new hardware, which partly explains their growing desire to consume South Korean content.

It is against this broader backdrop that cell phones in North Korea developed as a major means of entertainment to replace televisions and computers as media platforms. Cell phones' physical compactness and audio-visual processing capabilities made them the central portal to meet people's demand for free-flowing information and better-made media content beyond official North Korean propaganda. As cell phone models developed, even the limitations of the heavily surveilled intranet did not stand in the way, as foreign media nevertheless circulated offline. Thus, North Korean cell phones present a fascinating hybrid space where an electronic gadget meant to process online data is able to secure data from offline space through traditional means of person-to-person contact based on trust and secrecy.

Cell phones as physical gadgets have gone through notable changes in the new millennium. In the mid-2000s, Nokia phones were the predominant models.[71] Then came old Chinese handsets manufactured by ZTE and Huawei. But the state is hoping to reverse this trend of using foreign models. According to Kim Yonho, in April 2010, North Korea commenced the production of hand phone terminals as domestic demand for wireless communication rose quickly. "Although the regime intended to import and assemble parts from overseas (presumably from China), handset production was supposed to eventually become an entirely domestic operation. Within seven months, the Pyongyang-based Checom Technology Joint Venture Company started to produce hundreds of high-performance cellular phones each day, while also trying to customize their operating systems to satisfy local needs."[72] Even though the regime's desire to produce domestic terminals was high, the vast majority of the cell phones used around 2010 were still manufactured by Huawei, whose logos were replaced with North Korean ones.

In October 2011, cell phone model 1913 was introduced, with limited service provided only to the city where the phone was registered. This model supported only voice and texting capabilities, not video recording or data-transfer functions. Internal memory storage was limited to only ten to twenty megabytes without the blocked SD card slot. *Radio Free Asia* deduced "that the authorities decided to control information flow by allowing only basic functions on the phone."[73]

A major change in the function of cell phones took place around 2013, when the first smartphone, named Arirang, was introduced. Gang Jin-gyu notes that North Korea manufactured early models of Arirang with terminals from China in 2013, but after 2015, North Korea–made terminals were used.[74] On March 6, 2019, North Korea produced the latest model, Pyongyang 2423, with an "increased number of preloaded entertainment applications" and advanced features such as cordless charging, Bluetooth speakers, and a facial-recognition function using ultraviolet light in darkness.[75] The fancy model comes with a hefty cost of approximately 750 USD. Gang Jin-gyu notes how North Korean cell phone models are catching up rapidly with world standards: "In 2019, the difference in technology between South Korean smartphones and North Korean ones is not that big. The latter lags behind only one to two years."[76] As of 2019, there were some twenty brands in North Korea, with various designs and costs ranging from one hundred to 400 USD.[77] 2020 saw the release of the smartphone Jindalae, with voice and face recognition, fingerprint identification, and a mobile payment system uploaded. In 2022, a new model, Madusan, was released with four rear-facing cameras.[78]

Given that most North Koreans on average make less than fifty cents a month from their official workplace,[79] being able to afford a smartphone such as a Pyongyang 2423 comes with significant cachet. Smartphones are powerful symbols of owners' socioeconomic status and a marker of "conspicuous consumption,"[80] as Kim Yonho notes.

Prestige is another important driver for the popularity of cell phones among North Koreans. A man from Chongjin who defected in December 2012 said that cell phones had become so popular that a young man without a cell phone was not treated well and could not even find a girlfriend. "Considering the high prices of handsets, it is obvious that only those who 'regularly eat meat' can afford to buy one," he said. Even those without significant income are selling their assets or hard-earned crops to buy handsets to show off their own "wealth" or for their children who want to bond with their cell phone–using friends.[81]

Reiterating this point, Na Min-hui (female born in 1991 in Pyongyang who left North Korea in 2014 and came to South Korea in 2015) recalls how "some guys would just stick out their Arirang phones and pretend to make phone calls simply to show off their wealth when girls pass by."[82] Indeed, cell phones are objects of conspicuous consumption in North Korea, as another anonymous interviewee (male in his early thirties, born in Pyongyang, who left North Korea in 2017 and soon arrived in South Korea) attests: "I first used my cell phone in 2009, which my parents bought for me. It was mostly for showing off. I displayed it around my waist. There are many brokers in front of the cell phone stores, and they take care of everything. Laborers who cannot afford one will sell their rights for thirty US dollars. Starting in 2012, I started to carry three cell phones: one for business, another for talking to friends, and the third one for playing games."[83]

As can be gleaned from this interviewee, rapidly spreading cell phone usage called for an increased demand for cell phone sales and brokerage. Na further describes how a cell phone sales job is a desirable profession in North Korea: "I had a friend who was a phone salesperson. At age twenty-two, she was so well off, having multiple phones of the latest model in her bags and carrying bundles of money."[84] Choe Ju-yeon (female born in 1992 in Cheongjin who left North Korea in 2014), who worked as a cell phone broker in North Korea, provides a first-person account of how the profitable business of cell phone sales prospered under North Korea's unique system:

In the beginning, people could buy cell phones only from the government, but the sales took place strictly on designated dates, which created much inconvenience. This system created a pent-up demand, and during the interval, party leaders started to sell them under the table with a high profit margin. For example, if the official price of a phone was $200, then it could be sold for $300 underground. People would pay extra money since they could obtain phones right away as opposed to going through the proper government channel. If you go through a proper channel, it could take up to a whole month, starting with the application submission to the Department of Communication to waiting for the designated sales date. And even if you decide to wait for the department's review, your application could be denied if you don't have right connections, so people who either disliked waiting or did not have political ties bought their phones from individual sellers. Some people would pay extra to get good phone numbers that are easier to memorize. Especially those in business or party members would want easy numbers to memorize.[85]

Choe's interview ascertains the intense desire created around cell phones in North Korea, especially during the time of their initial introduction.

It is difficult to trace when various regions in North Korea first started using smartphones widely, but the general assumption is that great disparity existed in the way Arirang spread across North Korea. According to a former resident of Dancheon, South Hamgyeong Province, older models of flip phones were still in use by the vast majority of people in 2014.[86] Another anonymous interviewee (male in his thirties, neither from Pyongyang nor from a border region, who left North Korea in 2014), who owned a ZTE cell phone until 2014, recalls that in his town, only a limited number of people owned Arirang smartphones, and the screen was quite small, so Arirang wasn't seen as an optimal platform for media consumption.[87]

Around 2016, the number of smartphone users grew exponentially, and smartphones became popular graduation gifts; some even skipped meals to save money to buy them.[88] From the perspective of North Koreans, owning a smartphone is not just an act of conspicuous consumption but, more crucially, a marker of being a part of a broader world community; it is a statement about the owner's advanced worldview. Needless to say, this notion stems from the unsanctioned ways users adapt phones creatively rather than from the limited ways phones can be used officially in North Korea.

The officially sanctioned use of cell phones in North Korea is not limited to making domestic phone calls and sending messages but also includes the use of preloaded applications: Photoshop, video games, navigation programs, dictionaries, video chat, and the digital file containing the complete sayings of Kim Il Sung. In 2015, the state allowed the first commercial intranet and opened the first online shopping mall, called Okryu. Operated by the People's Service Bureau (Inmin bongsa chongguk), Okryu offers grocery, medical, and cosmetic products. Some restaurants also operate on Okryu, making it possible for customers to have a bowl of famous Okryu-gwan cold noodles delivered. The convenient service is made available only to a limited few in Pyongyang and Sinuiju; nonetheless, the widely circulated North Korean publication *Joseon nyeoseong* ran the short article "E-commerce" (Jeonja sangeop), which reads like a tutorial about the mechanisms of online commerce.[89] In the time of COVID-19, the state newspaper *Rodong sinmun* published on May 18, 2022, that in quarantine, it is advisable to maintain one's social relationships with others by exchanging text messages and phone calls.[90]

As versatile as the functions of cell phones are, the official ways they can be used are only scratching the surface, and the increasing use of foreign media via cell phones has made Kim Jong Un's regime quite nervous. Kim Yonho notes how, under the new leader, the suppression of cell phone usage has intensified: "One interesting finding is that cell phones function more as a personalized mobile entertainment device than a mobile communications device, especially among the youth. They usually carry their cell phones for taking photos and videos, watching videos, listening to music, and playing games. South Korean pop songs and dance videos transferrable from computers to handsets are particularly popular among young users. Cell phones have become an important part of the advanced media technologies that spread outside information to the youth. However, tightened censorship has intimidated people into refraining from enjoying foreign content."[91] The tightest possible control over who has access to the mass media has always been a serious concern for the North Korean leadership. For instance, individuals' access to printers has been restricted for fear that they might produce antistate materials in massive quantities, and it was Kim Jong Un's father who introduced 109 Gruppa to crack down on foreign-media consumption. Kim Jong Un tightened his grip even further: in 2013, he decided that individuals did not need the personal intranet, so it was prohibited, only to be allowed again in 2015. Modems with 56 Kbps were prohibited as well, only to be reallowed later. Under Kim Jong Un's rule, jamming of wireless signals and TV signals along the border intensified, and *noraebangs* (entertainment spaces where people can sing) were closed in 2018 to prevent the further spread of South Korean pop music. In December 2020, the North Korean government promulgated the Law against Reactionary Ideology and Culture (Bandong sasang munhwa baegyeok-beop) to tighten its grip on the spread of unsanctioned foreign media.

Most resettlers I personally interviewed resoundingly testified to how much more draconian the state crackdown on foreign media has become under Kim Jong Un's rule. Na Min-hui (female born in 1991 in Pyongyang who left North Korea in 2014 and came to South Korea in 2015), for instance, recounts a harrowing experience of being caught while watching South Korean media.

> I first encountered South Korean media via a wealthy friend whose parents traded with foreign countries. It's possible to talk about watching South Korean dramas with friends, but it's a completely different matter to share it with your friends, which requires trust. When I was nineteen, I copied South Korean songs to my friend. Unfortunately, she got caught and was sexually harassed by her captors. When I heard about this, I knew I was also in trouble and decided to commit suicide by swallowing a large number of sleeping pills. At that moment, I thought about my parents. I did not want to make them suffer because of me.[92]

Na's words show how the consequences of surveillance are so severe at times that they can cost one's life. Gang Na-ra (female born in 1997 in Cheongjin who left North Korea in 2014) vividly remembers how, in 2012, all the students from her high school were forced to witness a public execution of a man "whose crime was to circulate South Korean songs and dramas."[93] As widespread as the consumption of South Korean media might be, some distributors could meet deadly punishments like this if the regime decides to make an example out of them.

Na Min-hui (female born in 1991 in Pyongyang who left North Korea in 2014 and came to South Korea in 2015) further explains how the intensifying crackdown on foreign media stemmed from Kim Jong Un's need to win the hearts of the younger generation, who are less fearful and more willing to take risks to access foreign media:

> Just two degrees removed, one could get access to South Korea media [in Pyongyang]. In 2007–8, everyone who had money could bail themselves out of trouble [when caught]. But when I left North Korea in 2014, money was not a bulletproof solution. Kim Jong Un claimed that South Korean drama is like a weed, which has to be taken out by the root. He needs the younger generation's support. I think South Korean dramas circulate more broadly when the society is unstable and in flux. This is why Kim Jong Un constantly mobilizes people and makes them work harder so that they do not have time to think of anything else.[94]

With the introduction of video service on cell phones, the North Korean regime took a much more ironfisted approach to how the media circulated. Gim Ju-seong recollects that the regime was much stricter in censoring video content (MP4 files) than audio content (MP3 files), but this did not curb people's appetite for visual content from overseas: "My wife, who left North Korea in 2013, recollects that in marketplaces around that time, there were eight-gigabyte and sixteen-gigabyte USB drives loaded with forbidden content. Back then, people used to verify whether the flash drives were loaded with content by following the vendor to a secret place, usually the vendor's house, where the vendor would play the files on his or her computer. Nowadays, people can just connect the USB drive to their cell phones, verify the content, and make a purchase on the spot."[95]

Around 2012, USBs became the preferred portal to circulate visual media, since the content could be erased easily: "USB users noted their convenience not just because of their compactness, but because it was possible to delete sensitive materials without leaving a trace."[96] But with increasing creativity, smugglers used this to their benefit: they first uploaded dramas on USBs in China, erased them before crossing the border, and then restored the files using recovery software. Not to be outwitted, the North Korean state developed censorship programs to detect erased content if they capture

USBs on the border. To maintain full control of software circulating within North Korea, in 2021, the North Korean state promulgated the Software Protection Law, mandating that all software in use be registered with the authorities under the premise of "contributing to the development of software technology."[97] But the cat-and-mouse game will continue—the more intricate the surveillance, the smarter its circumvention; the more sophisticated the circumvention, the more ironfisted the surveillance.

Not only smugglers bring USBs and SD cards to North Korea for profit-driven sales. Refugees-cum-activists also create routes through which outside information can flow into North Korea. Kang Chol-hwan (Gang Cheol-hwan), who experienced North Korea's notorious Yoduk (Yodeok) Prison Camp as a child, settled in South Korea and became a fierce critic of the regime. His activist project includes stuffing auto tires with USBs loaded with South Korean media content and floating them along the river between North Korea and China (see figure 1.7). A similar approach is taken at the inter-Korean marine border, where Jeong Gwang-il (male born in the early

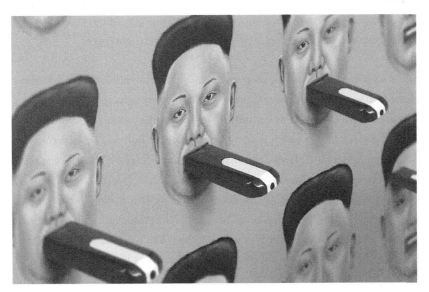

FIGURE 1.7. A promotional photo for the Human Rights Foundation's Flash Drives for Freedom campaign at the 2015 South by Southwest Festival. Used USB drives are collected and uploaded with outside information and sent to North Korea. Photo courtesy of Jeong Gwang-il. Reprinted with permission.

FIGURE 1.8. North Korean resettlers float plastic bottles filled with rice, money, and SD cards to North Korea, Seongmo-do, Ganghwa-gun, South Korea, May 2018. Photo courtesy of Jeong Gwang-il. Reprinted with permission.

1960s who worked in Pyongyang and left North Korea in 2003), who spent three years at Yoduk Prison Camp after being wrongly accused of being a spy, sends two-liter bottles containing 1.2 kilograms of rice, US dollar bills, and USB drives with files featuring South Korean political news across the ocean (see figure 1.8).[98] The selection of programs is carefully thought through before being uploaded and sent to North Korea. I met Jeong in Seoul, Korea, on December 14, 2019, for an interview about his operation: "When choosing what programs to send, I keep different viewerships in mind. What will women like to watch? What will young people like to watch? It's important that the drives we send become commercial products in the marketplace to be bought and sold so that they are more widely circulated. So I used to upload popular dramas along with documentaries about South Korea."[99] The work of sending foreign media to North Korea is done by others too. Students at the University of Halifax upload USB drives with documentation of their daily lives as college students and send them to North Korea in plastic bottles stuffed with rice.[100] Jeong Gwang-il notes that there is never any feedback as to whether the bottles reach their intended recipients. "The only proof we have of North Koreans collecting them is the reports from South Korean fishermen who witnessed how North Korean fishermen collected the bottles from the sea and loaded them into their boats. The USBs and SD cards smuggled across the North Korean–Chinese border yield much feedback, including the concrete request for certain items in the next order based on popularity. I even receive short video clips of viewers in North Korea actually watching the content I sent on the USB drive."[101]

Despite Jeong's concerns, there is proof that showcases how some of the content did indeed make it to the intended recipients in North Korea. According to Gang Li-hyeok (male born in 1987 in Bukcheon, Jagang Province, who left North Korea in 2013), he received quite a few South Korea–originated goods while serving in the North Korean army (2003–13) on the border island of Ganghwa—from leaflets, lighters, and keychains to food. But by the time he left the army in 2013, there were rice and USB drives containing files first showing South Korean news coverage of North Korea and then South Korean dramas. He recalls that those USB drives would eventually be smuggled out of the army base to the soldiers' families and be sold in the marketplaces.[102]

These little USBs can potentially become dangerous tools to dismantle the political establishment, but cell phones become even more subversive devices for counterregime activities when used to aid North Korean defectors. Cell phones serve as crucial means of survival, aiding would-be defectors from the planning stages to communicating with "brokers" (those who charge a fee to help North Koreans escape the country) when they reach China. Song Mi-na (female born in 1992 in Hyesan who left North Korea in 2013) was the first in her family to defect from North Korea. When she reached China, she sent cell phones to her family in North Korea to prepare them for their departure.[103] Likewise, Gang Na-ra (female born in 1997 in Cheongjin who left North Korea in 2014) received a phone call from a broker who connected Gang to her mother, already settled in South Korea, who convinced her to leave North Korea.[104] Like Yun Ji-o (female born in 1995 in Musan who left North Korea in 2015), who kept her cell phone all the way from North Korea to her final destination in South Korea and used it to communicate with her family already settled there, many defectors rely on cell phones to guide them along the treacherous route when constantly pursued by both the North Korean border patrol and the Chinese police.[105]

But if the intranet is all that is allowed in North Korea, how do North Koreans use cell phones to communicate with those outside the country? Those living in North Korea–China border towns, such as Hyesan and Musan, use smuggled Chinese phones to call China. These phones are used for a primitive but creative kind of international call known as a "cell phone kiss," devised by defectors to ensure that their remittance was well received by their family in North Korea. Remittances to North Korea cannot be delivered without the help of Chinese and North Korean brokers. These brokers, or "remittance helpers," play the role of telephone operators between the resettlers in South Korea and their families in North Korea. Kim Yonho lays out the mechanism in detail: "A call recipient in Haeju, South Hwanghae Province, 100 kilometers south of Pyongyang, goes to a broker in town, and using the Koryolink network, the broker calls a second broker in Hoeryong, North Hamgyong Province, a border city located opposite Jilin Province, China. As soon as the second broker receives the call, he calls the remitter in Seoul with his illegal Chinese cell phone. The second broker physically aligns the microphone of each phone with the earphone of the other phone so the remitter and the recipient can talk to each other and confirm the remittance."[106] Seo Jae-pyeong, secretary-general of the Committee for the Democratization of North Korea, notes that "when a real-time 'international' call is not possible, the recipient has the broker in town record a confirming voice message and send it to the second broker in the border area. Again, the second broker physically aligns the microphone of each phone with the earphone of the other cell phone, so the remitter can hear the recorded message."[107]

Without a reliable international banking system, for the remittance sender in South Korea, confirmation from the North Korean family is a necessary step to verify the receipt of funds. Due to dangers of surveillance and the high cost of cell phone minutes, family members cannot talk too much, but important information about South Korea flows into North Korea during that short period. Which information about South Korea would North Koreans trust more—that coming from the Kim Jong Un regime or that from their own family? It is difficult to know exactly how many calls are made this way, but with approximately 33,000 North Korean settlers in South Korea as of 2019 and North Korea's dependence on the remittance economy, it is reasonable to estimate that a considerable volume of phone calls takes place on a regular basis.

Due to the advantages of using Chinese cell phones for international call purposes, the majority of mobile phone holders in North Korea are in the China border region. Moreover, residents in the region use WeChat to communicate with South Koreans directly since "WeChat can evade North Korean government censorship."[108] Son Myung-hui (female in her midthirties, born in Dancheon, Hamgyeong Province, who left North Korea in 2007 and 2014) keeps in regular contact with her family on WeChat via brokers who record video messages from her family and then send them to Son when they reach the border city of Hyesan.[109] As recently as December 2019, a resettler family in South Korea used WeChat to communicate with their grandmother, who was left behind in a North Korean town near the border, to ensure that she had received money remitted to her. Although the original plan called for a confirmation via "live video chat," due to poor cell signals where the grandmother lived, an alternative model was used. Upon delivery of funds, the remittance broker showed the grandmother a recorded video message from her family in South Korea and had the grandmother record a video to be sent to them with a "confirmation of funds received." Then the broker sent out the video via WeChat as soon as he was able to get a better connection.[110]

Although cell phone towers erected by Chinese telecom companies in the borderland in effect facilitate North Korean residents' communication with China and beyond, Kretchun and Kim correctly note that the "use of illegal Chinese mobile phones is limited by geography, as callers must remain in range of Chinese mobile towers to receive service."[111] According to a male defector in his sixties who left North Korea in February 2010, there was no problem using Chinese cell phones in Onseong, Hamgyeong Province: "I used a Chinese mobile phone quite frequently. I brought one from China. There are mobile phones sold on the black market in North Korea, but I had a lot of friends who were Chinese guards. I just brought over a phone that had belonged to my friend. I would ask my friend to top up my phone, and I would be able to use it in North Korea."[112] Just like this man, those in the border region can use their Chinese cell phones to call abroad to check any international news—such as sanctions on and international aid shipments to North Korea—in order to predict the market prices based on supply and demand.

This is why I claim that the study of cell phones invites a paradigm shift in thinking about spatial hierarchy in North Korea, where Pyongyang has always occupied the center of political, cultural, and economic significance. With the introduction of cell phones, that order is being challenged as much smaller border cities, like Hyesan, Gilju, Onseong, and Musan, are able to offer more options for exchanging free-flowing information via international phone calls and faster access to goods from the outside world via China.

The study of cell phones also provides a unique framework to think about an emergent youth culture in North Korea, which will be fully investigated in the next chapter. But before concluding the overall history of media, marketization, and everyday experience in the new millennium, it is necessary to highlight the rising number of young cell phone users in North Korea. According to Kim Yonho, changes in cell phone registration rules greatly increased phone use among millennials:

> At the onset of cell phone use in North Korea, children and youngsters had to register under fake names because only the head of household and his spouse could legally use cell phones. As the demand for cell phones dramatically increased, even spouses were prohibited from registering for a while, due to handset shortages. However, according to defectors who regularly contact sources in North Korea, the authorities now [in 2013] allow the subscription of minors, although the registration procedure is more complicated. In these cases, the head of household needs to accompany the minor and submit additional paperwork to the CTMO [Communications Technology Management Office] for his/her application.[113]

As of 2019, it seems common for young adults and teens to own cell phones. O Cheong-seong (male born in Gae-song in 1992 who left North Korea in 2017) recollects, "When I joined the army at age seventeen, during the three months' training, many soldiers used cell phones to call their families. I also had a cell phone at that time."[114] Some users as young as thirteen or fourteen also have cell phones; according to Seo Hyeon-gyeong (female born in Hyesan in 2002 who left North Korea in 2016), there was a kid who had a cell phone in her middle school in the North Korea–China border city of Hyesan, although this is rather uncommon.[115] An anonymous resettler (male in his early twenties who left North Korea in 2016) notes that owning cell phones gives middle school students bragging rights, and students really have no need for cell phone usage other than playing games on them.[116] The decreasing age of phone users illustrates that North Korea is no longer alien to the rest of the world. Just as there are countless American students who are completely distracted by their cell phones in classrooms, plenty of North Korean students get engrossed in watching South Korean dramas and listening to South Korean music on their phones in the hidden corners of their schoolyard. The elders in both societies shake their heads with dismay, while those kids, in turn, feel frustrated by the outmoded generation.

TWO

The Rise of North Korean Millennials

In order to survive, one needs to think creatively.

—YUN JI-U (WHO LEFT NORTH KOREA IN 2015)[1]

Sitting across from me at a small coffee table one December afternoon in Seoul in 2019, an anonymous interviewee (female born in Hoeryeong in 1971 who left North Korea in 1998) speaks in an agitated voice: "At least when I was young [1980s] in North Korea, people received education. People were literate and could solve math problems. But nowadays, younger ones seem to be interested in money and money alone. They don't care about learning."[2] In a flustered voice, she shares a frank assessment of the North Korean millennial resettlers she encountered mostly in South Korea as pitifully lacking in education, having missed out on foundational opportunities to learn in their formative years. My interviewee is older than a typical millennial and has not experienced life in North Korea post-2000, but I lean closer to hear her out: "There was a famous song in North Korea, a film soundtrack that goes like 'gun in one hand and love in the other hand.' Nowadays, it will be more like 'money in one hand and love in the other hand.'"[3]

Talking to someone close to my age creates a feeling of rapport, although the circumstances of my coming of age in South Korea must have been quite different from this interviewee's experience in the North. Nevertheless, there is a common ground that connects us: we have a hard time understanding young people nowadays. I too often feel startled by their lack of broader interest as they cut corners in general education in pursuit of a narrow specialty to make themselves more competitive in the job market. The generational camaraderie can be quite comforting. But I soon remind myself that the natural affinities can also blind me from taking a more discerning look at North Korean millennials, who constitute extremely diverse groups. Are they really characterized by the pursuit of money alone, as my interviewee repeatedly claims?

Truth be told, marketplace activity has come to be of utmost significance to many millennials, so much so that even the best educated in North Korea choose to trade at a marketplace rather than pursue professional careers. Many of them shun government employment and careers in higher education—traditionally defined as lofty professions in North Korea—for more advantageous entrepreneurial opportunities. A former Pyongyang resident, Na Min-hui (female born in 1991 in Pyongyang who left North Korea in 2014 and came to South Korea in 2015), notes how "there were so many Kim Il Sung University graduates working in Pyongyang marketplaces. Even if they graduated from a prestigious university, making ends meet was hard."[4] Gim Ji-yeong (female in her early thirties, born in Hyesan, who left North Korea in 2012) herself was a graduate of Kim Il Sung University who decided to open her own restaurant in Pyongyang since "it was much more profitable than finding a regular job."[5] This tendency has been pervasive throughout North Korea and not just limited to Pyongyang. Choe Ju-yeon (female born in 1992 in Cheongjin who left North Korea in 2020) notes how "in Su-nam Marketplace, close to where I lived in Cheongjin, there were many Kim Il Sung University graduates, whose presence would invite murmurs from merchants: 'Oh my, what is the point of graduating from Kim Il Sung University if you are going to end up in a marketplace?'"[6] These elites-cum-entrepreneurs may present a curious case where prestigious educational background can no longer guarantee one's future in a society that still values education tremendously, but they should not be taken as representing the entire face of North Korean millennials.

This chapter traces the rise of North Korean millennials from all walks of life in relation to how the rules of the marketplace, supported by the fast-evolving media and technology, came to compete with the collective value system of the state. How did the millennials handle the clash between their individual needs for economic survival and prosperity and the collective ethos instilled by centralized state education? How did the harsh circumstances of the Arduous March, which dismantled the state education system to a large extent—especially for those who could not afford to go to school—teach them that individual survival was more important than the collective success of their fatherland? Finally, what roles do cell phones and other media technology play in navigating through these challenging processes?

In traversing the fine line between lingering ideological baggage from the past and being thrown into the brave new world to fend for themselves, many have cultivated a means to stay afloat, finding the right network to sustain their livelihood while mastering the evolving order of marketization and new media. Needless to say, this requires particular performative agility and resourcefulness on the part of millennials: walking through the uncertain space, they stage their dual allegiance to the rising materialism / new media / market network, on the one hand, and the Kim family worship / North Korean state / collectivism, on the other hand. Gravitating toward either extreme, economic or political, will lead to hardship and danger.

Following these multiple modes of existence leads us to the typical behavior of North Korean millennials, a glimpse of which surfaced in the previous chapter: weaving a flexible social network that requires tactful violation of socially imposed prohibitions, which in turn requires testing the limits just enough to evade punishment. While the state finds draconian surveillance indispensable for maintaining the fragile political regime, the resourceful millennials find it circumventable for the pursuit of alternative economic, social, and cultural interests. As a way to think through this process in theoretical terms, the chapter ends with an engagement with blockchain technologies and risk management that collectively speak to the complex needs of North Korean millennials to exist in multiple performative realities.

Unfolding the multilayered seam of such a performative strategy requires more than a simplistic investigation of what some scholars have referred to as a "hidden script"—a term to address North Korean citizens' surreptitious speech and behavior devised to elude state surveillance. As the resettlers' narratives featured in this chapter will illustrate, tracing the simultaneous performance of political loyalty for the state and practical pursuit of self-fulfillment demands an understanding of a particular kind of creativity that can only emerge under extremely repressive circumstances: a unique artistry of doublespeak, double vision, and double action, not entirely hidden, for the society to witness and some of its members to participate in. Pivotal to these considerations are a broader debate on the ownership of cultural content and the unique brand of creative networking around digital content particular to North Korean circumstances. In other words, this process is about rearticulating crucial features of today's ever-digitizing world crowded by the forces we refer to as networks, platforms, and virality.

Millennials from Many Walks of Life

"There are two '*dang*' in North Korea: Joseon Rodong*dang* [Korean Workers' Party] and *jangma*dang [marketplace]" is a popular saying in today's North Korea, which best captures the creativity involved in doublespeak and double action. In reference to the tension between maintaining political saliency and pursuing economic profit, Ralph Hassig and Kongdan Oh make a similar observation that "ordinary North Koreans have become 'socialists outside, capitalists inside' or 'daytime socialists and nighttime capitalists.'"[7] Such duality is a clear indication that the marketplace in North Korea can be neither reversed nor eradicated since the state itself has come to profit from its existence. While the state fills its coffers with tax revenue generated by market activities, the marketplace has come to support the livelihood of North Koreans in all aspects. As one anonymous interviewee (female born in 1994 in Musan who left North Korea in 2015) notes, "The only thing you cannot find in a North Korean market is a cat's horn" (in North Korean expression, a "cat's horn" refers to an object that simply does not exist in this world).[8]

The multifunctionality of the North Korean marketplace is as complex as the makeup of North Korean millennials, exposing their stratification viscerally, especially in terms of economic class and gender. As the flow of goods and information increased and flooded the marketplace, one can assume that some millennials—usually well-to-do ones—learned ways to express their individual desires for material goods and multidimensional information. At the same time, for less fortunate ones, the marketplace became another arena of struggle for survival, where they cannot apply the conventional rules instilled by the state. A paradoxical field where the millennial generation's profit-seeking market activities purportedly contradict the socialist state economy, the marketplace in the new millennium presents a battleground where a full-on collision between individuals' desire to choose a better option and many forms of state oppression unfolded.

A case in point, Gang Na-ra (female born in 1997 in Cheongjin who left North Korea in 2014) notes that one of the primary reasons for her defection to South Korea was to exercise freedom of choice, especially freedom to express herself through her body: "There is no freedom of hairstyle in North Korea. If you dye your hair brown, the Youth League [Cheongnyeon dong-maeng] will immediately catch you and force you to dye it black. I defected since I wanted to dress freely and travel freely."[9] Li Eun-hui (who was born in the 1990s in Kim Jong-suk Province and left North Korea in 2015) provides a similar account: "There was a strong regulation on what people could wear. Earrings could not be longer than two centimeters, and only married women were allowed to wear earrings. The Youth League would immediately crack down on any ostentatious clothing. My aunt used to smuggle clothing from China and there was one T-shirt with a photo of a young woman with wild disheveled hair. It looked very cool, so I wore it one day but was caught immediately and asked to take it off."[10]

These stories suggest how the appearance of foreign goods in marketplaces (hair dye, earrings, and clothing) prompted some North Korean millennials to seek free bodily expression, which nurtures the nascent desire for new information and a new perspective in order to see the world beyond the strictly guarded borders. An anonymous interviewee (male in his early thirties, neither from Pyongyang nor from a border town, who left North Korea in 2014) claims that his wish to receive a good education was what prompted him to escape to South Korea: "When in the North, I was able to secretly watch KBS TV station. What surprised me was their meticulous information sharing of traffic updates. When the weatherman announced that there would be traffic delays due to heavy snow, I was surprised to find out how such things can be regarded as news to them. In North Korea, it is common for trains to be delayed by a couple of days. So when I heard of such announcements about the traffic delays, I started to think about the social infrastructure in South Korea and how well established it must be."[11]

These narratives highlighting an active search for better ways of life are, however, counterpoised by less vociferous stories of the millennials who had no choice but to leave their homeland. North Korean millennials as a group are much more complex and fragmented than is revealed on the façade, and there is no consistent correlation between the exposure to foreign media and the increased motivation for defection. A resettler by the nickname Sunny (who was born in Pan-gyo, Gangwon Province, in 1996, grew up in Hoeryeong, and left North Korea in 2007) lived through harsh economic conditions in North Korea, selling corn and small firewood at a local marketplace to survive since she was seven years old. Although her family was impoverished, she had a chance to watch a popular South Korean drama, *Full House* (2004), while in the North. Although, it was not the glimpse of the outside world that motivated her to leave North Korea but rather her need to stay with her mother, who had left the country for China in an arranged marriage.[12]

Jo Ye-na's (female born in 1993 in Yanggang Province who left North Korea in 2012) story might shed light on what would be left of North Korean millennials without market entrepreneurship and the pursuit of individual interests. Since middle school, Jo carried the devastating brunt of economic hardship. She had to raise her younger sister in place of her mother, who spent all day at a marketplace to support the family. Economic hardship made her leave North Korea for China to make money and remit it to her family (2012–16). She kept sending money to her family even after arriving in South Korea in 2016.[13] Had it been possible for her to sustain her livelihood in North Korea, would she have left her country of birth? Had it not been for the forced withdrawal from normal life as a student, would she have chosen to be separated from her own family?

Involuntary border crossers are often young children who do not have a say in their parents' decision to leave North Korea, but in some extreme instances, even adults become mired in involuntarily defection. Bak Na-ri (who was born in Hoeryeong in 1990 and left North Korea in 2015) was working in the city of Cheongjin when, one evening, she suddenly received a phone call from her mother in Hoeryeong to come and join her immediately. Not knowing her mother's secret plan to evacuate the family from North Korea the following day, she left everything behind in Cheongjin, including her house, and joined her family in Hoeryeong. Only then did she discover the plan to defect.[14]

Bak Yeong-chan's (male in his twenties, place of birth unknown, who left North Korea in the late 2010s) story presents a rare case where an adult crossed the border unbeknownst to himself. While in North Korea, Bak was caught watching a South Korean drama and was sent to the notorious Jeongori Correctional Facility (*gyo-hwa-so*) in Hoeryeong. Although he was released after two years, Bak's father realized that Bak no longer had a viable future in North Korea due to this damaging criminal record. Desperately hoping that Bak would have a chance to receive a college education, his father decided to have the whole family defect without telling him of this life-changing plan. His father drugged him with sleeping pills and had other family members carry him into China. Bak woke up in China only to discover that he had crossed the line of no return. He eventually became separated from the rest of his family when they dispersed in an attempt to escape a crackdown by the Chinese police. He came to South Korea in 2016 alone, still bemoaning the involuntary separation from the rest of his family.[15]

Sometimes, involuntary border crossing is an immediate consequence of illicit-media consumption, which is strictly prohibited by the North Korean regime. Take, for example, an anonymous interviewee (male in his early thirties, born in Pyongyang, who left North Korea in 2017 and soon arrived in South Korea), who used to own a profitable billiard-room rental business in Pyongyang. He did not have any reason to leave behind his comfortable life but was forced to flee when authorities descended upon him:

I've been watching South Korean dramas on a computer since 2004 and had an enormous archive of South Korean dramas on my notebook. Then, a close acquaintance ratted me out to the authorities, and I was arrested by the police in 2016. When they caught me, they said they had never arrested someone with so many forbidden files in the past three years. I was taken to the police station at 2 a.m. and told that I would be handed over to the State Security Department [Bowuibu] at 7 a.m. It was a critical moment, which could decide life or death for me. I persuaded one guard to take me to my house with the promise of bribing him. When we went to my home, I gave him all the cash I had in the house and ran for my life when we came out to the dark street.[16]

The interviewee adds how other defectors get quite upset when they hear about his privileged life in North Korea and for misrepresenting the hardship others had to endure. As these accounts show, the North Korean millennial experience is multifaceted. North Koreans themselves acknowledge this and also see themselves as a discursive group divided by class, gender, education level, and place of origin.

While this chapter intends to fully acknowledge the stratification among millennials as diversifying microgenerations, when it comes to patterns of media use, one thing resonates strongly: millennials tend to use media in a more creative manner. Compared to other age groups, North Korean millennials generally are a more media-savvy and change-friendly demographic group, which makes them particularly susceptible to exposure to foreign media. According to Kim Yonho, who surveyed how North Koreans use their cell phones across the age group, "The defectors in their 40s and 50s that I interviewed tended to limit their cell phone use to voice calls and text messages. In contrast, defectors in their 20s said most youths tend to fully utilize the built-in functions that do not require extra charges. They carry their cell phones for show as well as for taking photos and videos, watching videos, listening to music, and playing games. They are even finding creative ways to use this new technology."[17] These accounts underline McCracken's observation on the cell phone's ability to open "an enormous world of experience."[18] For many North Korean millennials, they are a symbol of creativity and conspicuous consumption, serving as central props for performing their generational characteristics.

Since millennials and the younger generation tend to care more about the status claims they make by using cell phones in a recreational manner, they are more prone to be exposed to foreign media, including South Korean dramas, than older generations. Watching the programs does not remain an act of one-directional influence but becomes an act involving multidirectional networks bringing about the performance of social influence and change of cultural capital. As anthropologist Sandra Fahy notes of North Korean millennials, "Today's digital youth are learning from each other, improving their skills at selling and communicating, and understand the lure of capitalist desire, and how to create it in the other."[19] The meaning of "network," in this case, is not the online connectivity in our society but the intangible operations of the human network emerging around the creative dissemination and consumption of foreign media. No matter how subtle, these operations nevertheless reverberate resiliently in the lives of millennials via tangible offline spaces they build for recognition that is not entirely hidden.

Cryptolect, Antibehavior, and Playing with Forbidden Media

An equally important factor in forming social networks among North Korean millennials is the varying degrees of access to computer and digital technology. Park Eunhee (female in her twenties, born in Wonsan, who left North Korea in 2012), for instance, was surprised to discover how her friends freely used new terms such as "booting" or "file" when they tried to play a South Korean film saved on a USB drive. Compared to South Korea, where the infiltration of technology-related foreign words without translation is common, such neologisms had not been openly adopted in North Korea, and their circulation denotes the assumption that the listeners are in the knowing circle.[20]

Likewise, speaking in an alternate language is a common strategy to articulate one's belonging to a clique as it showcases subcultural knowledge and access to foreign media. For example, a common South Korean expression used by boys when they want to become intimate with girls, "Do you want to have *ramyeon* [instant noodles] with me?" became an adopted cryptolect (South Korean dialect and colloquial expressions) of seduction for North Korean youth as well.[21] Na Min-hui (female born in 1991 in Pyongyang who left North Korea in 2014 and came to South Korea in 2015) notes that "when a guy asks a girl, 'Do you want to watch South Korean drama with me?' that means he is intent on hooking up with her."[22] Coded language formed along the lines of foreign-media accessibility is a key component of forging new networks of alliance, making the status of individuals with access to outside information known among millennials. An anonymous interviewee (male in his early thirties, neither from Pyongyang nor from a border town, who left North Korea in 2014) claims that students in his high school all knew exactly whom to ask when they wanted to see South Korean dramas or other media: "Those who knew at least a couple of South Korean songs [and] those who have money to bail themselves out when caught" were natural candidates.[23] According to this interviewee, these people are similar to the South Korean concept of *inssa* (slang for an "insider") as they have significant social capital to attract others and forge a new human connection via sharing their media. There are commonly used phrases in North Korea—*nalari-pung* (in the style of a poser), *nolse* (player), *jom nonda* (knows how to party), *jom anda* (knows a bit)—to reference those who are in the knowing circle.

The practice of using coded language is quite similar to what British linguist M. A. K. Halliday termed an "anti-language"—a mercurial and ever-changing code that dodges any standardized meaning. According to Halliday, this kind of secret language is an inherent property of an "anti-society," which is "set up within another society as a conscious alternative to it. It is a mode of resistance, resistance which may take the form either of passive symbiosis or of active hostility and even destruction. An anti-language is not only parallel to an anti-society; it is generated by it."[24] To be sure, the aforementioned examples of cryptolect used by North Korean millennials do not—and cannot—represent their active hostility toward North Korea; if these terms become active agents of hostility, their users' safety is in jeopardy. Rather, the use of cryptolect borders on passive yet perceptible resistance against the stringent state measures that block the free flow of information. It certainly gestures toward what Halliday called "a society that is set up within another society," symbiotically coexisting within the wider social norms—in terms of not just how millennials form a special group within the broader North Korean society but also how various pockets of microsocieties exist within the millennial generation.

The nature of antilanguage as not entirely hidden has many precedents in history. One such case involves Rotwelsch, a Yiddish-infused coded language that vagrants and thieves have used in Europe since the Middle Ages. According to Martin Puchner, whose family history involves an intricate intertwining with Rotwelsch, "We create community with shared codes, but also by making sure that no outsider can understand them."[25] The limited shareability of the secret language, whether Rotwelsch or contemporary legalese, is what makes North Korean antilanguage function within selected circles. Gim Hae-suk (female in her forties, born in South Pyeongan Province, who left North Korea in 2018 and came to South Korea in 2019), who worked as an informant for the State Security Department (Bowuibu) while in North Korea, attests to this. She was a trader, whose husband crossed borders to

Russia and China for business, so she was naturally exposed to the realities of the outside world. She had a good political background and was recruited by the State Security Department to report those who watched forbidden media; in return, she would receive their protection in running her business. When asked if she was aware of any phone surveillance, she started to share her approach to remaining unharmed by phone tapping:

> I believe phones are tapped. I did not experience it myself, but I had an acquaintance whose daughter lived in China; she told me that volumes get lower when phones get tapped. So I asked the State Security Department whether phones actually get tapped. They told me that they don't surveil every phone but occasionally tap into the conversations of those who are under their close watch. So we often use coded language when speaking on the phone. For instance, you can call "Hyang-i" "Chorok" to hide Hyang-i's real identity. The more the authorities ramp up their surveillance, the smarter people get since they have to survive under that system. It's not surprising that North Korean hackers are so good.[26]

Stories like Gim's abound. According to Go Na-hae (female born in Dancheon, South Hamgyeong Province, who left North Korea in 2018 and came to South Korea in 2019), "VCD vendors would use coded language. If a customer asked, 'You got anything interesting?' they would respond, 'I do have something expensive.' They would also use 'I have something from below' to refer to South Korean media, whereas they just name Chinese or Hong Kong media as such."[27] An anonymous interviewee (male in his twenties, born in Yanggang Province, who left North Korea in 2020 and came to South Korea in 2021) tells us how official language of North Korea can also be deployed as a stand-in for an antilanguage:

> When people want to exchange their South Korean media files, they change the titles to North Korean titles. For example, [the South Korean drama] *Descendants of the Sun* would be referred to as [the North Korean film] *Mother's Happiness*. Both are about the military, so the conversationalist would guess what is really meant by this North Korean title. If they didn't get it, then I would give descriptions of *Descendants of the Sun* and ask, "There are such and such scenes in *Mother's Happiness*—have you seen it?" Then they would get that I was talking

about a South Korean drama. Or at times I would ask, "Is there something interesting to watch?" When I wanted to exchange US dollars, I would call it "Hyuna" [a typical girl's name] and call Chinese yuan "*samchon*" [uncle]. I would tell my acquaintants, "Hey, Uncle will arrive at your place in an hour. Receive him well." At first, my conversationalists wouldn't understand what I was talking about, but sooner or later, they got it.[28]

An almost identical example is provided by another anonymous interviewee (female in her midthirties, born in Cheongjin, who left North Korea in 2019 and came to South Korea in 2020): "When surveillance searches your computer, they can see the viewing history, and that's why we changed the titles to North Korean titles. For instance, [the South Korean title] *Fairy and Swindler* would be changed into [the North Korean title] *Springtime in Seokgaewul*. Even if the surveillance team catches you, they can't prove it, even though they know you watched it."[29]

Such various examples of antilanguage invite us to think more closely about the behavior of resistance and deviance or what could be called, for lack of a better expression, "antibehavior." As gleaned from Gang Na-ra's (female born in 1997 in Cheongjin who left North Korea in 2014) story featured at the beginning of this chapter, in acts of antibehavior such as wearing forbidden fashions, the body becomes a powerful medium to express the networks of inclusion and exclusion that are not entirely hidden from the eyes of society. If we were to extend the language practice to the broadly construed bodily practice, then antilanguage becomes one nodal point in the web of antibehavior.

The formation of class as related to access to foreign media and varying performance of antilanguage and antibehavior becomes even more stratified when gender dynamics come into play and influence the formation of millennials. In a country where patriarchy and gender discrimination still prevail, the proliferation of the market economy seems to have brought about small yet powerful ways to challenge the conventional gender norms. Men are the traditional breadwinners in North Korean society, but nowadays, a vast majority of marketplace workers are women. This is due to the fact that men mandatorily have to report to their jobs, most of which pay little, or face a heavy penalty. The logic behind such a practice is that all men should have employment in a socialist economy. Although some men bribe their employer to excuse themselves from having to report to work so that they can engage in significantly more lucrative market activities, this rule undeniably shaped the rapid rise of the female workforce in marketplaces. As Jeong Yu-na (female born in 1988 in Hoeryeong who left North Korea in 2008) notes, "The younger generation of North Koreans like strong women. This is a reflection of the *jangmadang* generation, who have seen strong mothers adapt to the marketplace economy to support their family. These strong mothers usually tell their sons to marry strong women who can fend for their family."[30]

Echoing the changes in gender roles, antilanguage started to capture the phenomenon of mothers becoming the true heroes in a desperate battle to keep the family alive. A well-known children's song entitled "We Are the Children's Union" was turned into a parody to reflect the reality of millennial North Korea. The original lyrics tout the young members of North Korean society, with "knapsacks" and "march to the training ground" standing as clear references to an important historic event in North Korea when the founding father, Kim Il Sung, set out to seek education in his youth.[31]

> Red scarves around their necks
> Knapsacks on their backs
> They march to the training ground.
> Praiseworthy, they are the children's union.

Retaining the same phraseological structure, the parody was created to reflect upon the heroes of the marketplace generation.

> Red wallet around her neck
> Knapsack on her back
> She marches to the marketplace.
> Praiseworthy is our mother.[32]

From unsung heroes to the true heroes, mothers and women of millennial North Korea have indeed gone through a transformation. Bak Hyeon-jeong (female in her thirties, born in Hyesan, who left North Korea in 2018) anecdotally affirms the sentiment captured in the song: "North

Koreans joke that they are reverting to a matriarchal society."[33] Bak's claim is not grounded on humorous exaggeration alone; millennials seeing their mothers become breadwinners of the family eventually might dismantle North Korea's rigid perception of gender hierarchy. Likewise, Fahy's research illustrates that economic pressure during the Arduous March and thereafter fell mostly on women, which made women consider men useless: "Men were no longer men but *mongmongi* (barking dogs) meaning noisy and demanding as several women reported."[34]

The doublespeak by North Korean millennials exemplified in the parody song as well as the derogatory reference to men is cogently performed so as to become legible at a social level. The relatability of the song is what makes the parody a type of antilanguage, a socially sharable mode of communication no matter how surreptitious the mode of circulation might be. In this regard, North Korean millennials live creatively *with* surveillance, not just passively *under* surveillance. Their life is a constant dance to dodge the direct scrutiny of the party and police while furtively making fun of them. Their creative response is tempered to be commensurate with the severity of the state surveillance.

Neither Entirely Hidden nor Entirely Trustworthy: Reacting Creatively to Surveillance

Creativity is not the mode of existence normally associated with a surveillance state like North Korea. Nor is it natural to link the sprouting North Korean market economy with the "creative economy"—a concept that has mostly been articulated and studied through the framework of affluent, hypertechnologized societies. Leading scholars of the creative economy, such as Richard Florida and Andrew Ross, focus on developed nations or thriving economic zones to flesh out how the rising class of creative workers and creative industries reshape the labor market and social distribution of wealth under neoliberal capitalism.[35] So what is the valence of discussing the creative economy in a place where the very basic freedom of speech is gagged?[36] And what kind of creative class can even emerge when the view of the outside world allowed to the public is systematically truncated?

The oxymoronic task of considering millennial North Korea in tandem with creativity and the creative economy is productive in showing that there is more than just one way of discussing creativity as mostly confined to the developed world. It makes outsiders, especially those living in liberal democratic societies, reflect on our own biases about whether creativity is a monolithic act not available to others living under different political regimes. There should be as many trajectories of creativity as there are diverse creative acts. Rather than defining "creativity" narrowly as producing something new, in a place like North Korea, where oppression is pervasive in every aspect of life, new ways of reacting by breaking social prohibitions or taboos demand a high degree of creativity and resourcefulness. Pertinent to this point, South Korean journalist O Gang-seon differentiates users from consumers, proposing that creativity in the new millennium lies within generating new modalities of shared and reciprocal experience among multiple users rather than a single inventor introducing a brand new product to consumers.[37] In O's opinion, the notion of creativity in today's networked society is more closely aligned with producing new modalities of communal experience, but in the case of North Korea, the emergence of creativity involves an extra step. To create a communal experience, participants first have to cultivate tactful skills to eschew impossible state policies, such as mandating men to report to the workplace, that hardly allow for economic survival. In an effort to capture the unique circumstances of North Korea while also considering the new modalities of creativity, I use the term "reactive creativity" to articulate the North Korean situation, where the state seldom hails innovative action as social virtue.

"Reactive" and "creative" conventionally are seen as diametrically opposed human attributes, but in North Korea, where daily life requires navigating through the maze of heavy restrictions imposed on information flow, one has no choice but to generate new ways of reacting. Starting from finding ways to obtain means of communication to learning new communication technologies that are not sanctioned by the state, North Korean millennials have to jump through many hoops and bend many official rules. Similar to how trickery is the chosen weapon of the powerless, as Michel de Certeau suggests, reacting creatively can take the form of deceptive strategy: "Power is bound by its very visibility. In contrast, trickery is possible for the weak, and often it is his only possibility, as a 'last resort.' . . . The weaker the forces at the disposition of the strategist, the more the strategist will be able to use deception."[38] Trickery as a means of passive resistance and of survival for the weak is a way for North Koreans to react to their oppressive daily reality in a creative way.

To this point, Kim Yonho notes how every aspect of cell phone usage involves creative thinking on the part of North Koreans, starting with how they dodge regulations to obtain means of communication: "As the number of subscribers increases rapidly, the number of booths selling used phones in the *jangmadang* (informal market) is also increasing at pace. Although repair services are authorized, transactions of used phones are illegal. The phones purchased at the informal markets are registered under bogus names, and, for their use, illegal top-up cards are also available at the booths."[39] Reacting to the impossible conditions of life invites creative measures that break taboos and prohibitions; daring to go against the punitive law and constant surveillance is at the heart of North Korean creativity.

There might be many tools—or trickery, if you will—for North Korean millennials to act out their divergence from the rules, but many of them center around cell phones. Used as conspicuous symbols of material means and cultural acquisition, cell phones often become the catalyst for breaking social rules, including cheating on exams, as in Kim Yonho's following story of a defector from Pyongyang: "In 2009 while taking senior examinations, students at Kim Il Sung University—the most prestigious university in North Korea—sent text messages to their friends outside asking for help. Their friends looked up the answers and sent them back in text messages. However, the professors detected this practice, and all of the students involved were punished. After the event, the University authorities banned cell phone use on campus."[40] Similar incidents of trickery related to the use of technology abound. In fact, there are too many to introduce in their full array, but Gim Ha-na's (female born in Hyesan in 1988 who left North Korea in 2014) following story sheds light on trickery as creative flair in handling the oppressed conditions of life:

> When I lived in Wonsan in 2009, many South Korean channels were captured on TV. Usually when people buy a TV, the local communications office comes out to fix your channel to just one North Korean channel. But I like to play with these things. When the person from the office came, he knew my father, so they started drinking. I like to play tricks

in general, and for this occasion, I opened the TV remote control and placed a tape behind the channel button to temporarily block the channel search function [from capturing Chinese channels]. I was able to fool the office and convince them that the channel had been fixed.[41]

Gim's story is amusing in that it openly flaunts her penchant for trickery, but in many other cases, trickery is the unavoidable means of subsistence. Creative trickery as a form of defying prohibition in North Korea has much to do with how cell phones are often deployed as a matter of survival, especially of economic survival.

For the vast majority of resettlers, the economic survival of their family members left behind in North Korea depends on their remittances. When resettlers in South Korea remit money to their family, the sender calls the receiver in North Korea with the help of a remittance broker who lends their cell phone to the receiver of the funds. Although such brokers charge approximately 30 percent of the total amount transferred, they make the transfer fast and efficient with the aid of cell phones. Due to the high cost and danger involved, the phone calls made to confirm the transfers normally cannot last more than five minutes. But this is the time when family members in North Korea are exposed to outside information from a reliable source—their own family members, as opposed to propagandistic government mouthpieces.

The behind-the-scenes nature of communication is what prompted South Korean political scientist Joo Hyung-min (Ju Hyeong-min) to use "hidden script" to refer to the small-scale murmurs that contradict the official indoctrination by the state. According to Joo, "hidden script" is the mechanism that exposes fissures and gaps between reality and the ideal. Eschewing both Antonio Gramsci's notion of hegemony as overestimating "the effects of ruling ideology" and major social theories on resistance that "focus too much on large-scale protests that pose 'a major threat to the state,'" Joo uses "hidden script" as a way to gauge how the "powerless" can harness a limited degree of power to express themselves.[42] Joo also uses the concept as a way to highlight the oppositional stance the scripts of the powerless take against the public script: "By definition, hidden transcripts are the antithesis to the public transcript of power,"[43] which resonates closely with what I have termed "reactive creativity."

At first glance, Joo's emphasis on the danger involved in free and open self-expression in North Korea might justify the use of "hidden." Indeed, for North Korean couples to watch South Korean dramas together means that they are able to claim private, albeit dangerous, moments. Li Wi-ryeok (male born in 1985 in Gimchaek who left North Korea in 2010) notes that this is an act of seduction for two reasons: "First, that means a couple is sharing a secret. Second, each drama has an emotional arc, and the couple is sharing that together in private."[44] Likewise, Li Ung-gil (male born in 1981 in Cheongjin who first left North Korea in 2003 and permanently left in 2006) started to share the smuggled media with his friend alone at first, but eventually their girlfriends joined them in their secret tryst.[45] While it is undeniable that the act of consuming foreign media is a cloistered moment hidden from the public eye, the adjective "hidden" does not acknowledge the fact that the script has to be understood at a communal level to a certain degree. In other words, the script has to be sharable by subcultural communities—and it is therefore not entirely "hidden."[46]

On the other hand, the term "script," primarily associated with written narrative, does not fully capture the range of performative repertoires, including the previously discussed antilanguage and antibehavior as embodied narratives, utterances, and scenarios. Particular gestures and grooming practices gleaned from the South Korean media become subtly visible in North Korea; therefore, "script" might potentially be flattening the performative potential of those bodily expressions. As the 2019 *BBC News Korea* survey of two hundred North Korean resettlers indicates, two out of ten emulated South Koreans by changing their clothing style. Some claim to have introduced South Korean content to family and friends, while some changed the way they talked to emulate South Korean colloquial language.[47] Jeong Yu-na (female born in 1988 in Hoeryeong who left North Korea in 2008) provides an empirical account of this survey: "Young people change the way they talk following the spoken language of South Korean dramas. We call young couples who watch South Korean dramas together [a] '-ji-ji' couple since North Korean sentences do not end with '-ji.' But South Korean sentences do."[48]

The subtle performances become legible when the members of the social network start sharing them and reenact things they have seen. The term "hidden script" risks dismissing the cogent legibility of the reactive creativity performed in its full complexity, layered with possibilities for alternations and mutations. Rather than seeing it through the binary oppositions of "hidden" and "public," or "backstage" and "front stage," I would like to think of reactive creativity as a rehearsal process of weaving networks with constantly morphing boundaries of inclusion and exclusion, in which the reactive response to surveillance becomes part and parcel of creative expression. Deeply entrenched in situational and relational possibilities and risks, it is a mode of making and breaking social networks in a highly volatile society.

The specifically North Korean way of constructing networks shares similarities to what we call "platforms" elsewhere (as in digital platforms, such as Amazon and Facebook). Although global platform companies are completely absent in North Korea at the moment, their mode of fabricating predetermined dynamics between the digital platform and its users, as pointed out by media scholars José van Dijck, Thomas Poell, and Martijn de Waal, presents an interesting point of comparison. "The term refers to a society in which social and economic traffic is increasingly channeled by an (overwhelmingly corporate) global online platform ecosystem that is driven by algorithms and fueled by data. . . . An online 'platform' is a program—marble digital architecture designed to organize interactions between users—not just end users but also corporate entities and public bodies."[49] If we take this as the standard definition of "platform," the North Korean version excludes the grand digital architecture as there is no true sense of an interactive online platform where massive amounts of information could be gathered through the voluntary participation of users to generate profitable big data. Unlike the rest of the world, the only digital architecture in North Korea is created by the state via intranet and state-run online stores, and participation in it is by no means voluntary.

North Korea is a rare case where the viral spread of media does not contribute at all to the creation of big data. So was it simply out of concern for the freedom of speech that the Google executive Eric Schmidt called for an open internet in North Korea when he visited the country in 2013?[50] In the world outside North Korea, where certain media content goes viral and creates trends on digital platforms, users' online activities generate valuable data for platform companies to trace and predict patterns of behavior. Approximating the typical dystopian novel where an omniscient Big Brother watches over every human desire and activity, big data rapidly became smart enough to predict our actions—a point that media critics such as Shoshana Zuboff have addressed extensively. In her seminal book *The Age of Surveillance Capitalism*, Zuboff warns about how big data accelerates the commodification of human experience: "I define surveillance capitalism as the unilateral claiming of private human experience as free raw material for translation into behavioral data. These data are then computed and packaged as prediction products and sold into behavioral futures markets—business customers with a commercial interest in knowing what we will do now, soon, and later."[51] Human lives become profitable mines for data companies, but what if the data transmission entirely evades the computation process—a unique situation that defines the North Korean reality? Can the spread of media via the exclusive human-to-human contact in offline space trickle down to the creation of big data that Zuboff sternly criticizes?

If the conventional notion of platforms and their data mining under surveillance capitalism cannot capture the unique circumstances of North Korea today, even more conspicuous differences exist in the mode of platform users' networking. In North Korea, the kind of networking that truly matters overwhelmingly takes place offline to evade data creation and tracing—as a matter of guarding personal safety and even life. The North Korean variant of a platform is formed spontaneously from the bottom up, without top-down digital architecture, around a small group of people who secretively confer in an offline space around shared interests in forbidden media. Hence "platform" in North Korea means something quite different than its conventional sense in our daily lives—something shaped through face-to-face human interaction around digital content that is hard to trace but nevertheless goes viral among a handful of users. Accordingly, instead of big data, small data, even microdata, emerge from the North Korean variant of the platform.

The social networks created on offline platforms—no matter how small or subcultural—require a great degree of what Joo aptly terms "reverse-reading." Joo notes that in North Korea, "when the government exhorts its people not to do something, it probably means that many North Koreans are actually doing it."[52] From secret watching of forbidden dramas to gingerly uttering coded language in public, the performance has to be communicated on a socially perceptible level. No matter how elusive the signals might be, they are nonetheless present—to be discovered and understood by those who share the same codes of bonding. Through a careful but resilient weaving of social networks, there are always creative means to perceive subtle points of connection despite—or because of—hyper–state control.

The pervasiveness of social surveillance ironically—and inadvertently—becomes a performative factor in forging alternative social networks. An anonymous interviewee (male in his early thirties, neither from Pyongyang nor from a border town, who left North Korea in 2014) notes how his parents' generation shares these media with relatives or business partners: "Since I lived far from the border region, the most prolific source of South Korean materials came from the surveillance organizations. Those who were supposed to surveil were the ones who were most exposed to South Korean materials, so when they saw something interesting, they would want to share the material with those close to them."[53] This account exemplifies how reactive creativity works in the most paradoxical ways, even through simultaneous acts of surveillance and consumption of forbidden-media products.

Network formation takes place discursively and on an individual basis but primarily among trustworthy family members and friends. Sense of trust is an important factor to determine whether North Korean millennials forge a secret network with others by sharing forbidden media. The 2019 *BBC News Korea* survey of two hundred resettlers reveals that the majority of them watched dramas with direct family members, followed by friends and neighbors.[54] When asked whom to trust when sharing forbidden media, Go Na-hae (female born in Dancheon, South Hamgyeong Province, who left North Korea in 2018 and came to South Korea in 2019) told me, "You have to observe a person over a period of time and notice the person's inclinations. When someone initiates a conversation about watching forbidden media, I become quite careful with that person. Even if it's someone you regard as a friend, it has to be either someone with a family member who left North Korea or someone with similar taste as mine."[55]

An anonymous interviewee (female in her thirties, born in Pyongyang, who left North Korea in 2008 and settled in South Korea in 2013) advances this claim further by probing into the fragility of trust: "In North Korea, you cannot trust anyone. No matter how close you feel to someone, you cannot make any political comments. If you have family secrets, you just don't share with anyone [outside the family]. When the government confiscated my business and my parents were persecuted, I had the urge to stab Kim Jong Il if I were in his vicinity. But no matter how strong the urge was, I did not tell my feelings to anyone."[56] Trusting family, friends, and business partners might be an intuitive part of social networking, but it is not to be taken for granted in North Korea.

Forging a network of trust in a surveillance society like North Korea is not simply for media consumption but, for some and of more significance, for sustaining a livelihood. Li Ung-gil's (male born in 1981 in Cheongjin who first left North Korea in 2003 and permanently left in 2006) following story represents North Korean millennials' bonding and their circumventive dance with the state prohibitions. Li recalls how he was able to smuggle VCDs from China that were loaded with foreign media thanks to a friendship he forged with a border patrolman in the town of Hoeryeong. Before Li became an active smuggler, he once got into a brawl with a heavily drunken patrolman in a local pub. After a bloody fight, they opened up their hearts and ended up becoming friends. When Li began his stealthy cross-border business operation, this accidental friendship provided a safety net, enabling him to cross back and forth to China through Hoeryeong under the watchful protection of his border-patrol friend.[57] While violating the state ban on foreign media, the members of this inner circle had to present a politically correct profile as citizens of North Korea in public space—a defensive maneuver to ensure their safety—while relying on their social network for their livelihood. Gang Li-hyeok (male born in 1987 in Bukcheon, Jagang Province, who left North Korea in 2013), who made his living in a marketplace, likewise notes the importance of trust in marketplace transactions: "You must have credibility to do business. If you have credibility, you can do business with just a phone call."[58]

Another anonymous interviewee (male in his twenties, born in Yanggang Province, who left North Korea in 2020 and came to South Korea in 2021) makes us realize that the sense of trust as socioeconomic capital is context dependent and varies considerably from person to person: "In the North, even if you don't have money, you can form your human network solely based on loyalty or rapport with someone."[59] However, the following anonymous interviewee (female in her midthirties, born in Cheongjin, who left North Korea in 2019 and came to South Korea in 2020) would disagree, claiming that trust has to be backed up by one's connections and financial means:

"One year before I left North Korea, I asked a friend who procured many South Korean dramas whether she was not afraid. Then the friend said to me, 'Since you have money, you can resolve this problem even if you're caught.' Generally speaking, $1,500 will solve your crime of having watched an entire series of a South Korean drama."[60] When I asked this interviewee what trust means in North Korea, she said, "Trust has everything to do with your capability. Simple trust between friends can solve nothing. But a friend with money can solve any problem."[61] The mode of interpersonal dynamics is not the only factor in determining who is trustworthy; money is another.

Trust is forged with many trials and hypersensitive caution since the formal structures of social interaction in North Korea involve competition with and criticism of one another. Li Hyeong-seok (male born in Pyongyang in 1984 who left North Korea in 2002) notes how school friends and workplace colleagues have a difficult time revealing their true inner thoughts since they are encouraged to constantly surveil one another for daily criticism sessions (saeng-hwal chong-hwa).[62] Li Ung-gil (male born in 1981 in Cheongjin who first left North Korea in 2003 and permanently left in 2006) confirms that unusually strong trust has to be established prior to sharing forbidden media. For instance, when he dated a police officer in North Korea, she first refused to hear about the South Korean realities from him, which were prohibited discussion topics in North Korea. But when their relationship became more intimate, they started to watch South Korean dramas, which eventually evolved into discussions of defecting to South Korea.[63]

However, feigned trust could lead to fatal mistakes. Li recounts such dangerous moments where unfiltered open communication could invite serious consequences:

> When I was serving in North Korea's draconian Storm Troop [*Pok-pung gundan*], a fellow soldier got drunk, bragged about the South Korean dramas he watched in China, and sang the drama's soundtrack. A few days later, he was summoned by the State Security Agency head in the unit, who interrogated whether he crossed the border to China. He persistently denied it and was able to save himself. After this incident, one of his fellow soldiers kept asking him about the South Korean dramas. The soldier realized that the curious guy was a hidden spy for the State

Security Agency, and he later told the rest of his friends to watch out for that rat.[64]

It is for this reason that an anonymous interviewee (male in his early thirties, born in Pyongyang, who left North Korea in 2017 and soon arrived in South Korea) took extra measures of precaution:

> I only shared dramas with very close friends. I witnessed too many times how one person's arrest led to multiple arrests. One friend of mine, to whom I copied and handed over the drama, got caught. As a result, I also got caught. During the police interrogation, that friend told everything about me. I was interrogated for ten days at the State Security Department and was jailed for twenty days, but I denied my involvement until the end. My father, who was a big shot in the military defense industry, helped me get out, but my friend went to a disciplinary camp [danryeon-dae] for six months.[65]

When I asked him what trust means in North Korea, he looked at me as if I was deranged or speaking of a word or concept that just does not exist in his world of experience.

Despite the broad experiential spectrum of how one sees the other as trustworthy, hard-earned trust leads to the formation of the North Korean variant of an offline platform, where the participants consuming and circulating the forbidden media share a sense of risk and credibility. But in the unfortunate event that they are caught by the authorities, the participants' various stations in life bring them different consequences. For example, those who are officially employed tend to receive less severe punishment than those who are unemployed. Choe Yu-jin's (female born in Hyesan in 1982 who left North Korea in 2020) following testimony notes how even the surveilling party is concerned with the disparity in punishments and wants to put up the best possible semblance of fairness in their surveillance and punishment practices:

> When the South Korean drama *Stairway to Heaven* became popular, I obtained CDs and watched all of them. Then I exchanged the CDs with our neighbor, who had *Autumn in My Heart* [Gaeul donghwa]. The neighbor unfortunately was discovered watching my CDs and divulged the source during interrogation, so I was caught. Since she was a minor,

she was sent to a juvenile correctional facility for six months, whereas I avoided arrest thanks to the bribe my father provided to bail me out of trouble. But the police urged me to go away for a while in order to give a semblance of fairness, so I went away for three months to live with my grandmother.[66]

The testimony speaks to the primary importance of trust and reliability in North Korean social interactions but also speaks volumes about the danger involved in what seem to be ubiquitous media-sharing practices to outsiders. As Kretchun and Kim note, "Foreign media is still too dangerous a topic to be discussed in public and is shared only with trusted friends and family, if at all."[67] Crucial to this process is that signals of safety and danger, rather than being hidden, should be communicated in a legible way so that individuals can make informed choices.

Although the rising popularity and wide availability of South Korean dramas in North Korea are undeniable, not all North Korean millennials have been exposed to forbidden media. Studies show that "approximately 88% of North Koreans who defect to South Korea had access to the forbidden foreign media in North Korea despite the risk."[68] Many resettlers, like Jeong Gwang-il (male born in the early 1960s who worked in Pyongyang and left North Korea in 2003), claim that "everyone in North Korea watches these foreign media,"[69] while O Cheong-seong (male born in Gaesong in the early 1990s who left North Korea in 2017) says that "it will not be exaggeration to say that all young people in North Korea would have watched South Korean film or drama at least once, if not frequently."[70] Nevertheless, we cannot generalize that the limited number of resettler testimonies represents the vast majority of millennial experience in North Korea.

Due to years of North Korean education that instills hostility toward South Korea, the North Korean youth interested in South Korea are those whose parents either are smugglers (*mil-su-kkun*), fun-loving people (*nolsae*) who want to enjoy international culture, or have money to bail them out if they are caught watching South Korean dramas. The lower the economic stratum, the less exposure they have to South Korean media. It is not rare to find a young North Korean resettler like Jo Ye-na (female born in 1993 in Yanggang Province who left North Korea in 2012) who "neither heard of, nor consumed Korean pop culture" since she was "struggling to make ends meet while in high school."[71] But even if they have means to purchase forbidden dramas and electronic gadgets to watch them, not everyone participates in the dangerous practice. According to a recent re-settler (anonymous male in his early twenties who left North Korea in 2016), he never watched South Korean dramas in the North, although he was from an economically sound background.[72] The most convincing conclusion to draw from these various accounts can be summarized by Na Min-hui's (female born in 1991 in Pyongyang who left North Korea in 2014 and came to South Korea in 2015) claim that "there are people who have never watched South Korean dramas, but there isn't anyone who has seen Korean dramas only once."[73] Some might never have had a glimpse of the forbidden media, but once they start, there is no way of stopping. Gang Na-ra's statement that "South Korean dramas are like drugs" is by no means hyperbole but a truthful reflection of the actual power that these programs exercise over their northern neighbors.[74]

Their attraction could be compounded by the fact that the dramas not only are forbidden but also feature taboo subjects. Na Min-hui (female born in 1991 in Pyongyang who left North Korea in 2014 and came to South Korea in 2015) makes a significant observation as to why the forbidden dramas have such a strong appeal for North Koreans: "I was surprised to see how people openly complained about their lives. Openly criticizing the society was something North Koreans would not dare to do. Even if life was hard for us, we had to declare that we were happy."[75] Kretchun and Kim take note of this sentiment when sharing their observation that in North Korea, "discussions with others about the outside world constitutes a significant path between media exposure and beliefs and attitudes."[76] For the vast majority of North Korean millennials, the not entirely hidden circulation of South Korean media is an enticing invitation to imagine the world beyond. What they see eventually becomes a part of their worldview, and the act of consuming unsanctioned media, in this regard, becomes not a passive reaction but an active gesture of creating visions of an alternative life.

Taking Risks with Viral Narratives

Over and over, we have heard from the North Korean resettlers themselves that sharing forbidden narratives through person-to-person transmission in North Korea involves a tremendous risk, even though that transmission takes place in a highly guarded manner with an intention of leaving no traceable online data. Best defined as "the qualitative perception of possible harm," risk evokes the uncertain consequences of present and future actions and anxiety-ridden measurements of their worth.[77] The risk factor is what qualifies North Korean millennials' reaction to the surveillance state as "creative," whereby forbidden media has become an indispensable catalyst in countering the monolithic ideology of the state. At least for the millennials, North Korea is built upon "the conjunction of risk and media/mediation," and "everyday life is replete with instances of such conjunctions."[78]

Media scholars Bishnupriya Ghosh and Bhaskar Sarkar poignantly observe that "a society in which the processes of modernization have proliferated and intensified risks comes to see itself over time as a 'risk society.'"[79] In millennial North Korea, circulation of forbidden media by a sizeable portion of the society certainly captures signs of social fragmentation, if not full-on modernization, but the scale of that social fragmentation characterized by increasing cracks and fissures in the state surveillance system calls for scrutiny of the emergence of a "risk society." The necessity to manage those risks in North Korea may best be understood in a partial analogy with blockchain technology, which ignited zealous responses from the millennial generation around the world for the degree of freedom it presented from power structures, especially the power structure of the state. Economist Robert J. Shiller captures this sentiment in more precise terms as regards Bitcoin, which has captivated millennial aspirations as the prime application of blockchain technology: "The Bitcoin narrative involves stories about inspired cosmopolitan young people, contrasting with uninspired bureaucrats," and "having a Bitcoin wallet makes the owner a citizen of the world and in some sense psychologically independent of traditional affiliations."[80] Taking risks, in this sense, becomes part and parcel to participating in this attractive new model of social interaction and hence is rationalized to a larger extent.

But blockchain technology works only fractionally in North Korea compared to the conventional way it works elsewhere. Typically understood as the linkage of an "uneditable, digital chain," blockchain hinges on the idea of "decentralized management" to "ensure trust, validity and usability."[81] Its central aim is to create an "immutable record that is consistent and chronologically organized, with all information and transactions shared between parties."[82] If blockchain technology's transparent and traceable person-to-person transmission is its philosophical backbone that generated the cryptocurrency craze, then the circulation pattern of South Korean media in the North presents its subversion—all in the service of protecting the secrecy of participants in transactions while sustaining their network. In order for the transfer of forbidden media to take place, the two involved parties have to verify their identities as trustworthy allies; as one anonymous resettler notes, "Everyone involved in secret sales transaction of forbidden media is linked to one another. There is a network here."[83] But as an attempt to diffuse the risk of being discovered, this verification process cannot and should not be recorded digitally and transparently, the way conventional blockchain transactions are recorded. The idea of person-to-person transmission is present in both cases, but they are clearly separated by the fact that the North Korean contact takes place exclusively in offline space, bypassing a digital footprint and thereby evading possibilities of state surveillance, whereas the conventional blockchain transactions take place in online space with clear digital traceability.

The nature of exclusive offline transactions, which create a halfway kinship with blockchain technology, is idiosyncratic since the North Korean case is a bizarre hybrid that combines contagious media frenzy with exclusive reliance on the limited channels of person-to-person contact. Such limited-scale offline contacts must be plenty in order to impact the society with virality. Shiller's thesis on the central power of narrative sheds light on how media contagion can take place even without the aid of an online network. For Shiller, Bitcoin is an iconic embodiment of narratives that evolve around the notions of anarchy, world citizenship, and a futuristic worldview: as a "contagious counternarrative" exemplifying "the impressive inventions that a free, anarchist society would eventually develop," Bitcoin presents a "pan-national narrative" that "no government can control" or "stop."[84] This is precisely why—that is, due to its embodiment of freedom from state power—it was seen as a religious cult in its inception stage. But as media scholar David Golumbia counters, "Unlike traditional cults, though, Bitcoin has no specific creed, no single geographic location and no truly identifiable belief system—other than Bitcoin itself."[85] It is for these reasons that Shiller thinks people enter Bitcoin transactions: "People often buy Bitcoin because they want to be part of something exciting and new, and they want to learn from the experience."[86] In North Korea, forbidden cultural content stands as a form of cultural cryptocurrency—an expensive, risky, yet exciting Bitcoin—which opens up the horizons of autonomy from the state while guaranteeing a degree of secrecy for users.

While blockchain technology is supposed to protect user information and data transferal, let's not forget that it can also be an ironic agent to enact power that it attempts to counter.[87] Historian Nishani Frazier articulates its ambivalent function as follows: "Blockchain embodies this tech duality and concomitantly stores within it the key to self-determination, sovereign identity, and community empowerment while divergently acting as an instrument for oppression."[88] Just as cell phones in North Korea figure simultaneously as enablers of state surveillance and creators of alternate social life, the sheer amount of effort to protect the identity of those involved in offline transfers of forbidden media ironically reaffirms—and facilitates—the operation of glaringly oppressive surveillance mechanisms. It may be akin to how racial minorities placed under heightened social surveillance in the United States deploy blockchain for self-protection against the racialized power structure, all the while enabling and protecting their social network, and emerge as sovereign political subjects. To cite Frazier once again, "Self-sovereignty is not just limited to identity. Its foundations lie in community control of information particularly in cases where the parties are not trusted. Blockchain technology similarly assumes distrust between parties, which is why it is both anonymous (identity by code versus personal name) and yet open for all to see (the public can chart each transaction or data block). As such, self-sovereignty and blockchain particularly operate well in relation to law enforcement where Black confidence is all but absent."[89]

As far-fetched as it might be to compare the US Black community to North Korean millennials, whose histories and access level to technology differ, both share a constant need to cope with structural surveillance.

The principle of blockchain, if not its technical operation, seems to play a similar function of creating networks while managing risks. In essence, offline versions of blockchain technology based on the need for security guarantee the promise of anonymity, and traceable intimate networks serve as a reasonable risk-management strategy for North Korean millennials who consume forbidden media.

On the flipside of risk management lies the uncontrollable virality of the South Korean narrative, and North Korean millennials' craze for South Korean media products is one emblematic extension of a broader global trend. Close analysis of South Korean media content will follow in chapter 3 and 4; here, its viral narratives show how members of the North Korean society forge liaisons. Viral media content impacts social relations and the modes in which social encounters take place. To this point, Tony D. Sampson notes how "virality is a theory couched in an ontology of relational encounter. . . . This can be thought of as a point of intersection at which biological desires, or basic survival needs, converge with much-needed social inventions and performances interwoven in the everyday mechanical habits of social encounter."[90] Whether online or offline, the relational intersections of media encounters are ultimately about the human desire to know the world beyond one's confines, which in the case of North Korea, often merge with "basic survival needs."

To Whom Do These Stories Belong?

The emergent knowledge economy raises questions about the ownership of digital content in circulation in a highly unique manner. In April 2003, North Korea joined the World Intellectual Property Organization, and its copyright law, article 5, clearly states, "The DPRK [Democratic People's Republic of Korea] shall duly protect copyrights belonging to corporations and individuals of a foreign country that honors the conventions or treaties that it has ratified."[91] But in reality, what kind of ownership can we discuss in the case of North Korea, where the vast majority of foreign media enters not through official importation with copyright clearance but through underground channels? And even when the state uses foreign media clips on their official daily news, fees are not paid either.[92] Because of North Korean users' pervasive use of foreign media without copyright considerations, it is easy to assume that intellectual-property rights are absent from the country. Quite the contrary: a close reading of widely circulated periodicals in recent years reveal that the North Korean state has been making consistent attempts to educate the general public about the emerging importance of protecting intellectual property (IP). Take, for example, the 2019 *Chollima* article "Intellectual Property Plays an Important Role in the Development of Society and Culture" (Sahoe-gyeongje-baljeon-eseo jungyohan yeokhal-eul noneun jijeok soyugwon), which states,

> We live in the age of intellectual property, when scientific technology and intellectual labor play a crucial role in socioeconomic development and well-being. So it is important for everyone to cultivate an exact understanding of intellectual property in order to advance scientific technology and the economy. Copyright law protects intellectual property and the rights of its creator. Traditionally speaking, property takes a material form and possesses certain economic value. . . . But with the development of scientific technology and economic activities, traditional notions of property have come to include intellectual property. Copyrights protect intellectual property concerning the creators' rights in the fields of science and technology, literary and artistic productions, patents and trademarks, and engineering plans.[93]

Just like *Chollima*, a journal covering a wide range of useful information intended for a general audience, *Joseon nyeoseong* set out to educate its general readership on the growing significance of IP: "Intellectual property rights protect not materials but intangible assets that are produced as a result of intellectual creation. But they are similar to property rights in that they protect the owner's rights to possess, use, and sell intellectual property. . . . Once a certain property is eligible for consideration to qualify as intellectual property, a state committee will review the case and have the property officially registered. After this process, the possession, use, and sales of intellectual property are subject to legal procedures."[94]

Given the heightened campaign to instill the significance of copyrights and intellectual property in the general public, it might seem odd that such top-down campaigns do not synch well with the actual grassroots-level uses of foreign-media products that constitute copyright infringement.

But because South Korean media, with extremely rare exceptions, are not supposed to enter North Korea in the first place, these media fall outside the scope of North Korean legal definitions and practices.

From Western viewpoints, the North Korean way of circulating unlicensed and illegally copied content constitutes intellectual-property infringement. Media scholars such as Zhang Weiqi and Mickey Lee label the North Korean practice "media piracy," noting that "the case of media piracy in China serves as a useful comparison [to North Korea]" because it indicates "how the inter-twined relationship between politics, the informal economy, technology, and culture has implications on the study of the Korean Wave in North Korea."[95] Zhang and Lee argue that pirated media products in China had an effect on shifting media consumption from the public to the private realm, which closely resonates with the media-consumption patterns in today's North Korea.

The illegality of copying unlicensed media content extends to hardware as well: the electronic devices with which North Koreans watch illegally copied content are also unlawfully supplied in many cases. According to Gang Jin-gyu, "due to sanctions, there is a limit to what North Korea can import directly. As a result, it illegally imports manufactured parts with copyrights infringement."[96]

In the strictest sense, it is indisputable that North Korea violates in-tellectual-property rights, but the case calls for a more nuanced reading of different ways intellectual property and copyright are construed in North Korea and elsewhere. As noted, the aforementioned article 5 of the copyright law of the Democratic People's Republic of Korea states that "the DPRK shall duly protect copyrights belonging to corporations and individuals of a foreign country that honors the conventions or treaties that it has ratified." But as Zhang and Lee point out, since "North Korea is not a member of WTO, the international community cannot pressure the country to open its media market or to observe Western-style copyright protection."[97]

Compounding this issue is the fact that North and South Korea under-stand the concept of "copyrights" quite differently. According to scholar of North Korean IP law Heo In, the South Korean copyright law, article 2, stipulates that "copyrights holder" refers to "the one who created the work"; the North Korean copyright law, article 3, on the other hand, specifies the rights holder as "the one who either created the work or the one who was transferred the creator's rights." To clarify, North Korea defines the copyright holder "not according to creator, but according to the one who inherited the creator's copyrights."[98] To this point, South Korean researcher Choe Gyeong-su provides a convincing reason the North Korean copyright law is not centered around creators: the state's strong grip on artists and creators, who are assigned to specific workplaces and receive wages from the state as a part of the collective workforce.[99] The location of rights rests with the place of origin in South Korea, whereas in the North, it rests with the place of the rights recipient, thereby placing more emphasis on the circulation rather than the originating point of rights.

If we take the two divergent definitions of copyright into consideration, for North Koreans, their consumption of illegally copied and transmitted South Korean media does not constitute a straightforward case of intellectual-property-rights infringement in the Western sense of the word.[100] Even more, would an average North Korean user of South Korean media be thinking of copyright issues? That is hardly likely. The unofficial circulation of forbidden media is often driven by an overwhelming sense of secretive curiosity, so much so that the viewers' sensitivity to risk and danger overwhelms any potential awareness of the copyright implications. It is difficult to simply impose the conventional perception of creators' rights onto North Korea, where abiding by strict laws often requires forfeiting the means to survive. In a society where even an eleven-year-old knows that "only those with a full stomach will preach socialist morality," can we truly expect the members to think of the legitimacy of illegally copied materials?[101]

So will media "piracy" (read "theft") remain a relevant concept in a place where the concept of rights lies not exclusively with the creator of the content but largely with the recipient? Turning back to Zhang and Lee's comparative discussion of China and North Korea, we see that the notion of piracy places much emphasis on the media recipient rather than the rights or intentions of the media producer in a way that transforms the identity of the recipient. Zhang and Lee veer away from the negative implications of piracy by highlighting the transformative reidentification of the media consumers:

> Importantly, the pirated foreign media change consumers' identity because piracy is a dialectical process of identification; on the one hand,

audiences are subject to the identity transformation influenced by for-eign culture, and on the other hand, they can actively select which part of the foreign culture and negotiate what aspects of modernity to indulge in. Piracy itself forms an underground subculture as copyrights laws can neither decide how foreign culture affects the society nor determine how people feel about the state control imposed on them. Unlike the public practice of watching state-approved film in a theatre, watching pirated media constitutes a private practice in which audiences experience the outside world through film—a mediated activity belonging to individual time and space.[102]

Piracy practices in North Korea are a crucial element enabling the transfer of media consumption from public space to private space, from mandatory activity to voluntary activity. Moreover, the impacts of media transfer are strong enough to raise questions about media consumers' agency, eclipsing the emphasis on creators.

To place this question in a broader global context once again, we can consider how the North Korean case of unsanctioned circulation of South Korean media, which emphasizes the collective over the individual and con-sumers over creators as agency and source of IP, strangely resonates with recent Western perspectives on the inevitability of copyright infringement due to the promiscuous nature of digital media itself. For instance, American legal scholar and political activist Lawrence Lessig views the current copyright cli-mate as an unavoidable and not always knowable entanglement of influences. Reflecting on his views, Dànielle Nicole DeVoss writes, "We currently exist in a *remix culture* of derivative works, a culture where everything and anything is up for grabs to change, to integrate, and to mash. This is accelerated by the personal computer and by digital networks, which allow us to more easily share, copy, download, and mix media."[103] Canadian legal scholar Anne-Marie Boisvert confirms this notion by characterizing the world in which we live as "both instantaneous and cumulative," where "everything ends up as odds and ends and debris to be glued back together, and thus begin anew."[104] These scholars come together in their shared skepticism about whether there can be something entirely new in the digital age to merit the strictest protection of punitive copyright protection. Can truly original creations be born out of so much preexisting information available at a click of a button? In this regard,

do the rampant media-piracy practices in North Korea not share commonal-
ities with such practices in the rest of the world, highlighting the weak logical
ground on which to argue for the pureness of IP?

Writer Lisa Samuels would share the sentiment of doubt presented by
Lessig and Boisvert, that there will be "benefits to be gained from giving up
the pretense that our production of ideas and words are original and that we
really acknowledge all our sources and are innocent of plagiarism, as though
it were possible to do or be either. Recognizing our own pieces of writing
as porous matrices of a continuing interchange, we would not, perhaps, be
so inclined to view each one as some last word."[105] Communication studies
scholar Kembrew McLeod would go further to warn us of the limitations
of the copyright law itself: "Worst of all, our freedoms are curtailed because
the law has expanded to privatize an ever-growing number of things—from
human genes to scents and gestures."[106] North Korean consumers of illicit
South Korean media are not bound by the restrictive IP-protection laws in
the West, but the cautionary warnings against the IP law and its smother-
ing of freedom closely resonate with how the sheer creativity involved in the
secret circulation of forbidden media makes us reimagine the agency of IP
as grounded in collective consumers, who add new meanings through their
creative modes of media consumption.

Activists such as Jeong Gwang-il (male born in the early 1960s who worked
in Pyongyang and left North Korea in 2003) would go further to take credit
for facilitating the circulation of South Korean media in unexpected territo-
ries. When asked about the infringement of the copyright on South Korean
materials he copies en masse and sends to North Korea, Jeong responded
with a touch of wry sarcasm: "I break the copyright law by illegally copying
the South Korean and foreign materials. So far, I did not get into trouble
with copyright holders. But what about it? Would the content creators not
be happy that we are promoting their work in uncharted territory?"[107] Jeong's
rebuttal, on the grounds of upholding his political activism, illustrates several key practices in media circulation in today's North Korea. As we have
seen, the North Korean patterns of media use showcase user- and circula-
tor-centered thinking, unlike the Western notion of intellectual-property
rights, which showcases creator-centered logic. Of four intellectual-property
types—copyright, patent, trademark, and trade secret—the circulation of

foreign media in North Korea is most closely aligned with the trade secret in that its circulation relies on secretive person-to-person transmission. For North Korean millennials, the acquisition of foreign knowledge that promotes media diversity is much more important than the strict observation of intellectual-property laws.

In the same spirit as the millennials in North Korea who often associate new media with trickery, transgression, and means to cope with the constant prohibition of outside information, Jeong's response reinforces that media circulation is a crossroads of contradictory notions of legality and creativity. Millennials in today's North Korea travel back and forth along those crossroads, carefully playing tunes of both compliance and transgression.

As a final point to highlight the resilient ambiguity of North Korean millennials, we turn to an anonymous interviewee (female in her midthirties, born in Cheongjin, who left North Korea in 2019 and came to South Korea in 2020), who ran a thriving business as a wedding planner producing wedding photos and videos that simulate South Korean dramas: "New couples would usually pay $200 for their wedding photo and video package. It's by no means a small amount [for North Koreans]. Clients would entrust me to create scenes similar to what they saw in South Korean dramas, so I would ask them to bump into each other by accident on a rainy day or 'discover' one another by chance while they are on a walk." Emulating South Korean drama became evident, and she concludes with a controlled chagrin: "The wedding business blossomed exponentially since the government did not touch it. But then Kim Jong Un started to regulate it since he saw it emulating corrupt capitalist culture too closely. And he killed it."[108]

But did the spark of creativity really die out just because Kim Jong Un wanted it dead? Did it not cause more unexpected venues of imaginative force to come into being? Limitations, at times, beget unexpected ingenuity. The anonymous interviewer reveals a fascinating glimpse into how the system of surveillance opens fissures and gaps for reactive creativity to emerge. The interviewee adds, with a sparkle in her eyes: "As I shot these wedding scenes often, they sometimes made me cringe [for their contrived nature], so I asked a friend of mine to write these scenes. My friend was a literature major at Kim Il Sung University and was able to write the scenes in more detail.

For a two-page scenario, she would charge fifty yuan, and I would use one scenario for ten wedding videos. Her dream was to become a writer, but it did not materialize. Writing these wedding video scripts perhaps was her way of flexing her literary muscle."[109] We might never get to know her name and her creative process, but one thing remains clear: the wedding-script writer gave a second life to a drama not originally intended for the newly-weds in the North, and the vignettes of love stories made in the South will create lasting memories of those embarking on a new journey.

THREE

This Story Is Ours

Long-standing cultural tradition in North Korea embraces illusory reality as a beacon to emulate. The realities in dramatic representation are more real than actual lives, and the belief in performed truth endows media with exceptional sociopolitical significance.[1] Such attitudes explain why the North Korean state is so sensitive to curbing the uncontrollable spread of forbidden media from the outside world. Perfectly aware that those media exert lasting influence on the way millennials formulate their perceptions of the realities beyond its borders, the state chases and persecutes the violators with all its might, whether the surreptitious viewers believe in what they see or not. That question of whether they believe in what they see elicits various responses from North Korean viewers, but all seem to agree that the act of watching illicit content is perilous.

Many North Korean resettler interviewees who frequently watch South Korean dramas testify to the centrality of the dramas in shaping their conception of South Korea. For example, Li Seo-eun (who was born in 1989 in Hyesan and left North Korea in 2010) recalls how she saw *Autumn in My Heart* for the first time in 2008 on a DVD player with her boyfriend: "There was nobody in my boyfriend's house. Still, he locked up all the windows and doors with metal locks and drew the curtains. I was hesitant to watch something that was forbidden, but when the drama began, I immediately became mesmerized. The Seoul accent struck me as a totally different language. I felt skittish and wanted to emulate that language."[2] The discovery of the Seoul dialect gave her an antilanguage to communicate in a secret network, as it has done for many other North Korean millennials.

The first wave of South Korean dramas to make it to North Korea at the dawn of the century had a lasting impact on countless North Korean millennials, so much so that many of them started to confuse the reality shown in the programs with the actual reality of South Korea. The identification with these dramas is so strong that when North Korean defectors resettle in South Korea, they sometimes have difficulty accepting the gap between real South Korean society and its portrayal in dramas. Song Mi-na (female born in Hyesan in 1992 who left North Korea in 2013) recalls, "Based on what I saw in these dramas, I knew that South Korea was a fancy place, but I was not sure whether to believe it or not. Nevertheless, when I came to South Korea, I somehow expected all men to look as handsome as those actors."[3] Li Eun-hui (female born in the 1990s in Kim Jong-suk Province who left North Korea in 2015) similarly observes that *Autumn in My Heart* featured a seaside two-story mansion. I thought that we would all end up living in such a place once in South Korea."[4] An anonymous interviewee (male in his twenties, born in Yanggang Province, who left North Korea in 2020 and came to South Korea in 2021) likewise notes, "When I watched South Korean dramas, I thought they were real. Having come to South Korea, I find the reality here is quite different. There are many difficulties and challenges [in the South]."[5] The primary reason for the discrepancy is North Korea's long tradition of upholding dramatic illusion as the beacon of truth to be emulated in real life.

While the far-fetched realities of the drama and actual life circumstances can only be perceived by the millennials who left North Korea and set foot in South Korea, those who have yet to face disillusionment see the dramatic new world as a model to emulate. More proactive drama viewers transform what they see into what they do. Gang Na-ra (female born in Cheongjin in 1997 who left North Korea in 2014) recalls that when *Boys over Flowers* became popular, girls in her school started wearing short-skirt uniforms like those featured in the show.[6] Others recall how *Stairway to Heaven* prompted young men to emulate the style of speech of Gwon Sang-u, a South Korean actor who became a heartthrob for young North Koreans.

While these interviewees' responses confirm their investment in the realities of the dramas they watched, others doubted what they saw on screen. According to an anonymous interviewee (female in her thirties, born in Pyongyang, who left North Korea in 2008 and settled in South Korea in 2013), "When I watched *jaebeol* dramas [like *Autumn in My Heart*], I felt that the story was not credible. Why on earth would a wealthy guy hang out with a poor girl? We have a North Korean saying: 'Magpies only hang out with magpies.'"[7] Another anonymous interviewee confirms this point (male in his early thirties, born in Pyongyang, who left North Korea in 2017 and soon arrived in South Korea): "The [South Korean] dramas I watched in North Korea were full of lies. Seventy percent of me was suspicious of what I was watching. If North Korean dramas are 99 percent lies, why would South Korean dramas be about truth? I just watched them for entertainment. But some people believe in what they see. Most Pyongyang residents watch them, but I don't think their worldview changes because of these dramas. It would be naïve to think so."[8]

Some interviewees are more ambivalent in their response when it comes to the veracity of what they saw. Go Na-hae (female born in Dancheon, South Hamgyeong Province, who left North Korea in 2018 and came to South Korea in 2019), for instance, sums up the in-between state of this divide: "People exchange thoughts when they watch South Korean dramas together. Everyone thinks differently. I [took the drama for reality and] thought that the wealth gap in South Korea is as big as that in North Korea. But my friend thought that what we saw was fictional because most dramas focused only on very rich people's lives."[9] This range of interview responses shows that the modes of reception for South Korean dramas are as diverse as their subject matter. Whether they believe in what they saw or not, all interviewees have a hyped awareness of the drama's impact on their own reality. If they were taking so much risk to see them, why should they not have such apprehension? In an ironic way, the North Korean authorities' absolute prohibition of the dramas created a heightened sense of their relevance to the realities of life in North Korea.

Taking a close look at the narratives presented by the forbidden South Korean dramas that have gained enormous followings in the North, this chapter traces how these dramas serve as significant platforms—here understood as offline communities that have coalesced around the secret consumption of shared content—and weave social networks not openly visible to the society but nevertheless able to change actual and imagined ways of life. The status of the platforms remains ambiguous due to the tactful use of cryptolect, which stands as a performative marker of social capital among millennials.

Drama Fever Sweeps the North

The first wave of South Korean dramas—miniseries of twelve to twenty episodes—emerged in the North around 2001. Six months went by without deep intervention by the North Korean regime. But as their popularity rose rapidly, the regime responded with measures to stop their circulation. An anonymous interviewee (male in his early thirties, neither from Pyongyang nor from a border town, who left North Korea in 2014) notes that in his town, there was virtually no restriction on watching foreign materials between 2001 and 2004. Only around 2004–5 did the authorities start to regulate the circulation of South Korean and American media due to their increased volume.[10] Li Ung-gil (male born in 1981 in Cheongjin who first left North Korea in 2003 and permanently left in 2006) notes that it was 2003 when he began his clandestine business of distributing foreign VCDs, illegally copied in his aunt's home in Yanji, China. He recalls how he had to exercise extreme caution after he witnessed the public execution of one of his business partners in charge of distributing his smuggled goods.[11] As the North Korean authorities have accrued experience in penalizing rule breakers over the past two decades, they have come up with a more sophisticated, prorated punishment system. An anonymous interviewee (female in her midthirties, born in Cheongjin, who left North Korea in 2019 and came to South Korea in 2020) notes how "punishment is determined by how many you've watched. Say you watched twenty episodes—you get your time by that number of episodes."[12]

Despite the constant surveillance and harsh punishment for watching South Korean dramas, there was no way for the North Korean regime to stop the proliferation of the forbidden media. Reacting creatively to the draconian surveillance, viewers took measures to ensure they outmaneuvered the watchful eyes, such as running two VCD players—one with official North Korean material and the other with a South Korean drama—so that when the censors cut off the electricity to trap the VCDs in the players for a quick surveillance, they could hide the player with the forbidden material and show the one with the proper North Korean material.[13] But not everyone was so tactful and creative, according to one anonymous interviewee (female in her midthirties, born in Cheongjin, who left North Korea in 2019 and came to South Korea in 2020):

> I watched so many dramas because a friend of my brother had many of them. South Korea has so much content, but in the North, they are hard to come by, so people tend to watch everything they can get their hands on. I watched too many, so I did not obsess over keeping those files since I could easily access them [if I wanted to]. But those who cannot let go of them keep their files, which is a way to get into danger. Usually young people have no fear, so they carry around four-gigabyte to eight-gigabyte cards in their phones. We preferred to watch the dramas on a small-screen TV—nine-inch to twelve-inch TVs powered by solar batteries.[14]

Another anonymous interviewee (male in his early thirties, born in Pyongyang, who left North Korea in 2017 and soon arrived in South Korea) notes how batteries played a role in the chosen device to play illicit media content: "I owned a smartphone in order to watch Korean videos. One advantage of watching videos on a smartphone is that the battery lasts longer. The portability of small screens, whether that be TV or cell phone screens, surely helps the viewers evade surveillance mechanisms."[15] In this case, the portability of the gadget enhanced the virality of its forbidden contents. Although unexpected phone surveillance was common and therefore imposed the danger of being caught with illegal SD cards loaded with South Korean media, cell phones also facilitated evasion of surveillance. Bak Yu-seong (male born in Hoeryeong in 1990 who left North Korea in 2007) remarks that "nowadays, people watch South Korean dramas on a flash drive or chips, so it does not produce any electronic waves. But in the past, when we watched them on VCD or DVD players, electronic waves would be detected by a surveillance machine, so we placed a bowl of water on top of the player as if we were performing an ancestral rite [*jesa*]."[16] Every medium comes with challenges for secret viewers of South Korean media, but the true lesson here is that there have always been risk takers who outsmart the authorities.

Of many dramas that started to circulate at the dawn of the millennium, several in particular resonated strongly with the millennials: *Autumn in My Heart, Stairway to Heaven, Boys over Flowers*, and *My Love from Another Star* (Byeol-eseo-on geudae), among others. According to *BBC News Korea*'s survey of North Korean resettlers in 2019, "Out of 200 respondents, 31 answered that *Autumn in My Heart* was their favorite," making it the most popular drama, while *Stairway to Heaven* was ranked the third most popular.[17] Although these shows feature different talents and production staff, they nevertheless share core traits that form the standard South Korean TV drama clichés: unrequited love between doomed lovers, triangular romances, a rich boy falling in love with a poor girl with a heart of gold, and escape from reality buoyed by the awe-inspiring power of money and consumerist pleasure. Never seen in the official North Korean media, these themes would make perfect elements for antibehavior in the eyes of the North Korean authority. But for young North Koreans, they mix exotic fantasy and escapism into an intoxicating potion.

There are countless accounts addressing why North Koreans are infatuated with these dramas, but focusing on how the evolving media technology influenced their circulation and viewing in North Korea is particularly fruitful for considering the role of technology in the lives of North Koreans. At the same time, the way major platforms of communication—computers, tablets, and especially cell phones—have appeared in these dramas over the years should be scrutinized in tandem with the cell phone's changing role in human relationships, especially how the latest technology is embedded in everyday life. The tenacious relationship between new media technology and the ability to shape one's fate might explain why contemporary dramas are much more popular than historical dramas among North Korean viewers.

For example, Li Su-ryeon (female in her thirties, born in Musan, who left North Korea the first time around 2007) notes how seeing cell phones in dramas increased her desire to participate in the media culture featured in the dramas: "While watching the South Korean drama *Glass Slippers*, I came to think of how I wanted to use cell phones like the ones drama characters use."[18] A similar account is shared by an anonymous interviewee (female in her thirties, born in Pyongyang, who left North Korea in 2008 and settled in South Korea in 2013), who had a chance to watch *Boys over Flowers* in China: "I thought of having a phone like those featured in the drama."[19] Accounts like these abound. Go Na-hae (female born in Dancheon, South Hamgyeong Province, who left North Korea in 2018 and came to South Korea in 2019) gives another: "When I watched South Korean dramas, it showed how everyone used cell phones. It was quite amazing to watch. I wanted to use those phones myself."[20] An anonymous interviewee (male in his twenties, born in Yanggang Province, who left North Korea in 2020 and came to South Korea in 2021) agrees. He noticed how cell phones in this drama were more multifunctional and used without restrictions: "When I watched *A Stairway to Heaven* in North Korea, I was already using a Chinese cell phone and noted how South Korean cell phones are so different. I thought to myself, 'They use cell phones so freely; wouldn't it be nice to be like that here?'"[21] Another anonymous interviewee (female in her midthirties, born in Cheongjin, who left North Korea in 2019 and came to South Korea in 2020), who started to watch South Korean dramas in her hometown of Cheongjin and continued in Pyongyang, where she attended college, is also envious of the easy access to cell phones featured in South Korean dramas.[22] Filled with challenging questions about one's sense of precarity in the fast-changing world, contemporary drama characters navigate their lives by using mobile technology and information flow. After all, the characters in Joseon dynasty (1392–1897) costume dramas cannot use cell phones to attack the same set of questions.

Amid the myriad of dramas that have captivated North Korean viewers, four—*Autumn in My Heart* (2000–2001), *Stairway to Heaven* (2003), *Boys over Flowers* (2009), and *My Love from Another Star* (2013–14)—stand out in particular for their sensational virality. They all unfold enduring love stories punctuated with desire for material affluence and power, but as looking more incisively into the dramatic events reveals, they introduce the current state of media and communication technology in the outside world to North Koreans. They provide opportunities for North Koreans to reflect on the considerable gaps between the communication technology (cell phones in particular) available in North Korea and that beyond their national border.

Thus, these dramas become a mirror that reflects how media and technology are interpolated into modes of being in the world and being connected to the world. With their tremendous popularity, they eventually became the not-so-hidden script for viewers to make sense of the fast-changing world, so much so that the risk-embracing mode of their consumption bordered on a creative act of weaving a unique variant of the North Korean social network, which operates in the twilight zone of state surveillance.

Tracing these dramas in chronological order will allow us to parse out the fantasy of free life that is closely married to cell phone usage and other related technological advances. Cell phones are often ingrained in the idea of individual subjectivity and mobility, which most North Koreans do not have a chance to openly express and experience in public life. But cell phones as devices of free communication are not merely confined to the fictional realm of "technotopia" in South Korean dramas. In everyday North Korea, they play an incrementally important role in advancing users' economic mobility (through marketplace activities) and physical mobility (through gaining information and arranging plans for defection). Lacking much access to available technology in their daily lives, North Korean viewers of these dramas are invited to witness the future where the technical possibilities of cell phones bring convenience to daily life, all the while becoming aware of how phones could be deployed for oppressive surveillance. If anything, the central lesson distilled from these dramas must be the paradoxical role of technology that both enables and constricts freedom.

Crash Landing on You (2019–20), which is the most recent production that I analyze in this book, in many ways, is a recapitulation of these dramas' reflexive ability to engage with the complexities of technology in North Korea. A metacommentary showcasing how the consumption of South Korean dramas within North Korea is a parabolic experience, *Crash Landing on You* exposes the double nature of media and technology as able to provide a means of surveillance and social connection. Circling back to how South Korean dramas were able to begin their unexpected second life in the North, this chapter shows that they have the unique capability to diagnose the past while delivering a prognosis for the future when the two Koreas will be able to communicate through shared media and popular culture.

Autumn in My Heart

Aired from September 18 to November 7, 2000, on South Korea's major terrestrial TV station KBS2, *Autumn in My Heart* was a domestic hit, with an average viewership of 38.6 percent and even reaching a peak viewership of 46.1 percent. Its popularity soon spread throughout Asia: although it aired on minor television channels such as BS Nippon and CATV from 2000 to 2002 in Japan, the drama enjoyed a substantial enough following to make the actors playing its main protagonists sought-after stars in Japan. The drama's success extended to Taiwan (2001), Hong Kong (2002), and the People's Republic of China (PRC) (2002), reaching viewership of over 40 percent.

After the drama became popular in mainland China, it gradually made its way to North Korea in the mid-2000s, signaling the beginning of the South Korean–drama fever that continues to this day. When the drama first came through the active underground trade channel between the two countries that started to change the economic lives of North Koreans around the turn of the new millennium, few would have guessed that this classic South Korean TV melodrama would captivate the hearts of accidental viewers in the North. Weaving the perennially popular theme of unrequited love into the central narrative, *Autumn in My Heart* revolves around an impossible love story between a young couple, Eun-seo and Jun-seo, who find themselves mired in the convoluted fate of birth secrets and potential incest. Jun-seo and Eun-seo grow up thinking that they are biological siblings, but the drama gradually reveals that Eun-seo was accidentally switched with Jun-seo's biological sister Sin-ae soon after their birth. When Eun-seo's real identity is revealed, Eun-seo and Jun-seo start to develop feelings for each other that transcend familial love. They are confronted with the difficult choice between platonic love and erotic love, but before they can fully realize their desire for each other, Eun-seo dies of leukemia, leaving behind the heartbroken Jun-seo.

Changes in fate and mistaken identity are timeless themes in world literature (think *The Prince and the Pauper*), but they have a particular resonance for Koreans. As subjects living in the forcibly divided nation, they are consciously and subconsciously haunted by the harrowing hypothesis of being born on the wrong side of the border. Such anxiety was fully explored in the

North Korean film *The Fate of Geum-hui and Eun-hui* (Geum-hui-wa Eun-hui-ui unmyeong). Released in 1972, the film presents a plot quite similar to *Autumn in My Heart*. Geum-hui and Eun-hui are born twin sisters but are separated during the Korean War, never to see each other again. Geum-hui grows up in North Korea, living a fulfilled life as an artist well cared for by the benevolent state, while Eun-hui lives a miserable life of economic and sexual exploitation in the South. Their parallel lives are analogous to the lives of Eun-seo and Sin-ae, who grow up in diametrically opposed environments: while Eun-seo is lavished with love and attention in a highly cultured family, Sin-ae endures poverty and abuse.

Autumn in My Heart does not presume fate to be permanently sealed but rather an unstable and fluid state to which every human being is randomly assigned. Just as Eun-seo and Sin-ae find themselves living each other's lives, can our fate suddenly change? But rather than galvanizing the myth of an individual who can rise above their predestined lot or reclaim the destiny wrongly taken away, the drama instead magnifies the fragility of human life with a sense of resignation: Could what we conventionally regard as the bedrock of life—parents, familial ties, and surrounding community—be false measures for identification that can suddenly shift overnight? North Korean viewers who see the sudden reversal of fortune for Eun-seo and Sin-ae might ask, What if I had been born in South Korea? What if my fortune was to be reversed like these drama protagonists? The doubleness of a Korean subject, having been randomly assigned North Korean or South Korean citizenship along the arbitrarily drawn border, stands on these shaky foundations, where an individual's biography and a nation's history intersect.

Although many North Korean viewers claim that they watched the drama for its "novelty" value, including its full-on emphasis on individual feelings and a scrumptious lifestyle, often construed as an escape fantasy, the drama's sensational success with North Koreans lies within the allegorical reflections of the history of the divided nation. Equally powerfully, the drama presents a foundational lesson about the rules of the marketplace, especially how human value is measured in monetary terms and human relationships, by market transactions. Given that the drama spread throughout North Korea in the early to mid-2000s, when the marketplace was proliferating, the hard lessons about money that it offered did not go unnoticed.

The open pursuit of individual economic mobility in North Korea cannot be discussed in public as it goes against the gist of the collective, socialist ethos; therefore, the drama provides much-needed antilanguage and antibehavior for North Koreans to process the importance of economic viability.

The drama is replete with moments immediately relatable to North Koreans, who suffer from an increasing gap in living standards; those who had opportunities to run a business in a marketplace grew exponentially wealthier than average North Koreans, who were left in painful poverty. Before the girls discover their true identities, impoverished Sin-ae jealously looks at the meat-filled lunch box of Eun-seo, who is surrounded by classmates openly expressing their envy. After Eun-seo and Sin-ae are returned to their biological families, Eun-seo struggles to make ends meet: in her early twenties she is nearly sold by her thuggish brother into marriage to a much older man, who promises to pay off the family debt—an attempt that Eun-seo successfully dodges. When Eun-seo's brother becomes aware that his sister is pursued by Tae-seok, a young and handsome heir to a hotel-business tycoon, he starts to ask for money from Tae-seok, whereby the practice of engaging in human relationship via monetary terms is confirmed once more. But the bluntest moment emerges during the following conversation between Eun-seo and Tae-seok. Deeply frustrated by Eun-seo's unreceptiveness to his love interest, Tae-seok resorts to his financial power when confronting her about her unchanging love for Jun-seo.

> Tae-seok. Love? Forget it. I will buy it. I will buy you. How much? How much will you take?
> Eun-seo. How much can you give me? I . . . I need money. I really need money. How much can you give me? How much can you give me? How much am I worth?[23]

This histrionic scene between two potential lovers is performed with a heightened sense of hysteria—with a generous dose of close-ups emulating the stormy dramatics of telenovelas—so much so that many South Korean comedians created parodies, providing a good chuckle for melodrama-jaded South Korean viewers. For North Koreans, however, Eun-seo's blunt talk of money confirms the continuity between the diegetic reality and the logics of the marketplace economy—a continuity that has come to define the millennial experience in North Korea. An anonymous interviewee (female in her thirties, born in Pyongyang, who left North Korea in 2008 and settled in South Korea in 2013) told me in an interview, "Eun-seo's open talk about money was not surprising at all. It's all the same in Pyongyang. The gap between those who have it all and those who don't is just too big. I was not surprised by the talks of money. People are the same everywhere."[24]

Perhaps *Autumn in My Heart*'s lasting power over North Koreans lies in how it mirrors the turbulent and ever-changing world for North Koreans, who now have to master the harsh grammar of capitalism. And this self-imposed learning process about the logic of money is what perhaps gives North Koreans a sense of cultural ownership of this drama. Unlike her usual self—virtuous in every possible way and uncompromised by the seduction of wealth—Eun-seo then takes a sudden interest in her monetary worth. Unbeknownst to Tae-seok, Eun-seo secretly suffers from leukemia, which demands expensive treatment she cannot afford. By expressing her ironic and sudden interest in the value of money, Eun-seo provokes difficult questions that resonate strongly with North Koreans—questions that cannot be openly discussed in public: What is the value of money in regard to human life? And what is the value of life in the face of money?

The scene not only shows Eun-seo's struggle to answer these questions but also lays the foundation for Tae-seok's character. Tall, handsome, carefree, and rich, he is uninhibited in pursuing what he desires. Nothing can deter him from acquiring what he wants, and Tae-seok deploys all the means he has to win Eun-seo's love, including the most powerful ammunition: wealth. But rather than making him a materialistic brute, the drama casts Tae-seok as a paragon of desirable masculinity. Just as Eun-seo's sudden interest in her own monetary value is justified, the romanticization of money enables Tae-seok to acquire true love. Gold begets a heart of gold.

Cell phones play a central role in romanticizing money, which is the primary force mitigating human relationships in this drama; cell phones expose one's true identity, even leading to the reversal of fate. Early in the series, Tae-seok, staying at his family resort, is intrigued by a phone operator, who presents herself as a thirty-seven-year-old mother of two children. This woman in fact is Eun-seo, who uses this false identity to fend off Tae-seok's romantic advances as he is already known as a notorious womanizer among hotel employees. Tae-seok decides to find out who this woman is by a technique identical to the "cell phone kiss" that North Koreans actually use to make forbidden phone calls beyond the border. Tae-seok uses the hotel room landline to call the operator, then uses his own cell phone to call an extra cell phone he carries. He then places the extra cell phone speaker on the landline receiver and walks from his hotel room to the operating station while conversing with the operator via his own cell phone. Just as Eun-seo might have served as the instructor of capitalist logic to North Korean viewers, Tae-seok, in this scene, might have taught viewers in the North how to stage creative treachery with cell phones to obtain what they desire.

Cell phones continue to be the central device for revelation as the drama progresses, exposing the power of technology as deeply implicated with monetary interests. Jun-seo and Eun-seo go on a secret trip, evading the watchful eyes of Yu-mi and Tae-seok, who are in love with each of them, respectively. What was meant to be a day trip turns into an overnight trip when a heavy downpour forces a road closure, barring their return to Yu-mi and Tae-seok. Eun-seo calls Tae-seok, and Jun-seo makes a phone call to Yu-mi with an obvious lie about the reason for their absence. But the secret lovers do not know that Tae-seok stopped by Yu-mi's house to inquire as to Eun-seo's whereabouts. Jun-seo and Eun-seo's lies are instantly revealed when Tae-seok and Yu-mi simultaneously receive phone calls about why their partners cannot return home that night.

As much as cell phones call for the revelation of truth behind deception, equally important is their ability to become powerful agents of surveillance. Shortly after Jun-seo and Eun-seo's lies are exposed, their relationship becomes known to their respective families, who dissuade the two lovers from further pursuing each other. Despite this opposition, Eun-seo and Jun-seo are unable to stop their growing feelings for each other and decide to elope to a remote place. On a faraway farm in a bucolic paradise, where they can be true to their feelings, they decide to turn off their cell phones and create a utopia of noninterference. Cell phones become duplicitous devices, enabling connection as well as disconnection in this scene. Likewise, in a later episode, Jun-seo and Eun-seo succumb to the pressures of the surrounding world, which does not welcome their burgeoning relationship. During a forced separation, in deep longing for each other, they reach out to their cell phones to hear their lover's voice, only to timidly withdraw from doing so. Cell phones become the incarnation of the absent lover, standing for the painful and futile pursuit of their passion. In the end, when Eun-seo discovers that she has limited time to live, the two overcome all opposition and decide to spend the few remaining days together. At this final phase, human-to-human contact replaces partial and incomplete connection through cell phones, setting cell phones as intermediaries to a true human connection. Eun-seo dies on Jun-seo's back by the seashore as he carries her to their favorite places filled with happy memories from childhood.

Autumn in My Heart paved the way for South Korean dramas to lift the psychological barriers between the two Koreas, but most significantly, it showcased how cell phones can emerge as convoluted mediators of human relationships: this advanced technology mitigates the users' connection to the world, with the cell phones serving as effective devices to make and break social networks, all the while acting as a potent means to surveil users. Despite all its trappings as a cliché-filled melodrama, *Autumn in My Heart* introduced the power of communication technology to North Koreans who had yet to see the widespread use of cell phones in their daily lives.

Stairway to Heaven

The original airing of *Stairway to Heaven* in South Korea in 2003 coincided with South Korea's rise as the key player in the global cell phone market. The country's foremost tech company, Samsung Electronics, launched cell phones that carried the title of "the world's first" around this time: in 2002, it produced the world's first video-recording phone. Not to be left out, Samsung's chief competitor, LG Electronics, launched phenomenally popular slide phones in December 2002 and released Korea's first phone with an embedded MP3-playing function.

As if reflecting on the latest trends in the cell phone industry, *Stairway to Heaven* features much more frequent use of the latest cell phones, such as folder phones, slide phones, and flip phones. But rather than being the simple parade ground for the latest technology, the drama presents scenes that tactfully mix modes of digital communication and person-to-person interfacing without the involvement of digital communication. This is done by the frequent juxtaposition of and interchangeability between mediated cell phone communication and physical copresence of conversationalists, which calls for closer scrutiny of how these modes of communication work symbiotically. For every crucial moment of plot development, the drama deploys cell phones as devices of double entendre, making and breaking the fate of its main characters.

Much like *Autumn in My Heart*, *Stairway to Heaven* relies on time-proven staples of South Korean melodrama: three star-crossed lovers, love bordering on incest, a rich and handsome guy falling for a less fortunate girl with a heart of gold, while his beautiful and wealthy fiancée is driven to madness with jealousy. The central storyline concerns the heart-rending relationship between Jeong-seo and Seong-ju, whose childhood friendship matures into love. Seong-ju grows up to be a dashing man who is about to inherit a business empire; in the meantime, Jeong-seo's father remarries a manipulative actress, who brings her son and daughter from a previous marriage, Tae-hwa and Yu-ri, into Jeong-seo's house. Tae-hwa soon falls in love with his stepsister, Jeong-seo, while Yu-ri becomes jealous and resentful of Jeong-seo's close relationship with Seong-ju. Infatuated with Seong-ju's wealth and power, Yu-ri torments her stepsister in every imaginable way. The tension between them takes a fateful turn when Yu-ri runs over Jeong-seo in a car accident, leaving her with memory loss. Capitalizing on this opportunity, Yu-ri ingratiates herself with Seong-ju and becomes nearly engaged to him while Tae-hwa starts a relationship with Jeong-seo, who knows neither her true identity nor her past. Eventually Jeong-seo recovers her memory, but she is soon diagnosed with terminal-stage eye cancer. Upon learning about Jeong-seo's condition, repentant Tae-hwa commits suicide in order to donate his retina to his beloved stepsister. Despite this sacrifice, Jeong-seo soon dies of cancer after a brief union with her true love Seong-ju.

The misdirected passion and unrequited love that create a messy entanglement of the protagonists' fates are punctuated by scenes that revolve around phone calls. The show regularly stages Jeong-seo and Seong-ju communicating on cell phones while being located within arm's reach. This distant mode of communication is performed when one of them is not aware of the other's physical proximity. The sequence that follows Seong-ju and

Yu-ri's engagement scene in episode 9 stages this irony most viscerally. When Seong-ju announces to the party guests that the woman he wishes to be with is not his fiancée, Yu-ri, but rather Jeong-seo, mayhem ensues, which culminates in Tae-hwa's arrest. Shocked by her conflicted feelings between Seong-ju's public confession of love and the arrest of Tae-hwa, who is deeply in love with her, Jeong-seo decides to follow Tae-hwa to the police station. Unbeknownst to Jeong-seo, Seong-ju trails her. There, he finds Jeong-seo crying in the dark stairwell waiting for Tae-hwa's release. Standing just half a flight down, Seong-ju calls her on a cell phone, and the two have a phone conversation with their backs turned to each other. But the reverse-angle shots with close-ups of their faces create an impression that they are having a face-to-face conversation. Upon realizing that Jeong-seo still has lingering feelings for Tae-hwa, Seong-ju tells her that although he wishes to be with her, he did not follow her. Seong-ju turns around to gaze at Jeong-seo's back, only to see her whole body shake with uncontrollable tears while she assures him that she is just fine. The dramatic irony arises from Jeong-seo's unawareness that the person she is conversing with on the phone is practically within arm's reach and that Seong-ju is able to perceive the gap between her voice and her bodily language.

But the scene does more than just highlight the irony: by framing Seong-ju's action as a gesture of love, it presents a foray into romanticizing the act of surveillance via cell technology. The cell phone conversation here highlights Seong-ju's omniscient perspective, allowing him to see Jeong-seo's vulnerability while her calm voice over the phone hides her actual devastation. Conversely, it accentuates Jeong-seo's partial vision that does not allow her to see Seong-ju's physical copresence. Her figurative blindness paves the way for the literal blindness that she succumbs to shortly after this scene. As Jeong-seo's ability to see ebbs away, she is cast as a highly eroticized object of surveillance.

The reversal of this scene resurfaces in later episodes when the two have a phone conversation separated only by a transparent window. Determined to marry Jeong-seo, Seong-ju chooses a wedding dress for her and waits for her at a café. Meanwhile, Jeong-seo visits a doctor's office and learns that she is becoming blind. Devastated by the news, she wanders the streets without returning to her appointment only to arrive at the café four hours later. There she sees distressed Seong-ju, upset with the long waiting, and calls him from outside the window. When she appears in front of him, Seong-ju closes his eyes like a blind man as a gesture to protest her tardiness. His closed eyes invite scrutiny, in effect drawing the audience to closely surveil this act. His unintentional mimicry of her actual blindness gestures toward subconscious empathy, allowing for the mirroring of identification to eventually frame the act of mutual surveillance.

Conventionally, surveillance is not associated with titillating romance, not to mention fatal love, in North Korea. Rather, it is a fear-inducing operation by the state power, halting discursive flows of information and exchange. What is striking about the popularity of *Stairway to Heaven* in North Korea is that it introduces a new equation of surveillance as a performative paradigm married to heartbreaking romance and creative modes of interpersonal communication. A direct subversion of the established conventions of surveillance, the drama opens alternative ways for North Koreans to look at surveillance outside the state apparatus, hence deconstructing their previous centralized notion.

Romanticized surveillance culminates in the final episode when Jeong-seo faces a death sentence as the cancer spreads to her brain. Seong-ju calls her from the hospital corridor while observing her just around the corner, unaware of his physical presence at that moment. She is not yet cognizant of her condition, but Seong-ju, who has just spoken to the doctor and learned the devastating news, suppresses his teary outbursts while trying to talk calmly to Jeong-seo. Inculcated with the desperation of true and—for the most part—unrequited love, the act of surveillance here takes on a highly eroticized patina. As devices of freedom and restriction, cell phones tie and untie the knots of each character's fate.

Over and over throughout the drama, the phones enunciate the identities of their owners. Deeply missing Seong-ju, Jeong-seo calls him just to hear his voice for a short while, then hangs up. But in order not to reveal her identity, she calls from a public phone, which leaves 000–0000 in Seong-ju's caller ID. Jeong-seo's wish to erase her presence in his life is symbolically captured in zeroes, but because of this nullifying caller ID, Seong-ju immediately recognizes the caller. The cell phone as a metaphoric extension of the owner is once again reaffirmed when Tae-hwa leaves a dried clover leaf inside

Jeong-seo's flip phone as a token of his love when he bids her farewell. In these moments, the phone stands as not simply a pale surrogate but a powerful extension of its owner. As if touching the beloved, Tae-hwa fondly holds the phone and carefully places the memento of his love as if to inscribe his feelings onto the gadget.

Similarly, money, not just cell phones, takes on a highly romantic character in *Stairway to Heaven*. If market transaction and wealth were sidebars of *Autumn in My Heart*, in *Stairway to Heaven*, they become more fully integrated into human relationships. Events in the drama frequently take place in Lotte Shopping Mall, a megacommercial center in the affluent Jamsil District of Seoul, where hundreds of high-end shops and restaurants appear alongside Lotte World, a fancy indoor amusement park. Developed amid the 1988 Seoul Olympic boom, the Lotte Shopping Mall and Lotte World still stood as a main commercial and entertainment hub in 2003. Seong-ju is cast as an heir to this business empire, pursued by both Jeong-seo and her gold-digging stepsister, Yu-ri. Although the drama presents how Jeong-seo's true virtue lies in her sincere pursuit of love, it does not make a secret of Seong-ju's wealth; rather, tremendous wealth is valorized as a part of his romantic appeal. Similar to *Autumn in My Heart* where one sister takes over the fate of the other, the quest for fortune—whether intentional or not—ends up reversing the fate of the two stepsisters, Yu-ri and Jeong-seo. Whereas Yu-ri's downfall lies in her greed, which prompted her to pursue Seong-ju even without genuine love, Jeong-seo truly wins over Seong-ju with her heart of gold. Once again, this drama weaves a comfortable symbiosis of romance and affluence, binding the irresistible allure of material wealth with fated love.

Autumn in My Heart and *Stairway to Heaven* frequently feature cell phones that had not yet been popularized in the North. North Koreans watched them on VCDs or DVDs as these dramas' circulation predated the common use of smartphones in both Koreas,[25] but viewers in the North were treated to the novelty of frequent and pervasive cell phone usage—the very reality that would saturate their country a decade later. While *Stairway to Heaven* has a very similar melodramatic plot to *Autumn in My Heart*, it uses cell phones in a much more indispensable way to punctuate the drama's emotional life: cell phones reveal the convoluted fate of key protagonists, who often miss crucial opportunities to fully connect to one another. These moments overlay many oppositions—analogue/digital, offline/online, and the actual/virtual—which the drama frequently deploys as metaphors for the crossed paths that allegorically extend to the divide between the South and the North. Given the central role cell phones play in the North Korean family's defection process, we can imagine how the phones' ability to make or break human relations speaks volumes to the North Korean viewers of this drama.

In the world of missed contacts and crossings, cell phones keenly expose how the performance of a partial vision leads to partial knowledge. South Korean drama producers might deploy cell phones as just another device in staging a melodramatic scene, but for North Koreans, they signify much more: although the circulation of this drama in North Korea predates the popular use of cell phones, the idea of cell phone conversation as a seminal moment to realize one's limited vision and knowledge about the world soon became reality. So did the pervasiveness of surveillance via cell phone technology. What comes across as a typical South Korean melodrama in effect ended up being a prescient tale for North Koreans—that the amazing wonder called cell phones would cut both ways to allow and restrict their freedom.

Boys over Flowers

In the six years between the airing of *Stairway to Heaven* and *Boys over Flowers*, much happened in the cell phone industry in South Korea and globally. The South Korean cell phone industry exerted much influence on the global industry as South Korean companies such as Samsung and LG became the industry leaders in manufacturing and sales of smartphones around the globe. Samsung in particular rose steadily to overtake Apple in global smartphone sales in the third quarter of 2011.[26] The airing of *Boys over Flowers* co-incided with the growing usage of smartphones and the subsequent soaring growth of the South Korean industry; each episode was poised to become the most boisterous billboard for smartphones.

It is not surprising that *Boys over Flowers* came to be recognized as argu-ably the most blatant advertising campaign disguised as a TV miniseries in half a century of South Korean TV history. From instant noodles to luxury cars, there was so much product placement that the drama violated South Korean Regulations on Broadcast Deliberation, article 46, on product placement numerous times, all of which was announced to viewers at the beginning of each episode. Leading this pervasive campaign was the Samsung Haptic Pop phone series, which came to be known by one of the protagonists' names as the "Gu Jun-pyo phone." Haptic Pop phones were introduced as a more affordable line in Samsung's popular Haptic phone series, designed to attract young consumers by keeping the price under $500. Through the effective product placement with *Boys over Flowers*, Samsung was able to flesh out the eye-catching design and the novel functions of text and video messaging, all of which combined to make cell phones the essential gadgets of the fashionable millennial generation.

But for young North Korean viewers who watched the drama in the early 2010s with just a little bit of time lag, it would have been hard to understand the full extent of the smartphone's multifunctionality. This depends on the time of consumption of these dramas. The earlier one watched the dramas, the bigger the technological gap. An anonymous interviewee (female in her twenties, born in Hyesan, who left North Korea in 2017) is a case in point: "I watched *Boys over Flowers* around 2015–16. This was the time when North Koreans also widely used cell phones, so watching how these protagonists used cell phones did not surprise me that much."[27]

Aside from the technological display, the drama was able to offer plenty of other visual pleasures. According to many accounts, North Korean millennial viewers promptly took notice of the ostentatious fashion statements of the main characters. According to *Radio Free Asia*'s report on September 15, 2011, "In the city of Cheongjin, many junior high school students emulated the hairstyles of the two leading male actors and named them after the characters, such as Gu Jun-pyo style or Yun Ji-hu style. What's more, a short plaid skirt featured as a part of a school uniform in the drama was named after its female protagonist, Geum Jan-di, and is a highly sought-after item among young women in the city of Hoeryeong—to the point that it is extremely difficult to find plaid-patterned cloth in the marketplace."[28] Over and over, the drama's popularity is attested by many resettlers. Li Hyang-mi (female born in Cheongjin in 1992 who left North Korea in 2013) is so deeply infatuated with the lead actor, Lee Min-ho, that she and her friends look down upon North Korean boys and treat them like little kids.[29] Na Min-hui (female born in 1991 in Pyongyang who left North Korea in 2014 and came to South Korea in 2015) attests to the drama's popularity by noting how "everyone watched *Boys over Flowers* in Pyongyang. One would be considered a spy if they did not watch it."[30] The drama's influence over the young and fashionable abound, as the following anonymous interviewee (male in his early thirties, born in Pyongyang, who left North Korea in 2017 and soon arrived in South Korea) would testify with a chuckle:

> I copied many fashion styles while watching *Boys over Flowers* and *Stairway to Heaven*. I noted how guys would have their hair long and wear waistcoats. They looked strange in the beginning, but the more I watched, the more fashionable they looked. Those guys were wearing long scarves, and I emulated how they tied them. Because of Lee Min-ho, I also watched *City Hunter*, where he appeared wearing dress shoes without socks, which I also copied. You can find all these items in marketplaces. Those merchants deal with specifically South Korean style. They also call you when they have new products, or if you give them an illustration of what you want, they will make it for you. So when I left North Korea, I wore a style that you cannot find in North Korea [so that I could pass as a South Korean in China]. But when I came to the South, I realized that the style went out of vogue already eight years ago.[31]

As much as fashion and hairstyles featured in the show indelibly became the textbook for North Korean millennials' antibehavior, so did stylish phones. In a way, the presentation of the body and tech gadgets has become the source of a viral network of influences—a process that intensified with *Boys over Flowers*. As an anonymous interviewee (female in her thirties, born in Pyongyang, who left North Korea in 2008 and settled in South Korea in 2013) notes, "When I watched *Boys over Flowers* in China, I thought of having a phone like those featured in the drama."[32] The point is confirmed once again by another anonymous interviewee (male in his early thirties, born in Pyongyang, who left North Korea in 2017 and soon arrived in South Korea): "I was mesmerized by how people used their phones, how they used their landline, and the many functions that came with the sets."[33]

The drama enjoyed great popularity in North Korea and circulated year after year, creating varying degrees of gap between the initial release date in South Korea (2009) and the varying points of circulation in North Korea. For the first wave of viewers who had yet to see smartphones in their daily lives, how much of these devices' multifunctionality could they understand?

If anything, the drama must have introduced the perceivable gap in cell phone technology between the two Koreas. North Korea had just established Koryolink in 2008, signaling the popularization of cell phones to come in the next decade. With the impending changes, the advanced cell phone technology in *Boys over Flowers* quite likely would have presented a fascinating point of attraction for North Korean viewers. Due to the technology gap, North Koreans first started to watch *Boys over Flowers* on DVD and then eventually switched to their smartphones. Gang Na-ra (female born in Cheongjin in 1997 who left North Korea in 2014), for instance, recalls watching the show with six to seven classmates by plugging a flash drive into her cell phone.[34]

The enduring popularity of the show can be accounted for on many levels—from conspicuous elements of visual pleasure to uncanny, novel technology—but at the fulcrum of fascination lies the strong endorsement of an emergent world order that prioritizes the power of money. In a 2013 article, "For the Eyes of North Koreans? Politics of Money and Class in *Boys over Flowers*," I note that *Boys over Flowers*'s central appeal to North Koreans is a harsh yet real lesson on plutocracy and the neoliberal economy—the very forces looming large in millennial North Korea. The drama's core message on the power of money and class hierarchy speaks strongly to North Koreans, who have to "endure as volatile subjects caught in between conflicting political and economic logics."[35] Of the manifold reasons for the drama's popularity, its open worship of money and limitless power resonated with the emergent entrepreneurial marketplace generation, who have come to depend heavily on means of rapid communication for their economic survival and success.

The show's central plot unfolds the improbable love between the tall and handsome heir to the most powerful South Korean conglomerate, Gu Jun-pyo, and a good-hearted girl, Geum Jan-di, with a humble background. Their happy engagement at the end of the miniseries follows a prolonged bitter struggle between the two. At the beginning of the series, Jan-di first bravely resists Jun-pyo, who incarnates the seductive yet tyrannical power that the drama presents as the preordained natural right of the wealthy. At a prestigious high school founded by his family, he reigns as a despot who knows no limits to his power. He torments anyone who disobeys him, but soon he is confronted by Jan-di, who puts up a good fight against his cruelty. For a while, Jan-di seems to successfully teach him a lesson or two about the dignity of the poor, prompting him to reconsider his belief in the unlimited power of money. But alas, their fight ends with just another validation of the almighty power of wealth. In a telling moment, money silences resistance:

> Jan-di. There is something you don't understand. Friends are not to be purchased with money but to be acquired by sincerity.
>
> Jun-pyo. There is nothing that cannot be won over with money. Tell me if there is. Do you really think there is such a thing that cannot be won over with money? If there is such a thing, name one thing, you commoner.
>
> Jan-di, *remains silent*.[36]

I have already read this confrontation as a blunt allegory of class conflict, which is prevalent in both Koreas. As "the intensified class struggle . . . peters out in the merciful face of the almighty power—be it the heroic leaders of the sacred state or the beyond-rich heir to the multinational conglomeration," we see the resurfacing of Korea's lingering class system, which came to an abrupt end at the dawn of the twentieth century.[37] Jan-di's character arc begins with unadulterated courage but ends with complicity, succumbing to the higher powers. Of all the dramas explored in this chapter, *Boys over Flowers* is by far the bluntest manifesto of plutocracy.

Without subtlety, wealth and power create a spectacular display of the humiliation and subjugation of the poor, which become magnified by how mass media and communication are used in the show. When Gu Jun-pyo's bludgeoning of fellow high schoolers starts to dominate the headlines of endless media outlets, Gu's mother steps in to mitigate the media frenzy. The ruthless leader of the Shinhwa Group, who knows nothing but ambition, reprimands her secretary for not having nipped the negative publicity in the bud. While doing so, she reveals the imperatives of open, public media: "Do you know why mass media is horrific? Because it's ignorant. Once it becomes madness, it gets out of control. No reason or common sense can curb it."[38] The condescending view expressed here resonates with the North Korean leadership's perspective on the mass media, where the draconian control restricts the free influx of information to the masses and that information is subject to an open appraisal. Needless to say, the regime does not allow any type of media—whether targeting the masses or a few interest groups—to run its course freely outside of the leadership's tight control.

For North Koreans, the real horrors invoked by the mass media lie not in the loss of reason, as Gu's mother describes, but in reason's complete openness to both good and bad news, traveling in real time to create synchronous impacts on the society. This point is validated over and over throughout the drama with the help of cell phones. When various items of gossip about Jan-di spread throughout school—whether it's a rumor about her pregnancy designed to tarnish her reputation or true news that she is dating Jun-pyo—they spread like wildfire via text messages that all the students share on their smartphones. For North Korean viewers to see smartphones become the conduit of virality must have been strange because, for them, user-generated transmission of news had been impossible to conceive of. The sense of ownership of knowledge, especially subversive knowledge, generated by a cell phone network had not yet been introduced to North Korea, but *Boys over Flowers* introduced the modes in which information can spread at real time without the intervention of the central state.

Bottom-up modes of creating and spreading information abound in the drama: Jan-di's younger brother, Gang-san, keeps updating his sister on the latest information about Jun-pyo and his friends. Much to the dismay of his mother, elementary school student Gang-san spends most of his time glued to his laptop. With irascible frustration, his mother reprimands her young son: "Why are you so attached to the computer? Does it produce money and rice?" Without a moment's hesitation, Gang-san confronts the question with unfaltering conviction: "Yes, it does. Money and rice come out of this!"[39] The seemingly benign banter between mother and son may present itself as just another mundane conversation typical of many South Korean family dramas. However, for viewers living in a closed society, like North Korea, the conversation makes an utterly loud claim for the power of information, or more precisely, having free and unlimited access to information—whether the right or wrong kind—becomes a source of empowerment. Gang-san's words ring a bell of truth for the marketplace participants whose livelihood entirely depends on access to technology and real-time exchange of information.

In the long list of the drama's many shortcomings (its blatant and tasteless commercial campaigns being just one), humorizing the terrors ignited by false rumors appears prominently. A key to this process is how surveillance is disguised as a manifestation of romantic interest. In the earlier phase of the drama when Jun-pyo launches a series of attacks on Jan-di, he sets up secret cameras around campus so that he can monitor every moment of her struggle. He enjoys the secret access to his victim from a luxurious private lounge reserved exclusively for him and his close friends. Ensconced on a plush leather sofa placed next to a well-stocked bar, pool table, and state-of-the art entertainment system, Jun-pyo, with great pleasure, surveils Jan-di's torment unfolding in real time. From cute pranks, such as littering the school swimming pool with yellow rubber ducks to keep Jan-di from practicing her laps, to cruel public bullying carried out on Jun-pyo's order, the tyrant watches it all, all unbeknownst to Jan-di.

The glaring contrast between the extremely well-guarded privacy of the surveilling subject and the naked exposure of the surveilled object highlights the haunting discrepancies in their power dynamics, but the drama deploys surveillance as a logical step to transforming Jun-pyo's love-hate relationship with Jan-di into passion. But unlike in *Autumn in My Heart* and *Stairway to Heaven* where surveillance assumes the tender gaze of the enamored, this show unabashedly discloses the sadistic pleasure of the surveilling gaze. Although it is hardly the show's intention, *Boys over Flowers* exposes the mechanisms of surveillance and the lopsided power distribution that defines the relationship between the surveilling and the surveilled.

Unexpectedly, the mindless entertainment drama that doubles as a commercial for cell phones also brings home basic phone etiquette for North Korean viewers. When Gu Jun-pyo is unexpectedly visited by his fiancée, Jae-gyeong, a wealthy and cheerful heiress whose marriage to him has been arranged, indignant Gu shouts out, "Did you boil your cell phone and eat it? Do you not know about the etiquette of calling someone and receiving permission to visit before actually showing up?"[40] In an uncanny parallel, this moment echoes the North Korean TV comedy sketch referenced in chapter 1, where a male passenger on the bus is frowned upon for having forgotten basic manners of using his phone in a public space. Likewise, sending too many unsolicited text messages invites scornful response. When Ga-eul's (Jan-di's best friend) unfaithful boyfriend attempts to break up with her, he notes, "Hey you, ugly, stop sending text messages. Because you keep sending an onslaught of text messages, my inbox is stuffed."[41] Although coming from a despicable character, the manners around texting are clearly communicated to viewers.

The drama's surprising ability to cross over to the forbidden land even caught the attention of its producers. The director of *Boys over Flowers*, Jeon Gi-sang, shares his insight on why the show crossed the inter-Korean border so easily and enjoys enduring popularity:

> I heard that [South] Korean dramas are intriguing [to North Korean viewers] partly because the story moves forward very fast. One of the advantages of watching Korean dramas is enjoying a wide variety of subject matters and to have a peek at a wide range of South Korean people's lives—fashion and food being cases in point. I think that's why it's popular. Since North and South Korea have been divided for a long time, both sides feel a strong sense of cultural alienation from each other. But someday, when Korea becomes reunited, I hope North Koreans won't feel so strange about South Korean culture. I believe this can be done by having North Koreans watch [South] Korean dramas: watching dramas will be akin to receiving an immunization shot for North Koreans, who will get acquainted with South Korean ways of life, such as clothing, food, and music.[42]

Conspicuously missing from the director's list of material and cultural influences on North Korean viewers are cell phones. Sooner than later, the drastic transformation of everyday life in North Korea brought about by the introduction of smartphones would hark back to the influence of the dramas on North Koreans' digital consumption. With the benefit of hindsight, can we not claim that *Boys over Flowers* prophesized to young North Korean viewers the consumptive pleasure and the binding power of money—often mediated through the literal usage of cell phones? Ironically, the story is not even South Korean: originally based on Japanese manga, the story was adapted into TV dramas in Taiwan, Japan, and South Korea.[43] When the South Korean producers of *Boys over Flowers* jumped on the bandwagon of such adaptation frenzy, they did not know that their version would traverse the DMZ as a parabolic narrative foreshadowing the reality that awaited North Koreans a few years down the road. Although the virality of online mass media featured in the drama does not exist in today's North Korea, viewers have been treated to a front-row preview of the ambivalent nature of technology—with its openness and its destructiveness fully entangled and obfuscating visions of the future.

My Love from Another Star

While *Boys over Flowers* is the most pan-Asian drama featured in this chapter, *My Love from Another Star* (originally aired in South Korea from December 18, 2013, to February 27, 2014) is by all measures the most commercially successful one to date. Its influence reached far beyond Korea, and it became especially popular in China to the extent that the PRC Nobel laureate in literature Mo Yan hailed its unique storytelling capability during the 2014 National People's Congress of the People's Republic of China.[44] A South Korean media outlet, *Hankook ilbo*, estimated the drama's economic impact on mainland China alone was equivalent to exporting twenty thousand Hyundai Sonata vehicles.[45]

But the true South Korean industry winner to parade its success was Samsung Electronics, the official sponsor of the drama. In 2012, a year prior to the airing of the series, Samsung became the number one manufacturer of smartphones worldwide: according to the 2013 fourth-quarter sales report, Samsung sold ninety-five million Galaxy phones, 39.7 million more phones than its competitors, the iPhone 5s and 5c.[46] The drama's transnational appeal resonated with Samsung's commercial success, whereby a strong identification between the show and the smartphone model was established to the point of identifying a phone with the iconic characters in the drama. Just as *Boys over Flowers* renamed Samsung's Haptic Pop phone the "Gu Jun-pyo phone," *My Love from Another Star* gave Samsung's Galaxy Note 3 a namesake moniker, the "Cheon Song-i phone," for the drama's female protagonist. The pink-color model that Cheon Song-i used became so popular that it took several weeks and months for customers to receive their orders. The drama not only lent itself as an arena for unabashed product placement but also came to construct a shared narrative about individuals' social and physical mobility, similar to how cell phones have come to tout their value in hyperconnected societies. In *My Love from Another Star*, cell phones became the grounds on which a character's identity was fully predicated.

The drama cemented its enduring success by continuing to use the time-proven formula of attractive actors, luscious visual design, and heart-wrenching love stories heavily sprinkled with comic zest. *My Love from Another Star*'s major narrative arc is built on the peculiar romance between two seemingly incompatible characters, Cheon Song-i and Do Min-jun. What happens when a beautiful but frivolous actress and a handsome time-traveling alien fall in love? Although presented as a shallow and vulgar celebrity at the beginning of the show, Song-i falls for the mysterious stranger, gradually revealing a deeper inner self that is capable of recognizing and accepting profound love. The drama situates their encounter in contemporary South Korea but eventually peels off layers of subplots to reveal that, unbeknownst to themselves, the two had already met and fatefully fallen in love some four hundred years earlier.[47] The drama evolves around the process of uncovering their past, culminating with them pledging eternal love as Do Min-jun returns to his planet. The epilogue reveals that Min-jun is able to visit Song-i only sporadically, marking their love story with ever more titillating entanglements of longing and separation.

Entwined with the heart-wrenching romance is the centrality of cell phones and surveillance technology, which play an ambiguous role, bringing justice to villains while exposing their frightening ubiquity in the daily lives of millennial subjects. Technology first exposes multiple schemes devised to harm Cheon Song-i and Do Min-jun and ultimately discloses the culprits to face due justice. Creating and breaking off human relationships in the drama is frequently mediated by the use of smartphones, which also appear as the crucial medium to showcase the consummate celebration of the individual and for self-promotion, which are considered typical virtues in a neoliberal society, like South Korea.

My Love from Another Star is the first South Korean drama to introduce to North Koreans how access to social media via smartphones can
serve as the central platform for social and physical mobility. The timing
of the drama's release coincided with the year when the first North Korean
smartphone, Arirang, was introduced to the North Korean market. In light
of these simultaneous developments, can we infer that *My Love from Another Star* facilitated North Korean viewers' consumerist desire for Arirang
smartphones, available for purchase at the market? And what accompanying
narratives and imaginaries emerged around smartphones as a result of the
sensational popularity of the drama?

An anonymous interviewee (male in his twenties, born in Yanggang
Province, who left North Korea in 2020 and came to South Korea in 2021)
shares how he enjoyed watching *My Love from Another Star* especially since
he was quite interested in cell phones and cars when he was in North Korea.
He notes a wide range of phones and cars feature in this drama and expresses
how he dreamt of having them someday.[48]

Not surprisingly, phones feature prominently in the show yet not necessarily as objects of envy but as the point of satire on materialism and vanity.
The multifunctionality of smartphones shapes the main arc of Song-i's character in the earlier episodes. Characterized by vainglorious self-absorption
typical of a megacelebrity, Song-i is constantly glued to her smartphone, im-
pulsively taking selfies and sharing them on social media for fans' approval.
With the intention of soliciting public affection, she posts a selfie holding a
cup of mocha coffee, featuring her flirtatious gaze and protruding candy-col-
ored lips accompanied by the caption "Thank you Mun Ik-jeom for introducing mocha to Korea!"[49] The caption would make native speakers of Korean
chuckle, immediately recognizing how the interchangeability of the quasi
homonyms "mocha" and "*mok-hwa*" and the stultifying wordplay fuel Song-
i's anachronistic ignorance. Mun Ik-jeom was a fourteenth-century diplomat
of the Koryo dynasty credited for bringing cotton seeds to Korea from the
Yuan dynasty. The Korean word for "cotton," *mok-hwa*, obviously sounds
similar to "mocha," but coffee was introduced to Korea much later, at the
turn of the twentieth century. Much to Song-i's dismay, her misuse of social
media invites nothing but harsh public ridicule. The drama comically—but
also poignantly—illustrates the cruelty of social media in terms of how

individuals' sense of their worthiness is constructed by how they are presented and perceived by other users.

Mocking of celebrity continues in the computer room, where a group of high school students are seen pasting Song-i's face onto a scantily clad woman's body; the giggling pubescent boys then discuss how they could photoshop her face onto a naked body to escalate the fun next time. The pervasive degree of bodily scrutiny enabled by digital technology in this drama is exposed through comedy, but these scenes, replete with irresistible humor, can also lay bare the workings of surveillance mechanisms forced onto other human beings. Do Min-jun also cannot evade the degree of public scrutiny brought on by technology. Min-jun's alien status—in the literal sense of the word—is marked by his use of outdated technology. Repeatedly in the drama, people call attention to how Min-jun still uses a pager instead of a cell phone. Is he literally an alien? When Min-jun capitulates and buys a cell phone upon Song-i's urging, smartphone technology, such as text messaging, becomes an unwanted burden for him. For instance, when he ends up sending an unintended text message to Song-i, he even uses his teleportation power to erase the message before she sees it. But the transition from a pager to a cell phone signals his integration into human society, where he eventually becomes more of an insider than an alien. In a country where open use of social media has yet to exist, it is curious to speculate how North Korean viewers, who watch this drama in a clandestine manner to evade surveillance from their own society, processed the marvelous technology's ability to facilitate public scrutiny in a supposedly free society like South Korea. And how do they process the significance of owning a cell phone as a signal for being integrated into the South Korean society when cell phones in North Korea are often used to break social prohibitions?

To add an extra layer to this paradox, surveillance is presented as a dual force capable of both destroying and saving others' lives. Showing its destructive power, the series presents a ghoulish vision of surveillance cameras and monitoring screens that litter nearly every place featured in the drama. Unlike *Autumn in My Heart* and *Stairway to Heaven*, where surveillance is carried out through the romanticized gaze of the lover, in *My Love from Another Star*, surveillance unveils a more harrowing vision of destroying others' lives.

This dark side of surveillance is closely associated with Jae-gyeong, an heir to a business conglomerate and an older brother of Hui-gyeong, who has been professing his unrequited love for Song-i for over a decade. Jae-gyeong deviously maneuvers through various surveillance technologies to silence his mistress, actress Yu-ra, whom he has no intention of marrying. When Yu-ra threatens Jae-gyeong with the public announcement that she might be carrying his child and demands that he marry her, Jae-gyeong poisons her and pushes her off the cruise ship where they are attending the wedding party of Yu-ra's colleague. The killing is disguised as suicide, for which the public blames Song-i, an open rival of Yu-ra in the acting world.

In order to defend Song-i from public blame, which quickly devolves into a cruel witch hunt, Do Min-jun retrieves the footage of the CCTV cameras on the cruise and saves it on a USB drive. Assuming that Song-i might have witnessed his crime and hidden the evidence, Jae-gyeong starts to surveil unsuspecting Song-i. As a part of this effort, in the name of an anonymous fan, he sends a large stuffed animal with a hidden camera to monitor Song-i's daily activities in her private residence. He also searches her condo for the USB drive. When he enters her building, he turns off the CCTV installed in the elevator with a twist of his ring, which functions like a remote control to the camera. Jae-gyeong deploys other tech gadgets, such as wiretaps and remote-controlled alarms, in his plan to eliminate anyone who stands in his way to inheriting his family's wealth. The visceral exposure of the surveillance operation in an affluent and technologized society is well documented in Jae-gyeong's schemes. Exposing the mechanism of an all-seeing eye is an open invitation for North Korean viewers to visualize and understand the anatomy of surveillance.

On the other hand, in keeping with the tradition set by the previously analyzed dramas where the act of surveillance was seen as an extension of love, Do Min-jun reaffirms how surveillance can be highly romanticized. To mark his special power as an alien, the drama presents him as possessing the ability to hear every sound from a distance, including that of his neighbor Song-i. When she moves into an apartment near his, he is unable to sleep because of her late-night drunken singing spree, which is her way of forgetting about online trolls who taunt her. Unbeknownst to Song-i, Do Min-jun becomes her inadvertent audience, and even though he is greatly tormented by the noise, his super hearing gives him close insight into the inner workings of his soon-to-be lover. Song-i becomes romantically interested in this possessor of supernatural-surveillance capability, thereby proposing a counterpoint to the vicious element of surveillance. Surveillance cuts both ways—as a means to bring destruction and as a form of love.

The use of media technology in this drama illustrates how it is inherently tied to the self-formation of central characters, even though that leads to paradoxes and conflicts: What is the main purpose of surveillance? How does it assume the faces of care and oppression simultaneously? These questions are a reflective mirror held in the face of North Korean viewers, although in passing, North Korea is humorously evoked in this drama. Before falling in love with Min-jun, Song-i mistakes him for a diehard fan stalking her when she steps into an elevator in their residential building. Not knowing that Min-jun lives next door and has every right to use the same elevator, she abruptly reprimands him that he should not spend his time and energy so futilely in pursuit of celebrities. When Min-jun silently ignores her, embarrassed Song-i challenges him: "You really don't know who I am? Did you come from North Korea? Are you an alien?"[50] Whereas her open confrontation of Min-jun's alien status by invoking North Korea points to Min-jun's true identity, the reference nonetheless shows truthful assumptions about the country's complete segregation from the rest of the world. Although merely a passing incident where North Korea is deployed as a light joke to reveal Min-jun's disconnect from society, the reference ignites a spark of curiosity as to whether dramas such as *My Love from Another Star* reaffirm our notions of North Korea as "another star," completely isolated from the rest of the world and segregated from a broader network of information flow. The answer to that question is elaborately contemplated in *Crash Landing on You*, which emerged six years later, after *My Love from Another Star* was aired to much fanfare.

Crash Landing on You

Crash Landing on You makes a clear departure from *Autumn in My Heart*, *Stairway to Heaven*, *Boys over Flowers*, and *My Love from Another Star*, which were made primarily for the South Korean domestic audience but ended up influencing an unintended audience in the North. From its inception, *Crash*

Landing on You had North Korea written all over it: from a dashing North Korean protagonist to the realistic set design capturing North Korean locales, the drama took the imagined North Korean audience's perspective into serious consideration.

Aired on the South Korean cable channel tvN from December 4, 2019, to February 16, 2020, and later made available for streaming on Netflix, this romance comedy features the unlikely love story between a South Korean conglomerate businesswoman, Bak Se-ri, and a North Korean company commander, Li Jeong-hyuk, hailing from a powerful political family. Their uncanny love story begins with Se-ri's accidental landing in North Korea when a strong storm carries her paraglider from the south side of the DMZ into the north. Jeong-hyuk and his four retinue soldiers hide Se-ri from local surveillance and prevent her capture by the North Korean authorities, eventually enabling her successful return to South Korea. Later, Jeong-hyuk and his retinue reunite with Se-ri in Seoul when they are sent on a special mission only to experience another painful separation afterward. The drama nonetheless ends happily with the two lovers continuing with their relationship as they reunite in Switzerland every summer.

The premise of the story, as fantastical as it appears, does not confine the plot to the realm of the uncanny but converses closely with the realities of millennial North Korea. To ensure the veracity of the North Korean life featured in the drama, the production team invited North Korean resettlers to join the creative team: Gwak Mun-wan, who graduated from Pyongyang University of Theater and Film, joined the chief screenplay writer, Bak Ji-eun, as an assistant writer; and Gim A-ra (female born in Hoeryeong in 1991 who left North Korea in 2003), a North Korean resettler-cum-actor, was invited to play a minor North Korean character in the show. Numerous recent resettlers joined the production as consultants as well; Gang Na-ra (female born in 1997 in Cheongjin who left North Korea in 2014) was one of the eleven resettlers who helped the production team understand the differences between the Kim Jong Il era and the Kim Jong Un era.[51] Bak Yu-seong (male born in Hoeryeong in 1990 who left North Korea in 2007), another consultant, thinks that most details in the drama, such as the exterior look of the North Korean houses, appear quite authentic.[52] Gim A-ra recalls how stepping onto the set made her shiver as she felt she was stepping into an actual North Korean village:

"I had goose bumps when I saw the tower at the center of the village display-ing the phrase, in red letters, 'The great comrades Kim Il Sung and Kim Jong Il are forever with us.' This is something that can be seen everywhere in North Korea."[53] By resorting to the knowledge of North Korean resettlers, *Crash Landing on You* was able to concoct a strange mix of quixotic plot and authen-tic-looking spatial settings, so much so that Han Song-i (female born in 1993 in Hyesan who left North Korea in 2013) claims that "North Koreans would be surprised to see the show since its set is just like North Korea."[54]

The verisimilitude of the set design is only the first item that approxi-mates the North Korean reality. More foundationally, the drama presents an intimate report on the sweeping social changes that flooded North Korea in the new millennium—pervasive foreign culture, especially South Korean dramas, material goods, and marketplace transactions—and how their in-filtration was mitigated by the newly introduced media technology that in-evitably invited draconian surveillance by the state. New media platforms and content in particular propose ways of translating the seemingly alien cultures of the two Koreas, exposing, at times, seams of uneven translation and, at other times, a more fluid rapport and mutual understanding.

The first episode of the drama features how Se-ri desperately tries to run across the DMZ to return to South Korea, evading a close chase by Jeong-hyuk, who was assigned to patrol the northern part of the DMZ. She runs right across the North Korean watchtower guarded by Gim Ju-meok, Jeong-hyuk's subordinate. The viewers witness how this post guard, who is sup-posed to keenly surveil the area, which is highly critical for national security, is entirely carried away by *Stairway to Heaven*. Engrossed in the drama with swelling tears, Ju-meok is unable to see beyond his computer screen.

A North Korean soldier watching a South Korean drama while serv-ing might appear an improbable scenario, but an anonymous interviewee (male in his twenties, born in Yanggang Province, who left North Korea in 2020 and came to South Korea in 2021) says that such things happen within North Korean army units. When asked his impressions of *Crash Landing on You*, he noted,

What was real about the drama was the village scenery. [It is] also true that one can watch South Korean dramas in the North Korean military.

But low-ranking soldiers cannot watch since there is no safe place for them to watch, and they don't have time to do so. Only those with time and power can do it. I also watched and got caught many times, but I was able to bribe my way out. If you are caught watching South Korean dramas within the military, the level of punishment will be much higher than in society. So in my estimate, around 20 percent of the military might have access to South Korean dramas.[55]

The drama's metacommentary on the enthusiastic reception of South Korean dramas by North Korean viewers—even in a strictly controlled environment, like an army unit—appears in the very first episode to frame the drama's central logic on media and technology: that it may offer a way out of the unbridgeable military and political gap that engulfed the two Koreas in decades of extreme hostility.

The drama features how North Koreans who are exposed to South Korean dramas can serve as translators in their own right—as intermediaries between two opposing worlds that hardly interface in reality. Indeed, when Se-ri goes into hiding in North Korea, Ju-meok becomes her designated translator, interpreting her South Korean vernacular and behaviors, which are incomprehensible to most North Koreans. He teaches North Korean soldiers how the protagonists in South Korean dramas avoid crisis by feigning to be lovers—a tip Jeong-hyuk successfully puts into use at a later point when he attempts to help Se-ri escape North Korea but ends up being caught by the North Korean border patrol. He also translates North Korean slang for "fib" (*burai kkaji-mara*) into a South Korean counterpart (*ppeong-chida*) for Se-ri's comprehension. When Jeong-hyuk and his retinue come to Seoul in the second half of the series, it is Ju-meok who is able to navigate through the heart of the enemy line most comfortably, thanks to his colloquial knowledge of South Korean society gleaned from watching their popular dramas. In a way, Ju-meok's familiarity with the South Korean dramas uniquely positions him as the decipherer of the incomprehensible cryptolect—both linguistically and behaviorally—accentuating the influence that South Korean dramas and foreign media have come to exert in North Korea.

Not stopping there, *Crash Landing on You* advances the notion that being fluent in the cryptolect is a talent that merits a hefty reward: before Se-ri departs from North Korea (the first of many attempts that fail in succession), she hands out rewards to Jeong-hyuk's subordinate soldiers who helped her remain in safety. Se-ri gives Ju-meok a "Passion for South Korean Pop Culture Award"[56] and asks him to make a choice between an immediate monetary reward or a special lunch date with Choe Ji-u, the female protagonist of *Stairway to Heaven*, with whom Se-ri claims to be acquainted. Even though the possibility of having this lunch date is close to zero due to the division of Korea, Ju-meok chooses it over the monetary prize without a moment's hesitation. But his unlikely dream of meeting the beloved star beyond the DMZ becomes a reality when he is sent to South Korea on a mission to assist Jeong-hyuk and bring him back to North Korea.

South Korean dramas—both actual drama productions (*Crash Landing on You* in this case) and metacultural references within dramas (*Stairway to Heaven* as a drama within the drama)—wield special power in encouraging Koreans from both sides to assume alternate perspectives on the other. *Crash Landing on You* is intended for a North Korean audience—whether the resettlers in South Korea or those in North Korea—who watch South Korean actors play North Korean characters, as much as for South Koreans, who see the drama as a translation of North Korean culture. As the assistant writer Gwak Mun-wan (male in his fifties who settled in South Korea in 2005) makes clear, the drama primarily caters to the South Korean viewership: "Writers always take into consideration the perspective of the audience. The overall perception of South Koreans is that not everyone sees North Korea as the enemy."[57] The drama invites the spectators to see North Korean life through the eyes of the South Korean Se-ri, who gives them a crash course on how the seemingly impenetrable country has been mired in rapid marketization and information exchange. For the vast majority of South Korean viewers who have not followed the recent transformation of North Korean society closely, the drama offers a glimpse of a place conventionally portrayed as hostile terrain.

Just as South Korean dramas serve as a medium to reflect upon this entangled network of seeing oneself through the alienated gaze of the other, cell phones also play a double role of facilitating self-reflection and surveillance of the other. The drama presents cell phones as helpful and dangerous because their usage can cut both ways: freeing users from the constraints of the society while also exposing them to a greater degree of surveillance. While the drama supplies no shortage of instances of surveillance of all types and manners, surveillance by cell phones becomes most central to exposing the paradox of technology.

Similar to the way *My Love from Another Star* showcases the detailed mechanism of surveillance, *Crash Landing on You* captures how technology defines the anatomy of all-seeing eyes. In fact, *Crash Landing on You* intensifies the surveillance mechanism and posits it at the center of the narrative arc. When Jeong-hyuk brings Se-ri to Pyongyang in preparation for her escape from North Korea, he checks all corners of her hotel room for bugs. He finds plenty of small devices hidden under the lampshade, in the ceiling lights, and in corners of the bed for viewers to see. He tells her that surveillance devices are ubiquitous in North Korea—a lesson Se-ri remembers and applies later on to debug another house she visits. The drama additionally provides numerous examples of how surveillance works in North Korea. For example, when Se-ri first arrives at the border town where Jeong-hyuk is stationed, she is subject to a sudden accommodation inspection (*sukbak geom-yeol*). In a country where the freedom of travel from town to town is allowed only with permits, a routine inspection is often performed to catch illegal visitors who have not officially registered their travel with local authorities. During the inspection episode, one local resident gets caught using a South Korean rice cooker hidden behind a curtain when the electronic gadget sends out an automatic announcement in a South Korean phrasing and accent.

The drama presents the speaking rice cooker as a wonderous anomaly to the drab North Korean kitchen setting. Its strangeness is accentuated not simply by the automated announcement delivered in a South Korean accent but also by its technologically advanced features. To fully sketch out the context of this scene, we must note how the North Korean media have been introducing technologically advanced kitchen gadgets as natural fixtures of the utopian future. For instance, a 2015 article titled "Smart House Appliances" recounts, "A recent exhibition titled 'Kitchen in the 21ˢᵗ Century' staged by a certain country showcased the future trend of kitchenware. . . . Tableware made of nano materials will automatically detect whether they contain food or not. They are able to change shapes and provide ideal temperature according to the food they contain. . . . We will also be able to see doorless refrigerators that can create a protective door out of air pressure, not permitting warm air to filter inside."[58] The tone of the article is consistent with the heightened extolment of technological wonders that has flooded North Korean media in the new millennium. The mysteriously erased identity of the exhibition host ("a certain country") is a subject of speculation, but it could easily be South Korea given its reputation as one of the leading manufacturers of home appliances. It is no wonder that the North Korean authorities strongly condemned *My Love from Another Star* for painting North Koreans as mere admirers of South Korea's material wealth (more on this later), which is most acutely captured in this scene.

Although it is strictly forbidden, the local residents in the drama do not hold back from using products manufactured in South Korea. In marketplace scenes, South Korean products are called "stuff from the village below" (*nam-jjok-e-seo on mul-geon*),[59] concealed from public view, tucked on the lower shelves behind curtains, and frequently bought and sold at higher prices than North Korean merchandise by well-to-do residents. According to Han Song-i, the degree of surveillance depicted in the drama is real and ubiquitous, so much so that if North Koreans were to view it, they would find that all kinds of surveillance portrayed in the drama have a parallel in reality.[60]

Crash Landing on You reveals the most explicit performance of surveillance through the character Jeong Man-bok, an employee at the State Security Agency assigned to eavesdrop on the border-town residents. Described by one of Jeong-hyuk's soldiers in derogatory terms as someone working as surreptitiously as "birds during the daytime and rats during the nighttime,"[61] Man-bok faces a conflicted assignment of having to eavesdrop on Jeong-hyuk, whom he deeply respects and hopes to protect. Man-bok reluctantly carries out his mission on the orders of his superior Jo Cheol-gang, a corrupt State Security Agency officer who wants to destroy Li Jeong-hyuk and his family. The drama shows Man-bok working in a dark, cave-like office littered with headphones, wires, and recording devices. There, he constantly monitors every move made by Jeong-hyuk and the strange and secretive female houseguest—a scene reminiscent of the Ministry for State Security *Hauptmann* (captain) in the 2006 German film *Das Leben der Anderen* (The lives of others). For resettlers, this scene presents a startling situation that they know exists in North Korea but did not have a chance to see with their own eyes. An anonymous interviewee (female in her thirties, born in Pyongyang, who left North Korea in 2008 and settled in South Korea in 2013) recounts, "We say in the North, 'Birds listen to your daytime conversation, rats listen to your nighttime conversation.' One out of five in North Korea is an informant."[62] Likewise, Bak Yu-seong (male born in Hoeryeong in 1990 who left North Korea in 2007) notes, "In North Korea, I knew that I was being listened to but never actually witnessed someone do it. So when I watched the scene in the drama, it was really fascinating to note how surveillance actually takes place. In North Korea, if people say wrong things, they will disappear the next day. People would say that every household is bugged with devices as tiny as needles."[63] These words illustrate how self-censorship was as effective as being censored by others, which is enabled by the idea of a ubiquitous, all-seeing eye.

Emphasizing the duality of surveillance as watching both the other and oneself, paranoid Man-bok becomes conflicted, struggling between his official assignment to eavesdrop on Jeong-hyuk and using other means of technology to help the man he is supposed to surveil. Man-bok passively reacts to the directives of his superior, who is eager to find evidence to destroy Jeong-hyuk, but he soon transforms his mission into a project to realize his true intention of helping Jeong-hyuk. Man-bok's reactive creativity enables him to feign his official duty while finding ways not to perform it. When Jo Cheol-gang calls Man-bok for Jeong-hyuk's latest moves, Man-bok lies, saying that no special moves have been detected. He holds his cell phone with trembling hands as if it can hear his own lies. As a means to snitch on someone as well as to free Jeong-hyuk from the watchful eyes of his political enemy, cell phones are highlighted as central in the paradox that the characters living in a surveillance state are faced with on a daily basis.

Cell phones' duality is exposed in another incident in North Korea when a swindler businessman named Gu Seung-jun uses his phone to record Se-ri's voice. Seung-jun is a fugitive pursued by Se-ri's half brother, Se-hyeong, who lost a substantial amount of money on his fraudulent scheme. Seung-jun ends up in North Korea in order to evade menacing debt collectors sent by Se-hyeong. In North Korea, Seung-jun runs into Se-ri by chance and learns that she is trapped there, unbeknownst to her family, who assume she is dead when she goes missing after the paragliding accident. In order to provide proof that Se-ri is still alive to her half brother, Se-hyeong, Seung-jun secretly records a conversation with her on his cell phone, intending to negotiate with Se-hyeong. When Seung-jun learns that Se-ri is not wanted by her half sibling, who sees her as a threatening rival to inheriting their father's wealth, Seung-jun rekindles feelings for her (they had previously been on a blind date in South Korea) and pursues her romantically.

The double-edged nature of cell phones as a means to connect and to surveil also plays out in South Korea, where phones are used to make secret recordings of private conversations. Se-hyeong, who resents his father's decision to designate Se-ri as his heir, conspires to destroy her when she successfully returns to South Korea. With the help of Jo Cheol-gang, who comes to South Korea to catch Se-ri, Se-hyeong plots to eliminate her. When Se-hyeong and his wife discuss the plan, Se-ri's cell phone secretly records their conversation, which is used later as evidence to incriminate them. Cell phones can be used as surveillance tools but also as a means of bridging the separated. The phone's ability to ignite and fuel romance is confirmed once again when Se-ri heartbrokenly bids farewell to Jeong-hyuk as he returns to North Korea upon completing his mission to destroy Cheol-gang. Soon afterward, Se-ri falls into a despondent state. But much to her surprise, she suddenly receives text messages from the departed Jeong-hyuk, who has programmed his messages to be sent over the course of the following year. The drama shows exhilarated Se-ri receiving birthday messages and Christmas greetings from absent Jeong-hyuk as cell phone technology becomes the prime facilitator of their romantic relationship.[64] Despite the fact that North and South Koreans cannot communicate openly with one another, the text messages make Se-ri feel that Jeong-hyuk is still with her, much the same way resettlers sustain their ties to their separated kin in the North.

Although the drama did its best to present rapport between the two divided nations and apply even criticism to both Koreas—North Korea for the lack of freedom and South Korea for its ruthless capitalism—it did not escape the wrath of the North Korean government. The official North Korean internet press, Uriminzokkiri.com, published a scathing critique of the recent South Korean media products that dramatized events in North Korea. Although the article does not mention *Crash Landing on You* by title, it criticizes those who "profit from the tragedy of division" and declares that "the South Korean government and production companies who insult our bright society by distorting it will have to pay the price for depicting their kinsmen in a vile manner."[65]

To be clear, the North Korean regime was not the only critic of the drama. While most resettlers were impressed with the verisimilitude of the set design, some shared their discomfort about the misrepresentation of the realities in the North. One anonymous resettler (male in his twenties who left North Korea in 2011) wonders if the screenwriter ever did any research: "The story has no plausibility. It would not be an overstatement to say that the drama beautifies North Korea. The reality in the North is much grimmer [than depicted in the drama]."[66] Others state that the authorities in the North could condemn the drama for its depiction of poverty in North Korea, far from its proclaimed status as paradise: unpaved roads covered in dust, provincial residents having to raise hens and pigs inside their apartments to make ends meet, and frequent loss of electricity even in fancy buildings in Pyongyang, all of which are taken nonchalantly by residents as routine interruptions.

In the eyes of the North Korean authorities, perhaps the most insulting aspect of the drama is how it showcases the poverty of North Koreans. When Jeong-hyuk's soldiers reunite with Se-ri in Seoul, Se-ri offers them a safe place to stay in her palatial penthouse, the opulence of which prompts disbelief from the Northern visitors. Gender dynamics not so subtly come to play in this scene: Pyo Chi-su, one of the soldiers who has shown much hostility to Se-ri during her stay in North Korea, looks up to the skyscraper she owns, and Se-ri notes that the *"eminai"* (a derogatory term for woman) did not fib about her wealth.[67] When Se-ri reunites with Jeong-hyuk in Seoul, she takes him to a fancy boutique, where she showers him with luxurious garments she likes. Jeong-hyuk, who belongs to the highest elite circles in North Korea, is diminished into a fashion doll Se-ri toys with, canceling the authority he assumed in North Korea. Se-ri is not only South Korean but also a woman who steps in to patronize North Koreans during their stay in South Korea, which bodes ill for North Korea's long-standing culture of misogyny. By positing Se-ri as the agent of material power, the drama advances a thesis that marketization and southernization are interchangeable processes—which also become aligned with feminization.

But Se-ri is not the only financially powerful woman in this drama. She has a counterpart in the North, Go Myeong-eun, who is the general manager of Pyongyang's fanciest department store. She is working hard to marry her daughter, Seo Dan, to Jeong-hyuk and uses her wealth to materialize her plan. Myeong-eun claims proudly, "I am the one whose hands touch all the dollars in Pyongyang."[68] A strong and financially powerful mother without a husband, she faithfully embodies the ideal motherhood of the marketplace generation. Desirable North Korean femininity in the new millennium is defined by how quickly women can learn the rules of the marketplace, which is valorized through the figures of smart businesswomen from both Koreas.

In a society where dramatic illusion is more important than reality, disavowal of the belief that North Korea is the best place on earth could truly hurt the viewership in the North, which likely would have prompted the North Korean government's hostility toward the drama. But their negative reaction to the drama's popularity in the South—and possibly in the North—raises the questions, Do the conversations between the ideal version of North Korea and its realities, between the South's perception of the North and the North's self-perception, have to be left to the millennial cultural translators? Shall the twain never see eye to eye at an official level? Only the passage of time will reveal the answers, but for the time being, media technology in the form of cell phones might be the only agent capable of mitigating the discrepancies between the two worlds while playing the paradoxical dual role to surveil and to connect.

All in all, contemporary South Korean TV dramas were well poised to gain tremendous popularity in North Korea. Their sustained and repetitive narrative on communication technology and the realities of the market economy influenced the North Korean viewers, often countering the official state ideology. Due to these dramas' seriality, with each episode ending in a cliffhanger, North Korean millennials watched them more extensively than other media products, such as news, films, music videos, or variety shows, which will be discussed in the next chapter.

As many interviewees attest, the dramas' enduring appeal might lie in the differences they offer: the exotic variations of the Korean language, the novel subject matters (romance, love, and focus on individuals), and glimpses of life beyond North Korea all fuel the escape fantasies of those jaded by the North

Korean propagandistic clichés. As Ahlam Lee points out, "an unknown free world . . . capture[s] North Koreans' attention, and can possibly change their perceptions about the authoritarian leadership and political system of their home country."[69] But overshadowing this obvious point are undeniable similarities between North Korean life and South Korean dramas: emphasis on a family-centered life and the importance of class origin (political background in the North and economic background in the South). Sunny Yoon's claim that "North Koreans are connected with South Koreans emotionally, as the people share the same history, language, and seven decades of ideological tension between the two Koreas" resonates with this point.[70] But to top it all, the evolving technologies regarding cell phones and other related media featured in South Korean dramas eventually became realities in North Korea, all the while offering an important lesson on how surveillance can appear as both care and oppression.

FOUR

Visions and Sounds to Change Lives

On April 7, 2015, *Radio Free Asia* reported that six young North Koreans were put on a public trial held in front of the Hyesan Movie Theater in Yanggang Province. Citing an anonymous local informant, the news outlet said that these young folks were discovered secretively watching the South Korean film *Promise* (Yaksok). All six turned out to be friends, who had attended the same junior high school. For their varying degrees of transgression, the former classmates ended up receiving different sentences: from six months of forced labor for those who had full-time employment to one year for those who were unemployed. But the longest sentence, two years of forced labor, was reserved for two individuals: the one who possessed the film on a USB drive and the other who organized the secret viewing at his house.[1]

Released in South Korea in 1998, *Promise*, in 2015, was virtually forgotten in the place of its birth, but it still had life strong enough in North Korea to tempt viewers to risk their safety. The friendship among the participants could have given the violators trust to cross the forbidden line, but the true irony of this story glares in the location where the trial took place. I have written extensively on how movie houses in North Korea have served not just as places of entertainment but more as political shrines, where people's ideology and sociality are forged so they become proper citizens of the North Korean state.[2] The heyday of the North Korean film industry under the patronage of the cinephile leader Kim Jong Il in effect ended the Arduous March. Film theaters, once a central nodal point of North Korean communal life, turned into a pale backdrop for punishing young citizens, who would voraciously watch anything other than homebred films.

Unlike the serial South Korean TV dramas built on cliffhanger endings, which force North Korean viewers to expose themselves to prolonged danger, films are far shorter in length and thereby enjoy a particular advantage. More crucially, due to the necessity of creating popular appeal and easy accessibility, South Korean TV dramas are more restricted in their genres and subject matter. This translates into a diversity of film genres and subjects not paralleled by the TV shows; North Korean viewers of South Korean films are treated to an expansive array of themes that would be unsuitable for family-friendly home screens.

In addition to their wide thematic spread, South Korean films' unabated self-reflection about the ailments of the society provides additional attraction for North Korean viewers. Na Min-hui (female born in 1991 in Pyongyang who left North Korea in 2014 and came to South Korea in 2015), for instance, thinks that the most impressive aspects of South Korea media are its freedom to criticize everything, its bold attitude, and its fierce tone: "I thought it was brave to showcase criticism of all these aspects [of the society], which cannot be done without confidence. I was shocked to watch *The Attorney* [Byeon-ho-in, a 2013 South Korean film about a human rights lawyer, who defends innocent civilians against a military dictatorship]. A single lawyer can wage a battle against a whole country!"[3] A rapidly transforming society, like North Korea, needs self-reflection more than other places, but since social circumstances do not allow for it, surreptitious viewers in the North find powerful alternatives on the forbidden screen.

Curious North Korean viewers tend not to discriminate between various genres of South Korean films as the opportunities to see them do not come every day. From films that center around the contentious relationship between North and South Korea—such as *The Taebaek Mountains* (Taebaek sanmaek; 1994),[4] *Shiri* (Shwi-ri; 1999), and *JSA* (2000)—to more recent films—such as the sci-fi-fantasy-thriller *Along with the Gods: The Last 49*

Days (Singwa hamkke, in-gwa yeon; 2018) and the Oscar-winning *Parasite* (Gisangchung; 2019)—South Korean films that circulate in the North tend to attract the inquisitive gaze of the audience.⁵

This chapter begins by addressing several films that enjoyed popularity in the North, with a particular emphasis on how they mirror the realities of millennial North Korea. Continuing the previous chapter's discussion on the ways exposure to a variety of media types is propelled by the changing nature of media technology, devices, and the human-to-human networking possibilities in the North, the analysis of films is followed by a discussion of songs, variety shows, and news coverage from the South to trace the increasingly diversifying media consumption by North Koreans. If TV dramas' fictitious narratives are their prime appeal for North Korean viewers, then the documentary nature of news coverage and reality shows present a stronger semblance of authenticity. Songs, on the other hand, offer an alternative emotive experience for a broad swath of North Korean listeners, adding new routes of media circulation among various microgenerations of millennials.

Cathartic Identification with Violence

The vast majority of South Korean TV dramas center around the safe and benign themes of friendship and romance, making them conducive to family-friendly home-theater screens. TV dramas' relatively tame nature is often not amenable to graphic depictions of raw violence or sexual encounters, and for this reason, sensational scenes are more likely to prevail on film screens than on TV shows. By many accounts, raw depiction of violence in South Korean films is one of the main attractions for North Koreans. Li Ung-gil (male born in 1981 in Cheongjin who first left North Korea in 2003 and permanently left in 2006) notes North Koreans' double penchant for gangster films and good fights, as if confirming the natural kinship between the two: "North Koreans really love gangster movies. When a fight breaks out in North Korea, they fight really tough."⁶ North Korean people's awareness of and exposure to violence seem to create a particular attraction point. Gim Hae-suk (female in her forties, born in South Pyeongan Province, who left North Korea in 2018 and came to South Korea in 2019) remembers watching the South Korean film *My Wife Is a Gangster* with great interest: "I recall how the sequel to this film featured South Korean gangsters expanding their influence outside Korea. In North Korea, gangsters expand their power to China. I was impressed that South Korean gangsters are no joke."[7] Similar testimonies associating the graphic depiction of violence in South Korean films with the violence-filled reality of North Korean life abound. Gim Ha-na (female born in Hyesan in 1988 who left North Korea in 2014) recalls,

> In 2009, I worked in a trading company, which had rights to develop a gold mine. While working there, I witnessed a rough gang fight over the developing rights between my company and the military. The military sent some one hundred people with plywood, who started smashing down everything they saw when they entered our turf. They knocked down literally everything. It was shocking to see such violence in reality—a kind of violence I had only seen in South Korean films. When I watched South Korean gangster films, I wondered how and why there were so many gangsters in South Korea, but that kind of violence was now unfolding in front of my eyes [in North Korea]. What I saw was a lawless society of capitalism rather than an orderly socialist society that school taught me about. None of the perpetrators were punished. . . . It's worse than capitalism. At least in the South, if people die, there are consequences for the violators, but in North Korea, nothing like that happens. If you are in the business of gold trading in the North, the entire family of traders are often killed by thieves who take everything from them.[8]

Similarly, an anonymous interviewee (female in her thirties, born in Pyongyang, who left North Korea in 2008 and settled in South Korea in 2013), who ran a restaurant business in Pyongyang in the early 2000s, recalls how business owners who took out loans to open their businesses committed suicide out of extreme fear of gangster debt collectors: "Officially there are no gangsters in North Korea. But in reality, they do exist. When people cannot pay off their debt, gangsters take away their house and cripple them. Some even poison debtors. In North Korea, the fist has precedence over the law. I think such reality makes South Korean gangster films quite popular in North Korea."[9]

These words viscerally reveal North Korean society under the massive transition from the state-planned socialist economy to a profit-driven market economy—the process of which cannot be explained by North Korea's official self-eulogy as a socialist paradise. Although the pressures to reckon with its failures simmer under the social surface, North Koreans cannot discuss their own societal failures as openly as these South Korean films can; hence the North Korean viewers' attraction to South Korean gangster films can be explicated by the vicarious identification between the North Korean daily reality and the South Korean filmic reality. For North Korean viewers, the South Korean gangster films littered with unfiltered violence cathartically speak to their own reality, which will never be represented in their official media.

There might be a predetermined correlation between the viewers' gender and their preferred film genres, but gangster films appear to be popular among North Koreans regardless of gender.[10] According to Gim Tae-hui (female born in the early 1970s who settled in South Korea in 2007), "North Korean women like melodrama and sweet romance, but there are many who also like action films. I personally recall being a big fan of action films."[11]

Many North Korean resettlers mention how productions that center around an organized crime unit, such as *The Generals' Son* (Janggun-eui adeul; 1990), *Two Cops* (1993), *My Wife Is a Gangster* (Jopok manura; 2001), and *Family Pride* (Gajok-eui yeong-gwang; 2002), resonate strongly with viewers. Of these films featuring various subgenres (historical gangster films or gangster comedy, for example), *My Wife Is a Gangster* occupies a unique place due to its emphasis on the reversal of traditional gender roles. When the film was first released in South Korea in 2001, it attracted more than five hundred million viewers—an indisputable commercial success for South Korean films at the time. A lowbrow comedy capitalizing on a parody of the macho gangster world, the successful film launched sequels to transform *My Wife Is a Gangster* into a franchise.

While most gangster films posit women as trophies to be won by the alpha-male figure, *My Wife Is a Gangster* reverses the genre convention to project a female character as the repository of unbridled violence and vengeance. The popularity of the film in North Korea is no doubt closely aligned with the millennials' gender perceptions, where strong women prevail as the providers for their family. In this regard, it is beyond coincidence that the chief producer of the film, Yi Sun-yeol, sent the film posters and press materials to

North Korea via Hong Kong in an effort to screen the film in North Korea, although the plan was never realized.[12]

My Wife Is a Gangster begins with the very dramatic entry of the character referred to as Big Brother, whose fighting skills, according to the narrator, "may put Bruce Lee to shame."[13] The opening sequence shot in dizzying camera movements introduces a slender and androgynous figure of Big Brother (played by equally androgynous actress Sin Eun-gyeong) as she enters to rescue a member of her gang being attacked by a mob of rival gangsters. Moving artfully and effortlessly under the pouring rain, Big Brother saves her gang member using just small scissors. Fighting with this tool found in everyday domestic life, she fends off thugs armed with knives and hand axes, defying the gender hierarchy of the gangster world.

The reversal of traditional gender roles continues throughout the film. When one of her subordinates brings a new fellow to join her organization, she coolly dismisses him to the kitchen, which is meant to be a great insult for an aspiring gangster. The irony of gender reversal becomes most conspicuous when Big Brother is urged to get married by her sister—the only person Big Brother seems to truly love and who she keeps close to her heart. Bending over backward to please the only person she deeply cares for, Big Brother finds a docile man who does not know of her gangster identity and pursues a marriage of convenience. During the honeymoon, when the husband attempts to get intimate with the bride, Big Brother gives him a black eye and presents him with an ultimatum that he will no longer see the light of the world if he attempts to touch her without permission—all amid the topsy-turvy portrayal of the traditional gender roles the main characters have been assigned.

The timing of the film's release in 2001 might explain why cell phones and other communication technology do not appear frequently. This was still an early phase of cell phone adoption in South Korea, but the film features several scenes in which the use of cell phones makes a notable statement about the public etiquette involved. In a scene leading up to Big Brother's wedding, her subordinates go to an electronics store to shop for Big Brother's new household. There, one of the gang members receives a phone call, and his crude, loud voice resonates throughout the store as if accentuating his thuggish traits. Just like the North Korean comedy skit introduced in chapter 1, which extols the public etiquette of using cell phones, this scene in *My Wife Is a Gangster* invites frowns and thereby highlights the inappropriate use of the phone as it perturbs others in public space.

More visceral critique of cell phone usage enters the film in the most intrusive form of privacy invasion. The film features a short scene in which Big Brother's most trusted lieutenant is engaged in an intimate act with his girlfriend in a dimly lit hotel room. Placed on the bedside table, his cell phone starts to ring, and the lieutenant has no choice but to answer it since he knows that the call is coming from his boss. The lieutenant picks up the phone while still engaged in the sexual act with his girlfriend, all of which is transmitted to Big Brother on the other end of the line. Although the scene can easily be dismissed as a vulgar cliché suitable for *The Sopranos'* gangster genre, it also calls attention to the mounting interconnectedness between cell phones and surveillance. Cell phone owners cannot escape being connected to the world, even in the most primal and private moments. Cell phones allow probing into every and any part of users' lives, in effect serving as the faithful medium of surveillance. The violence of such intrusion is materialized in the presence of the ringing cell phone, which, in 2001, was entering the lives of South Korean audiences in growing numbers—a reality that North Korean viewers would only experience a full decade later.

The popularity of violent films in North Korea can be explicated on many levels—primarily as a reflection of their own social violence but also as a vicarious outlet for repressed subjects living under the paradoxical symbiosis of extreme state control and prevailing social violence. Violence arises when systematic social order cannot be implemented, and private citizens have to take matters of justice into their own hands. For North Korean viewers of foreign media who lead a double life as docile subjects of the state and as rebels who defy the law, violence appeals as a fantastical solution that operates outside the state system. As a possible remedy to address problems that mushroomed in places where the state failed, violence is available to any and all, both men and women, dealing with crucial life matters. The harsh lessons the millennial generation learned to survive and prevail reverberate in the popular reception of *My Wife Is a Gangster*, where women are in charge of their own fate, even if that means resorting to ferocious destruction.

Cell Phones as Nuclear Weapons

Released in South Korea nearly two decades after *My Wife Is a Gangster*, *Parasite* (2019) was a triumphant celebration of the hundred-year history of Korean cinema and received the highest international accolades, including the Palme d'Or and four Oscars. Apart from the fact that both films enjoyed considerable commercial success in South Korea, comparing the two at first comes across as a highly contrived exercise: whereas *My Wife Is a Gangster* purportedly plays up the B-rated sensibilities of gangster comedy, *Parasite* entered a list of signature Bong Joon-ho (Bong Jun-ho) films that double as art-house cinema and commercial megahits.

The North Korean reception of these two films could not have been more different. While *My Wife Is a Gangster* was introduced and circulated voluntarily through a network of people and by word of mouth in a bottom-up manner, *Parasite*'s international success was immediately recognized from the top down by the North Korean authorities. *Joseon sinbo*—an official mouthpiece of the North Korean state published by a pro–North Korean *zainichi* (ethnic Koreans who reside in Japan) organization, General Association of Korean Residents—praises the film as the "visceral exposure of South Korean reality," which centers on "the disparity between the rich and the poor and the class struggle."[14]

Within North Korea, the film's phenomenal success was not reported directly to the public. But curiously enough, immediately trailing the Oscar win of *Parasite*, *Tongil sinbo*, the official North Korean weekly newspaper, featured special coverage of director Bong Joon-ho's maternal grandfather, writer Bak Tae-won, who defected to North Korea during the Korean War, highlighting the North Korean leaders Kim Il Sung and Kim Jong Il's praise of his novels on Joseon-dynasty peasant revolts.[15] The article does not mention Bak Tae-won's link to *Parasite*'s director, and hence the comments can be seen as a compromise gesture in the hope of taking some credit for the film's success while not acknowledging South Korea's cultural triumph openly.

North Korean resettlers offer an intriguing reading of the film. Gim Ga-yeong (female born in Hyesan in her twenties who left North Korea in 2012), for instance, could not understand the film at first but came to comprehend it better the second time: "The film reminded me of when I first came to

South Korea. In North Korea, I had some foundation to build my life, but in the South, I had to start all over, empty-handed. That's why I felt like there were affinities between my life and the lives of some characters in the film, although our life circumstances might look quite different. . . . [I]t was gratifying to see a film that seemed to have reflected upon lives [of the disenfranchised]."[16] Gim's observation touches upon one of the most conspicuous themes of the film: the dire economic struggle of the poor; she further points out that North Koreans who see this film would not believe in the visceral depiction of poverty since North Korean viewers have become thoroughly accustomed to seeing prosperous South Korea on screen. Another resettler, Jeon Hyo-jin (female in her midtwenties who left North Korea in 2013), reaffirms Gim's observation: "When I was in North Korea, I thought of South Korea as some kind of heaven where money grows on trees. If North Koreans see this film, they will learn that even in heaven, some are well off and some are not, but they would get to learn a lot about the South Korean reality."[17]

Foreign media joined North Korean resettlers in taking note of the increasing wealth gap and the ensuing social divide. As the *New York Times* article "'*Parasite*' and South Korea's Income Gap: Call It Dirt Spoon Cinema" made clear, the film indeed highlights the grotesque distance between the rich (allegorically referred to as "gold spoon") and the poor (referred to as "dirt spoon") that has come to define the ailments of postwar South Korean society.[18] Cinema scholar Kim Kyung Hyun (Gim Gyeong-hyeon) likewise places *Parasite* in the natural genealogy of the director's filmography: "Ever since his first film, *Barking Dogs Never Bite* (*Pŭrandasŭ ŭi kae*, 2000), Bong Joon-ho has been fascinated by the vacant spaces left behind by the frenzied pace of Korean modernization. The countryside is beyond repair, cities exhibit the monstrous destruction of ecological harmony, and dark secrets often lurk in basements and rooftop spaces."[19] The chiaroscuro created by the gap between the spectacularly rich and the ones fallen behind in rapidly modernizing South Korean society might resonate well with most North Korean resettlers who see themselves as the shadows of the hyped prosperity to which they have been transplanted.

The film is about a strange symbiosis of three families, all living under the roof of the Park family's magnificent contemporary-style mansion. As the CEO of a global IT company, Mr. Park has a retinue of house staff composed of a housekeeper, a driver, and a series of tutors—all jobs eventually filled by Gi-taek's impoverished family members. Through a series of lies and trickery, Gi-taek's family gradually infiltrates Mr. Park's household: Gi-taek's son, Gi-woo, forges a university diploma and becomes an English tutor to Mr. Park's daughter, Da-hye, who is in high school; Gi-woo then introduces his sister, Gi-jeong, as a foreign university student named Jessica, who becomes an art therapist to Da-song, Mr. Park's second-grader son; Jessica, in turn, frames Mr. Park's young male driver as a sexual pervert and replaces him with her father, Gi-taek; Gi-taek tricks Mrs. Park into thinking that the housekeeper, Mun-gwang, has tuberculosis and replaces her with his wife, Chung-suk (played by Jang Hye-jin, who also played a Pyongyang department store manager in the TV miniseries *Crash Landing on You*). Due to meticulous planning, the Park family is unaware that their new tutors, housekeeper, and driver are family members who have replaced their predecessors via deceitful maneuvering.

The artful ruse contrived by Gi-taek's family brings us to de Certeau's notion of trickery as the only weapon the powerless can possess. Without any means but the ability to create lies, Gi-taek's family comes to live symbiotically with Mr. Park's family as parasites. The deception is their only means of survival against the tide of harsh economic polarization. In order to make ends meet, Gi-taek's family has to tread a tricky line between truth (of the heartless realities for struggling families) and lies (about their own identities to enter Mr. Park's household). The film reveals that Gi-taek has a long track record of failure with various small-business attempts, dragging down his family to the lowest economic level; a roach-infested semibasement that becomes vulnerable to street urination and flooding seems to be their final destination, out of which it is nearly impossible to climb.

But what seems to be the lowest depth of Gi-taek's semibasement has an even deeper nadir beneath it: the hidden basement in Mr. Park's house. Gi-taek's rising and falling fortunes are allegorically captured in the spatial design of the film, which deploys a vertical hierarchy with extensive use of stairs dominating the scenes. The film comes to a turning point when the banished housekeeper, Mun-gwang, returns unannounced to the house one night. At that moment, Gi-taek's family is having a rowdy brawl in Mr. Park's living room, littering its lavish table and wooden floor with Mr. Park's expensive liquor and snacks while Mr. Park's family is away on a camping trip. Gi-taek's family, openly enjoying themselves as a family in the house as if it is their own, is startled when the doorbell rings ominously amid the pouring rain.

The close-up of Mun-gwang's beaten-up face appears on a small screen of the door security system. A seasoned housekeeper who used to look elegant and authoritative when she worked for Mr. Park's family now turns up as a grotesque figure; rain soaked with bruised eyes and a forced smile, she begs Chung-suk to open the door for her, lying that she left something behind. The following sequence is a speedy unfolding of shocking revelations and reversal of fortunes. Mun-gwang happens to have hidden her husband, Geun-se, in the secret basement of the house. Pursued by violent loan sharks after having lost his money in an unsuccessful business venture, Geun-se had no choice but to hide in Mr. Park's basement, where Mun-gwang had secretly provided him with basic sustenance while she worked for the family. But due to the sudden layoff, Mun-gwang had no choice but to leave Geun-se trapped in the basement unattended.

Until this moment, the existence of this basement is unknown to everyone, even to Mr. Park, who is the second owner of the house. Only Mun-gwang, who started out as a housekeeper for the original owner, who built the house, is aware of it as a space meant to provide the rich with security in the event of North Korea's invasion and/or a loan shark's pursuit in the event of the house owners' business failure. She tells Chung-suk in a rapid succession of words that the original builder was somewhat embarrassed by its existence and therefore did not tell Mr. Park when he sold the house. Chung-suk is shell-shocked when delirious Mun-gwang leads her down the steep stairs to the deepest abyss of the house.

This is the moment when North Korea comes to the surface of the film as a titillating subplot. While Mun-gwang hysterically begs Chung-suk to take care of her husband in the basement and not report his presence to Mr. Park's family, Gi-taek, Gi-woo, and Gi-jeong, who have been eavesdropping on the conversation in shock, accidentally fall down the stairs to the bottom of the basement—this time, much to the surprise of Mun-gwang. Suddenly, Mun-gwang comes to understand that Chung-suk, the new tutors, and the new driver are all family members who have been parading as strangers to

Mr. Park's family. Realizing that Gi-taek's family has been equally parasitic to Mr. Park's family, Mun-gwang takes out her cell phone and shoots a video of Gi-taek's family all rolling on the basement floor, entangled in pain from their fall down the stairs.

Mun-gwang then threatens to push the send button to send the video to Mrs. Park, which will reveal their true identity. Mun-gwang has Gi-taek's family kneel down on the floor with arms raised in punishment. While they have no choice but to follow Mun-gwang's orders, Geun-se, who is holding the phone, makes a peculiar analogy in his deliriously comical voice: "This button is just like a missile button. They [Gi-taek's family] are so powerless at the threat of pushing the send button. It's just like the North Korean missiles' launch button." As if triggered by her husband's comparison, Mun-gwang suddenly blurts out the following lines in the intonation and cadence typical of a Pyongyang news host: "Today, our Beloved Dear Supreme Leader Comrade Kim Jong Il shuddered with shock and rage when he watched the video recording of a swindler family's vile provocation. . . . Our Great Supreme Leader sent his directives to stuff the crazy family's putrid snout with the last existing nuclear missile as an effort to denuclearize the Korean Peninsula."[20] The speech is accompanied by unmistakable gestures of a North Korean propagandist, inviting viewers' curiosity about why and how the film came to deploy North Korea as its not-so-hidden fault line. Following the reference to the North Korean nuclear crisis, this volatile moment, charged with high-flying tension between the two parasite families, leads to explosive physical violence and their mutual demise.

In an interview after winning the Palme d'Or, director Bong brushed off the North Korean reference as merely a widespread laughter cue in South Korea: "You shouldn't construe that scene as a serious message about North Korea. Quite the contrary, it's just a joke."[21] Although Bong hoped to dismiss the moment as typical North Korea–related humor pervasive in South Korea, Darcy Paquet, who supplied the film's English subtitles, reveals that this was also the moment that the director was most concerned with getting the translation right.[22] For a director known for his meticulous planning of details that define every inch of his film, North Korea obviously cannot be just a passing reference.

This curious moment elicits varying responses from film viewers. Go Na-hae (female born in Dancheon, South Hamgyeong Province, who left North Korea in 2018 and came to South Korea in 2019) shares her thoughts on the moment when the North Korean dialect appears:

> I was quite surprised to see it, but I also wondered if someone from such a low social stratum has time to bother with North Korea. The film was interesting, and I did not think ill of it. But I think when North Koreans watch it, they could be critical of this moment because even though life is hard for them, they do not openly criticize the regime. If North Koreans watch films with any moment illustrating critical views of North Korea, they will face grave consequences. I know of people who send South Korean dramas that the North does not approve of on USB drives. Sending forbidden media is just like killing the recipients. I know that some folks sent *Parasite* to the North.[23]

On the other hand, one South Korean blogger attempts to make sense of this crucial scene by noting that "the North Korean dialect reminds us that in no other place on earth does the class divide exist as stringently as in North Korea."[24] While this reading is sensible, it overlooks the irony that the main battle takes place not just between the rich and the poor—conventional counterpoints for class struggle that North Korea often promotes—but, more importantly, between two struggling families. What I see as the most poignant connection to North Korea in this scene is its deployment of cell phones as weapons that cut both ways: a prime device of surveillance is also a necessary means of bailing oneself out of dire hardship.

Gen-se is right to see a cell phone as a nuclear weapon—one so powerful that it can bring about a grand demise to both Mun-gwang's and Gi-taek's families. Prior to this moment, the film unveils how Gi-taek uses his cell phone to prepare for Mun-gwang's dismissal from the Park household. He secretly follows her to a hospital, where she receives an allergy treatment, and takes a photo of her in the hospital waiting room to convince Mrs. Park that she has tuberculosis. Here, the cell phone becomes Gi-taek's prime means of surveillance and distortion of truth while providing an opportunity for his wife's hire. Just as when Mun-gwang later uses the video recording of the Gi-taek family to crawl out of the abyss of the house with her husband, cell phones facilitate the rise and demise of the powerless.

As an enabling device of social mobility as well as downfall, the cell phone's paradoxical role in *Parasite* resonates strongly with the situation in millennial North Korea. From the very beginning, the film establishes the logic that having access to cell phones is empowering. Gi-taek's two children are introduced to viewers in the opening sequence as they try to capture a free Wi-Fi signal with their cell phones, climbing up to the highest spot in their filthy semibasement house. They search for the Wi-Fi signal to secure their livelihood, such as finding out about their job-application results (which starts with part-time jobs of folding pizza delivery boxes and later develops into their employment opportunity at Mr. Park's house). The poor family in the film is portrayed as not having access to basic internet service, which is paralleled by their lack of a sanitary living space. The opening montage advances the view that having Wi-Fi access is a basic human right, analogous to having access to clean water or air. For North Korean viewers, who also search for connecting signals, Gi-taek's family's struggle for Wi-Fi would present a documentarian moment rather than a moment of mere cinematic humor.

The cell phone's ability to provide a ladder to climb the social strata is countered by its dark side as a powerful tool of surveillance. Adding to Gi-taek and Mun-gwang's aforementioned use of cell phones to knock each other down from the ladder, cell phones' ability to provide effective surveillance without the knowledge of the surveilled creates a twisted reversal of fates. Mun-gwang, for instance, returns to Mr. Park's house to save her trapped husband precisely because she knows when Mr. Park's family will be out; it turns out that Mun-gwang still exchanges text messages with Mr. Park's son, Da-song, who tells her that the family will be on a camping trip to celebrate his birthday. Mun-gwang surprises Chung-suk by calling her by name, also something she learned from exchanging text messages with Da-song. In order not to be captured returning to the house, Mun-gwang cuts off all the CCTV power lines surrounding it, mirroring the elaborate trickery that Gi-taek's family uses to achieve their goal.

In a way, Mun-gwang's meticulousness stems from the powerless subjects' desperate efforts to remain afloat. Poor they may be, but they see much more than the rich merely in order to survive; the film consistently presents the economically empowered subjects as blind to their surroundings. Even in the deep basement of the house, Gen-se is all too well aware of Mr. Park's success as a CEO of a globally renowned IT company, often comically chanting "respect" to him from the basement. Mr. Park, on the other hand, does not know of Gen-se, not to mention the existence of the basement in the dark belly of his own house. The irony intensifies when we consider that Mr. Park's company produces goggles for VR technology, which is supposed to open up a new field of vision. Nonetheless, it is the parasitic subjects who possess the power of surveillance (or, in this case, what scholar-artist Steve Mann terms "sousveillance").[25]

Parasite, in a way, is a scathing parable on the expansive vision of the powerless. But it goes further to show how that astute trickery inevitably brings about the mutual destruction of the host and the parasite. Whether the director intended it or not, cell phones reveal the not-so-hidden truth about the impossible symbiosis between the parasite and the host—or between parasites. Thus, the film provides a warning about the North Korean reality in which cell phones may create unprecedented lateral networks while also being capable of destroying them with increasing surveillance power. It is also a cautionary tale about the harshly divided social strata, where those who have nothing but trickery to offer take enormous risks to survive. They do this merely to exist—no grand revolutionary plan to subvert the social order is in place—but their landing point sinks them further into the abyss and into despair. Unlike *Boys over Flowers*, where the logics of money are articulated by the rich and upheld as the norm, *Parasite* presents a bleak vision of the stratified society as somewhere that nobody can claim the moral upper hand.

Lyrics and Rhythm to Touch Young Hearts

Just as South Korean films are embraced for their thematic variety not usually found in South Korean TV dramas, popular songs from South Korea resonate with North Koreans, with a unique appeal not found in other media types. The versatility of this music characterized by wide-ranging styles and lyrics—from the latest BTS songs to oldies but goodies that have stood the test of time—provides a broad sonic spread that captivates listeners in the

North. Perhaps due to their easier accessibility when compared to moving images, South Korean songs entered deeply into North Korean lives even before the arrival of films and TV dramas.

North Korean resettlers testify to receiving varying degrees of punishment when caught listening to South Korean songs. An anonymous interviewee (male in his twenties, born in Yanggang Province, who left North Korea in 2020 and came to South Korea in 2021) notes that the punishment is prorated depending on how many songs the violator listened to.[26] Han Song-i (female born in 1993 in Hyesan who left North Korea in 2013), on the other hand, notes that "there are regional differences when it comes to crackdowns. Boys in Yanggang Province were sent to a juvenile correction facility when they were caught listening to South Korean songs."[27] Elsewhere, the same transgression could result in a mild reprimand. Gang Na-ra (female born in 1997 in Cheongjin who left North Korea in 2014) recalls how she sang South Korean songs while playing piano at her performing arts high school, which never failed to invite punitive responses from teachers.[28] Choe Yu-jin (female born in Hyesan in 1982 who left North Korea in 2020) also reports evading direct punishment:

> When I was a junior high school student, I listened to the South Korean singer Yun Do-hyeon on my MP3 player. But instead of just listening to it silently, I sang along loudly while not being aware that I was singing along. My supervisor caught me at that moment and asked what song I was listening to. I could not confess that I was listening to a South Korean song, so I improvised a lie that it was a popular song from Yanbian, China. When the supervisor asked me to replay the entire song, I knew I was in serious trouble, so I kneeled in front of him and asked for forgiveness. The supervisor asked where I got this MP3, and I lied again and told him that I bought it at a marketplace not knowing that it was preloaded with the forbidden songs. The supervisor said he would let it go if I destroyed the MP3 on the spot, so I stepped on it and smashed it.[29]

Choe, at that moment, was being recruited to join the so-called Fifth Department (O-gwa), a subdivision of the Korean Workers' Party where pleasant-looking young adults from families with immaculate political backgrounds are recruited and trained to serve the party leadership and the Kim family as secretaries, typists, and waitstaff after graduation. The supervisor was personally in charge of recruiting and grooming Choe, and in order to fulfill his duty of ensuring her entry to the Fifth Department, he intentionally turned a blind eye to her transgression.

If Choe saved herself thanks to her political capital, those who have financial means tend to fare well since they can bail themselves out when caught. Jeong Shi-u (male born in 1991 in Pyongyang who left North Korea in 2017), for instance, notes how his close friend "fell asleep while listening to a South Korean pop song and was reported to the State Security Department, but he was released after paying a $1,200 bribe."[30] But in some unfortunate instances, money cannot provide a complete solution; even a wealthy Pyongyang citizen like Jeong had to leave North Korea because someone he trusted told on him for possessing thousands of South Korean programs, including the singing contest show *Immortal Songs: Singing the Legend* (Bul-hu-ui myeong-gok).[31]

Those who are unfortunate enough to have neither the political nor the financial capital simply take the beating, quite literally. An anonymous interviewee (female in her midthirties, born in Yanggang Province, who left North Korea in 2018 and came to South Korea in 2019) shares her account of being caught in the grip of surveillance:

> I mostly listened to South Korean songs on my cell phone. My phone had a small memory, so I could not watch dramas on it. First, I started listening to MP3 files, but later, I switched to USB drives. I had about 260 files of [South Korean] songs saved in memory sticks and cards that I kept at home. In the beginning, I did not know they were South Korean songs, nor did I mark the names of singers. But you could seriously get into trouble. One time, I was hanging out at my friend's house listening to music when the surveillance team suddenly descended upon us. They beat me because I swallowed the card in front of them.[32]

For more proactive types, merely listening to the forbidden songs is not enough; they go on to create their own versions and often pay the price for it. An anonymous interviewee (female in her thirties, born in Pyongyang, who left North Korea in 2008 and settled in South Korea in 2013), who attended Pyongyang College of Theater and Cinema, shares, "During my college years, there was a classmate who was a music genius. He made songs that sounded like South Korean ballad songs—you know, songs that cap-tivate your heart right away, songs that speak about dreams and love. His songs gained wide popularity beyond our campus. One day he disappeared, and classmates started to whisper that the State Security Department took him for interrogation. But then he appeared again. I don't know what really happened, but in reality, individually created songs like those cannot exist. All publicly circulated songs have to be sanctioned first."[33]

Nevertheless, as much as there are ways for a surveillance team to crack down on violators, even more ways exist to remain stealthy and enjoy the South Korean pop music. The cat-and-mouse game gets smarter each time it is played. For example, an anonymous interviewee (female in her thirties, born in Pyongyang, who left North Korea in 2008 and settled in South Korea in 2013) recounts, "All kids from affluent families had MP3 and MP4 play-ers. National security agents all wore civilian clothes and surveilled young students all the time. They would take our earphones at random and listen to what was playing. We knew about such surveillance, so we lined up the playlist with South Korean and North Korean songs. When our music play-ers were taken, we played the North Korean songs."[34] Gim Jun-hyeok (male born in 1991 in Pyongyang who left North Korea in 2010) also comes from a highly privileged family in Pyongyang, with a father who runs a business of renting out boats along the Daedong River that runs through the capital city. "The ride takes about two and half hours," recalls Gim. "During that time, passengers sing along to South Korean songs saved on a USB drive. But before they return to the dock, they erase all the recorded songs from the USB drive" to avoid trouble.[35] As noted, it is common to use USBs to listen to South Korean songs, but most North Korean listeners in recent times purchase memory cards loaded with South Korean songs and use their cell phones to play them. O Cheong-seong (male born in Gae-song, left North Korea in 2017) remembers how "Samsung MP3 was popular in his junior high school (Gae-seong Foreign Language School)" and he was exposed to Korean songs during those school years.[36]

By all accounts, songs enjoy much broader appeal compared to other media types. Choe Ju-yeon (female born in 1992 in Cheongjin who left North Korea in 2015) recalls, "I listened to South Korean music. My favorite genres were ballad songs and trot songs. I loved trot songs especially. When I was ten, at home, we had a CD that featured popular South Korean singers, like Na Hun-a, Seol Un-do, and Tae Jin-a. I memorized all Ju Hyun-mi's songs."[37] Choe clearly knew the origins of these songs, but at times North Korean listeners do not realize where the songs originated. Gim Ha-na (female born in Hyesan in 1988 who left North Korea in 2014) confirms the point: "I was seven when my aunt played South Korean songs for me for the first time. Back then, I did not know anything—neither their titles nor their origins. I just sang along."[38] Li Eun-hui (who was born in the 1990s in Kim Jong-suk Province and left North Korea in 2015) likewise states that "listening to South Korean songs was regarded as basic entertainment. It was so prevalent that when I was in college, directives forbidding songs by Jang Yun-jeong, Na Hun-a, and Hong Jin-yeong were sent from the top. In North Korea, people do not know the names of the singers and just listen to songs, but since the directive specified the names of those South Korean singers, it piqued our interest, and we started to search specifically for their songs."[39] As Li's words reveal, the North Korean authorities' overreaction and overcontrol backfired, revealing the national origins of what was previously perceived as politically innocuous. Once the origins of the songs became clear, they took on subversive political meaning, as an anonymous interviewee (female in her thirties, born in Pyongyang, who left North Korea in 2008 and settled in South Korea in 2013) notes about her most beloved song: "Yi Jeong-hyeon's 'Change' was my favorite song, The lyrics 'Change, change, change the entire world' strongly appealed to me. There were so many restrictions and contradictions in North Korea, such as how women should always look prim, how people should always care immaculately for the portraits of the leaders, and so on. We could not even chew gum in Pyongyang. There was no freedom at all, but these South Korean singers seemed so free."[40]

Some South Korean singers have been invited to the North for official concerts—whether it is due to the considerable popularity South Korean singers have enjoyed throughout North Korea is unclear—but recently, in April 2018, following the short temporary thaw in the inter-Korean relationship, a delegation of South Korean pop singers performed in East Pyongyang Grand Theater. Artists representing a wide variety of popular music in the South—Jo Yong-pil, Li Seon-hui, Baek Ji-yeong, and K-pop girl group Red Velvet—performed to a full house of 1,500 Pyongyang citizens, presided over by the North Korean leader Kim Jong Un himself.

The inclusion of a K-pop group in the lineup of South Korean singers was not new. The history of cultural exchange between the two Koreas harks back to 1985 and occurred quite regularly throughout the 1990s and 2000s. But given that 2003 was the last time K-pop groups, such as Baby Vox and Sinhwa, performed in Pyongyang, the 2018 appearance of Red Velvet was surely the first time that a K-pop group had been invited to perform under Kim Jong Un's leadership. Red Velvet's appearance is read as an intentional move on the part of the North Korean leadership to proclaim its cultural openness to outside influence. But this choreographed event showed its limits when the live audience put on their stern faces in line with the tradition of showing no open support for the pop culture of the proclaimed enemy state. Though the reality is that K-pop has been enjoying stealthy yet increasing popularity among North Korean youth, the concert was not made available to the vast majority of North Koreans. But those not invited to the live performance still found ways to watch it by obtaining illegally copied USB drives that featured the recorded version, produced by the South Korean broadcasting station MBC.[41]

A K-pop girl group's performance in itself is a far cry from any political statement, but the fact that it provided an occasion to activate a hidden network to spread their recording presented a political threat to the regime. The preemptive measures to conceal the performance from the broader public, more than anything else, prove how strong the new network of sharing forbidden information is in North Korea. For this reason, only a few are allowed open access to K-pop under exceptional circumstances, such as the limited number of Pyongyang citizens in 2018 or the North Korean female ice-hockey players who were invited to form one united Korean team with the South Korean players for the 2018 Pyeongchang Winter Olympics. Bak Jong-a, a South Korean member of the united Korean women's team, reveals that the team listened to BTS's "Fire" or Red Velvet's "Red Taste" (Ppalgan-mat) during their training sessions and discovered that the North Korean team members soon became used to the music.[42]

For some, simply listening to K-pop and watching music videos are not enough. They go further to perform the roles of various K-pop artists. Han Song-i (female born in Hyesan in 1993 who left North Korea in 2013), a self-proclaimed *nolsae* (North Korean slang for a "player"), notes, "I really loved Girls' Generation while I was in the North. I played the role of the leader of the group, Yun-a, whom I adored. I brought a group of friends home, and we danced along with the Girls' Generation music."[43] Han's words illustrate how K-pop's appeal to North Korean millennials might lie in its ability to foster a particular kind of sociality. In addition to the conspicuous lure of high style, fashion, and feeling cool, K-pop embodies camaraderie specific to the young generation. Just as K-pop became a popular cultural phenomenon among a global audience with a unique showcasing of the relationship among band members often predicated on kinship terms—such as designating the oldest member as *mat-hyeong* (the oldest brother) and the youngest as *mak-nae* (the youngest sibling)—North Korean millennials' fascination with K-pop spills into the realm of forging relationships beyond their socially sanctioned circles through carefully devised role playing. As seen in Han's case, participating in K-pop culture creates an alternative way to imagine kinship and sociality, quite similar to the way global K-pop fandom operates.

While K-pop might appeal to a particular age group of young North Koreans, it is by no means the dominant music genre for North Korean listeners. Soft, melodic songs with heart-wrenching lyrics tend to resonate more closely with a broad range of demographics. Jeong Si-u (male born in 1991 in Pyongyang who left North Korea in 2017), for instance, notes, "North Korean listeners like South Korean songs that are comforting. They cannot understand rap music easily."[44] A similar account is shared by an anonymous interviewee (male in his early thirties, born in Pyongyang, who left North Korea in 2017 and soon arrived in South Korea): "I liked uplifting, fast-tempo songs. Lee Jeong-hyeon, Tae Jin-a, and Kim Gunmo were my favorites. On New Year's Eve, I would get together with friends and sing these songs with a guitar accompaniment. I am not too crazy about rap songs."[45] It is reasonable to surmise that the traditionally popular songs are typically not the latest K-pop or hip hop; ballad and trot songs—among them, the original soundtracks of widely viewed TV dramas—are the most popular.

This could be in large part due to the generational divide that grows with morphing technologies and modes of media consumption made available to various generations at the time of their youth. Gweon Seol-gyeong (female born in Onseong, Northern Hamgyeong Province, in 1982 who left North Korea in 2007) makes a pertinent point: "My generation primarily used to watch dramas on VCDs, but recent North Korean defectors watch many variety shows and know so much about K-pop groups."[46] With the transition in media formats comes the transition in what types of media are popular. The diversity of South Korean music genres that circulate in North Korea is due to the fact that K-pop emerged recently, claiming the hearts of the younger generation, whereas the enduring popularity of the South Korean dramas, most of which feature balladic songs as their original soundtracks, enables the lasting popularity of ballad songs. This accounts for the simultaneous coexistence of various genres and why singers such as Jo Yong-pil, Choe Jin-hee, Lee Seon-hee, Tae Jin-a, and Kim Geon-mo have been most welcome voices to North Koreans. Of the varied lineup for the 2018 East Pyongyang Grand Theater concert, Baek Ji-young's "Don't Forget" invited arguably the most enthusiastic response. The original soundtrack for the 2009 South Korean hit TV drama *Iris*, "Don't Forget" (Itji mal-a-yo), left such an impression on the audience that even Kim Jong Un allegedly showed interest in the song and asked many questions about it.[47] Some of the lyrics are as follows:

> Tears muted my voice,
> And I could not say the words:
> We loved each other,
> But we now bid farewell.
> Although living in separate places,
> We are under the same sky.
> Forget me not.
> Forget me not.[48]

The heart-wrenching lyrics of unrequited love and separation may universally apply to any context, but those North Koreans who were introduced to the song via the drama *Iris*—which centered around special agents from both Koreas trying to stop international-espionage schemes of starting the

second Korean War—would know well that the lyrics resonate closely with
the North-South relationship. The universal appeal of emotional reflection gains special resonance when a broader historical perspective comes
into play.

The dual appeal of lyrics that touch upon personal and historical entanglements plays out again in Gim Gwang-seok's celebrated song "A Letter
from a Private" (I-deung-byeong-ui pyeonji). According to a 2018 *BBC
News Korea* survey of fifty-one North Korean resettlers, this was one of
the most popular South Korean songs, closely trailing An Jae-uk's "Friend"
(Chin-gu).[49] A legendary figure in South Korean music history, Gim
Gwang-seok secured immortality as a "singing philosopher" of contemporary South Korean life. Of his many songs, "A Letter from a Private" runs
deeply through the souls of both North and South Koreans, who still face
division that mandates male citizens serve in the military during the prime
of their youth. The lyrics express,

> Bowing deeply to parents to bid farewell,
> The day I left home to join the military post by train.
> Something lingers on in the heart,
> Still, everything feels new from a blade of grass to a face
>   of a friend.
> It starts anew, my life in youth.
>
> Dear friends, don't forget to write me
> So that I won't forget our joyful days.
> Your warm hands as the train approached,
> How you disappeared as tiny figures as the train
>   moved away.
> It starts anew, my dream in youth.[50]

The lyrics capture the young male subject's moment of departure for military
service; the personal pain of leaving youthful life behind to fulfill military duty
overlaps with the national pain of facing the gash of division. The song was
used as the original soundtrack for *Joint Security Area* (Gongdong gyeongbi
guyeok; 2004), a quintessential movie that masterfully depicts the tragedy of

the Korean division on the most personal level. But even for North Koreans who have not seen the South Korean film, the song is quite familiar as it is often sung when North Korean men join the military. Known by a slightly different title ("Sang-deung-byeong-ui pyeonji"), the song is widely believed to be of North Korean origin.[51] The sacrifice made by the young men of both Koreas in the face of lingering national division is captured in the form of slow communication—that is, handwritten letters that symptomatically tell how disconnected they are from the rest of the world once they join the army.

An Jae-uk's sonorous ballad titled "Friend"—the most popular South Korean song in North Korea, according to the 2018 *BBC News Korea* survey—highlights the way people connect to one another in trying times. But unlike "A Letter from a Private," which expresses the isolation of youth serving in the military in the form of letter writing, "Friend" addresses a similar struggle of youth by means of a phone call:

> I called you suddenly on a trying day
> And cried silently while you listened to me.
> I took you for granted for being always by my side,
> I am thankful and regretful. . . .
>
> When the world tumbles, we toast
> And say that our days will come.
> Facing you and holding your hands,
> I can put the world filled with fear beneath my feet.[52]

The song significantly begins with a phone call to a friend, a means to genuinely connect to the beloved and trusted confidant. The singing subject's way to seek unconditional love and support, the call reaffirms pure friendship that highlights the universal human connection by transcending any particularities of time and space. Unlike various ways phones have served as prime means of surveillance in North Korea, "Friend" overshadows the dark side of new communication technology by accentuating the human rapport that can be enabled by phone calls.

As the title of the song suggests, friendship is a significant mode of social relationship. For those members of the society who are constantly pressured to surveil and report on one another, An's song resonates deeply with the primal human desire to support one another. Choe Ju-yeon (female born in 1992 in Cheongjin who left North Korea in 2015) recalls, "My favorite song was An Jae-uk's 'Friend.' I learned it with a friend, and together we memorized lyrics written in small letters in a tiny notebook. But when the surveillance team came to our house during the routine search, they found that notebook with the South Korean lyrics and took it away."[53] People living under conditions where it is difficult to satisfy basic social needs, such as having friends of their choice, may crave friendship more than those who have freedom to forge their network. Their humanity is validated in lyrical forms, defying the inhumanity of the system in which they find themselves.

Offering a different kind of social experience based on community support and friendship networks—whether vicariously (via their representations in lyrics) or literally (via sharing with a deeply trusted network of friends)—the songs offer intense, albeit brief, versions of human bonding even in the face of the most draconian surveillance mechanisms. This sentiment is best captured in Jeon Hyo-jin's (female born in 1987 in Hyesan who left North Korea in 2013) recollections: "During my high school years when students were sent to the countryside to help with farm work, classmates played South Korean songs, and we sang along when there was nobody watching us."[54] Whether in North or South Korea, strong emotional connections by sharing rhythms and lyrics can never be stopped—no matter how forceful the surveillance may be.

Variety Shows and Various Networks

South Korea in the new millennium has become a stronghold of variety shows that have gone viral across Asia.[55] Generally known as *yeneung* in South Korea, the versatile genre encompasses everything from a mock Olympiad of K-pop idols to gregarious quiz shows. In South Korea, *yeneung* is a media development that boomed in the new millennium, but it is hardly the domain of only millennials or Generation Z since there are plenty of productions that cater to all generations of viewers.

Media scholar Grace Jung identifies excess as the key characteristic of *yeneung*, which accounts for its distinctive kitsch sensibilities: "*Yeneung* programs that emerged in the new millennia are characteristically excessive in materiality; there is an excess of postmodern materials such as plastic for props, set design and costumes, as well as frequent use of cellular devices for tag-team games (therefore more use of postmodern 'material' such as 3G, 4G and LTE data)."[56] *Yeneung* relies heavily on cellular devices, including cell phones, surveillance cameras, and wireless service, which champion South Korea's status as a stronghold of information technology. The recent boom of South Korean variety shows in North Korea signals the latter's awakening to the presence of these technological possibilities outside the country. The voracious consumption of media featured in South Korean *yeneung*, in this regard, may be as important as the lighthearted humor that *yeneung* champions as its focal point. According to Jung,

> "*Yeneung*," which literally translates into "entertainment," is used interchangeably with "variety show" among Korean viewers and producers. Korea began to adopt American reality TV as a format in 2009.[1] With that said, reality TV is also "a particularly mercurial and polysemic genre."[2] The transnational genre mashup of reality and variety program elements has birthed a new form of programming in Korea referred to as *gwanchal yeneung*, which literally translates into "observational entertainment." *Gwanchal yeneung* is a hybridization of the reality show and variety show, thus becoming the reality-variety show.[57]

As Jung points out, the genre itself is multifaced, reflecting the variegated voices and needs of the ever-stratifying society of recent years.

Of the many *yeneung* programs that circulate in North Korea, two productions deserve particular attention for their coverage of a diverse generational spread and particular dynamics of gender: broadcasting station KBS2 TV's *The Return of Superman* (Seupeomaen-i dolawatta; 2013–present) and the cable channel tvN's *Grandpas over Flowers* (Kkotboda halbae; 2013–15, 2018). Both are phenomenally popular *yeneung* programs that have captured

1. Dal Yong Jin, *New Korean Wave: Transnational Cultural Power in the Age of Social Media* (Chicago: University of Illinois Press, 2016), 59–63.

2. Toby Miller and Marwan Kraidy, *Global Media Studies* (Cambridge: Polity Press, 2016), 159.

the characteristics of millennial South Korea, such as the rapidly transforming nature of patriarchy, ageism, and women's economic agency and performance of domestic labor—all of which are defining characteristics of North Korean millennials and millennial North Korea as well.

Airing since 2013 on KBS2 TV, *The Return of Superman* has enjoyed lasting popularity in South Korea. The show's visual pleasure lies in the challenges inexperienced dads face in looking after their little children, usually under age five, without help from their spouses. Traditionally regarded as a woman's job, childcare has not been seen as in the domain of men's work for a long time in South Korea. The show casts celebrity dads—actors, singers, comedians, announcers, and sportsmen—who would normally be consumed with their busy career. The premise aims simultaneously at the exposure of the dads' comical ineptitude at the parental job and the inevitable rearrangement of traditional gender roles.

A novelty for South Koreans, the show's format also appeals to North Koreans. According to Gweon Seol-gyeong (female born in Onseong, Northern Hamgyeong Province, in 1982 who left North Korea in 2007), recent resettlers she encountered in 2018 claimed that *The Return of Superman* enjoyed popularity in North Korea.[58] The show's appeal for North Koreans is multifold, but most obviously, the situation where mothers are absent from the domestic space speaks volumes to the North Korean millennial reality. Mothers of the *jangmadang* generation were largely missing from home in order to provide for the family, while their fathers mostly worked at official government-assigned jobs, receiving only symbolic pay. The show also highlights the universal experience of parenthood: the infinite challenges of looking after young children are relatable regardless of the stark differences in the political systems and economic structures between the two Koreas. Parents—rich or poor, experienced or not, North Korean or South Korean—dote on their children and care for them to the best of their ability.

But the primary point of attraction that *The Return of Superman* provides for North Koreans must be the intimate glimpse into South Korean domestic life. The show supposedly provides a documentarian presentation of the South Korean household: North Korean viewers get to see how South Korean apartments are laid out, what furniture families typically use, what snacks they give to their children, what toys children play with, and what home appliances are used in people's daily lives.

Of all the electronics featured in the show, cell phones occupy an important place in everyday communication. Just as TV dramas provide a sneak preview of the latest South Korean cell phone technologies that have yet to arrive in North Korea, *The Return of Superman* demonstrates various functions of new smartphone models. The show often features moments when dads video chat with their spouses while watching the kids so that the kids can talk to their missing moms. One of the show's guests, Do Gyeong-hwan, calls his wife to connect her to the kids, who are out camping.[59] Similarly, Sam Hamington, an Australia-born TV celebrity who married a South Korean wife and now resides in South Korea, also uses a video call to connect his children with their mom.[60] Family video chats like these are reminiscent of the previously mentioned phone calls that take place during the confirmation of remittance when resettlers send money to their families in the North. But due to poor connections and the dangers involved, those illicit calls usually do not last long, so they tend to be voice calls rather than video calls. Even though North Korean residents are allowed video chats internally within North Korea, they are well aware of the potential surveillance that can monitor their conversations anytime. Coming back to *The Return of Superman* with this in mind, we are confronted with a similar question: How free from surveillance is South Korea?

Viewers get to witness intimate family connections via smartphone video chats that are enabled by the ubiquitous presence of cameras. In fact, the show makes no secret of the fact that cameras are omnipresent. They are installed at every eye level, from ceiling view to children's eye level, measuring every move and every reaction of the featured children. Halfway revealed and halfway covered in white cloth, the cameras are hidden but not quite hidden, sticking out from playhouses, trees, and fireplaces, all reminding us that the surveillance of everyday domestic life is an inescapable reality.

The show features moments of surprise when children outmaneuver the system of surveillance. In one of the episodes, Gary's son, Hao, is tasked with finding chocolate hidden in the house. After making many futile attempts, Hao comes up with the idea of asking the cameraman to find and show him the footage capturing his dad hiding the chocolate.[61] Fully aware of the omniscient presence of the camera and its ability to document every move made in the house, Hao takes advantage of the surveillance system to fulfill his objective. In another episode, three-year-old Geon-u likewise walks right into the cameraman hiding in a playhouse and takes the man's colorful baseball cap to play with. Similar to how North Korean phone users outmaneuver the surveillance system with their creative reactions, these little children use the rules of the game to their own advantage.

Even without the ubiquitous presence of cameras in *The Return of Superman*, which is indispensable for generating enough footage to create a reality show, the overwhelming use of technology in everyday life in South Korea creates digital footprints that eventually turn into a prime mining field for corporations to generate profitable big data. Consumer choice in an affluent market economy often parades as political freedom that differentiates free marketplaces from the rest, but nevertheless, these marketplaces become prime factors that invite surveillance by corporate powers that no individual can escape.

Grandpas over Flowers is a travelogue of much older generations: senior citizens in their seventies (the so-called silent generation) and their travel assistants in their forties (Generation X). The show's focus on premillennials can be construed as a close reflection on the aging society that South Korea has become in the twenty-first century. The exponential increase in the number of senior citizens presents one of the biggest problems for South Korean society today, with widespread gerontophobia increasing the poverty of senior citizens that cripples their well-being and the dismantling of the traditional family structure, which took away the aging population's guaranteed system of support by the younger generation.[62]

With a touch of lighthearted humor, the show disguises these real social problems by turning them into a source of amusement. A sardonic homage to the KBS TV miniseries *Boys over Flowers* (2009), the title of the show places an immediate emphasis on the elderly as the main protagonists. Its usual guests are Li Sun-jae, Shin Gu, Bak Geun-hyeong, and Baek Il-seop, whose average age was seventy-six when the first season of the show commenced in 2013. Cast as the mature counterpart of four dashing male protagonists in *Boys over Flowers*, they traverse the world as backpack travelers with a limited budget in search of adventure and discovery. Throughout four

seasons, which feature tourist locations in Taiwan, the United Arab Emir-
ates, France, Greece, Spain, Germany, Austria, and the Czech Republic, the
elderly guests are accompanied by a younger "porter" (*jim-kkun*), Yi Seo-jin,
who was a forty-three-year-old actor when the show began in 2013.

Much of the show's attraction emerges from the interpersonal dynamics
among the senior guests, all of whom started their celebrated acting careers
nearly half a century ago. Presenting an amusing counterpart to the camaraderie among young friends who enjoy singing or dancing to K-pop music,
how these aged celebrities forge interpersonal relationships evokes much
laughter; the process is no less amusing than that of their younger counterparts. Actor Baek Il-seop in his seventies is referred to as *mak-nae* (the
youngest) among the fantastic four, being expected to do chores for other
actors who are a few years senior to him. He is relieved from his onerous
mak-nae status when Yi Seo-jin joins the team as a dedicated porter, which
could be read as a simulation of the time-honored tradition of the younger
generation's respect for and caring of the elders—a tradition that is all too
quickly vanishing in today's South Korea.

The show's attraction to North Koreans might best be explained by the
resettler Jeong Gwang-il (male born in the early 1960s who worked in Pyongyang and left North Korea in 2003), who has been carrying out an operation
to send USBs in plastic bottles to North Korea: "I send *Grandpas over Flowers* to show North Koreans how old people in the South can freely travel
and be active, which is far from the realities of North Korea."[63] According to
Jeong, the realities that the elderly citizens face in North Korea are far worse
than the South Korean counterpart. With their basic mobility severely
curbed (it is difficult to find elderly people freely roaming on the streets of
Pyongyang) and faced with dire economic hardship like the vast majority of
North Koreans, the North Korean senior citizens can hardly afford the kind
of worldly sojourn that *Grandpas over Flowers* presents.

The show is not only about South Korean senior citizens but also about
South Koreans' ability to travel the world and gain access to the supposed
backstage reality of the places they travel. The mobility that travel embodies
ultimately points to freedom, which, the show makes clear, is enabled by
financial backing. One of the elderly guests, Shin Gu, articulates this when
asked about the meaning of travel in episode 1: "When we were young, we

were all consumed by making ends meet. Traveling was a luxury that we could not afford. All we did was just work hard. With time, circumstances improved, and now we are able to travel, but we have also become old."[64] Likewise, in episode 1, the eldest of the grandpas, Yi Sun-jae, jokes when asked about what comes to mind when thinking of backpack travel: "Backpack? I think of the Korean War. During the war, I carried a bag of rice for my family."[65] Traveling the world for these grandpas marks a clear departure from the past tragedies of the Korean War and the ensuing economic hardship that consumed so much of their youth. In an odd generational interconnection, these South Korean grandpas' life trajectories overlap with that of the current North Korean millennial generation, who have aspirations that their challenge-ridden youth will mature into more prosperous senior years.

Nonetheless, *Grandpas over Flowers* is not a wanton celebration of South Korea's affluence of today. One of the focal attractions of the show is how the group travels through famous tourist destinations on a limited budget. An intentionally curtailed budget is an often-used premise for many *yeneung* programs. Managing expenses—usually in the form of pinching pennies—is left to the Gen X porter Yi Seo-jin, an obvious reversal of roles between parents and children.

Typical dynamics between parents and children are formed around a scenario of frugal war-generation parents teaching their wasteful Gen X children how to be economical, but *Grandpas over Flowers* draws obvious pleasure from having the younger generation play the role of responsible budget managers while the elderly travelers indulge in pleasures of discovery and spending. By staging the reversal of roles, the show makes a case that generational divides do not essentially stem from biological age groups but rather from performed identities. In episodes in Dubai and Greece, Yi Seo-jin is joined by another "porter" assistant, Choe Ji-woo, a popular actress who achieved fame as the protagonist of *Winter Sonata* (Gyeo-ul yeon-ga) and *Stairway to Heaven*. The scenes between the two often feature a quarrel over small amounts of money to keep the travel budget intact, with Yi Seo-jin reprimanding Choe Ji-woo for having treated herself to too many scoops of ice cream.[66] The stereotypical frugality usually reserved as a key characteristic of the war generation is staged here by the much younger Generation X and millennial actors.

For North Korean viewers, the humor stemming from having the two wealthy young celebrities pinch pennies might be lost, but one message is loudly communicated despite the cultural differences between North and South Korea. More than anything else, *Grandpas over Flowers* is a laudatory validation of South Korea's globality—South Korean citizens' presence in the world as a form of freedom of mobility. The first episode features a preliminary meeting of the staff and guests in a Seoul café to discuss the concept of the show. A producer uses a globe to show where the grandpas will be going, providing visions of the world and their ability to make choices for their travel. In season 4, episode 9, the group dines in a Korean restaurant in Prague, owned by an overseas Korean.[67] In *The Return of Superman*, South Korea's globality also takes the form of the world coming to South Korea. The Hamington family as well as soccer player Bak Ju-ho's family are mixed race from international marriages, with the former featuring the union between an Australian husband and a South Korean wife and the latter featuring a South Korean husband and a Swiss wife. These two *yeneung* shows take South Koreans' mobility not just as their premise but also as the very condition of life in the twenty-first century.

Here, mobility is in large part enabled by the connectivity that cell phone usage guarantees. Before season 4 of *Grandpas over Flowers* commences, the guests gather at the Incheon International Airport to depart for their various destinations in eastern Europe. Then, in season 4, episode 1, Yi Seo-jin, the designated porter, is handed a Berlin hotel address—their first lodging upon arrival. While sitting in the airport, Seo-jin immediately starts to search his cell phone and accesses a local Berlin map.[68] As he is the designated travel guide, his habit of using a cell phone to navigate through foreign cities intensifies as the journey unfolds. Upon arrival in Berlin, Seo-jin and the staff use a laptop computer to search for nearby restaurants and check their online customer ratings.[69] These moments showcase how cell phones and other electronic gadgets enable global connectivity—something that is forbidden for North Koreans just as free travel is forbidden for them both domestically and internationally.

Although these shows champion South Korea's presence in the world, enabled by mobile gadgets, the flipside is the dangers of technology that permit all-seeing surveillance. The ubiquitous camera presence fosters intimacy and irony between the viewers and the filmed subjects by frequently using the format of a secret camera (*molae kamera*). Just as cameras littered around the domestic space in *The Return of Superman* open up an intimate gaze into South Korean households, *Grandpas over Flowers* uses hidden cameras to present a close perspective on the actors' private lives.

Cameras are placed at the filmed subjects' eye levels to introduce an immersive experience for viewers. This practice starts with grandpas packing their bags before their travel. When Yi Sun-jae, for example, packs his bag before departure, the camera is set at his eye level, opening up a probing perspective into his household. In South Korea, Yi Sun-jae is known for his time-honored portrayal of an authoritative father figure, but the camera reveals him obediently listening to every order from his wife, who endlessly commands him around the house to bring various things for packing. In the process, the details of his household—not only the gender dynamics but also the layout of his apartment and the objects that fill the space—are disclosed to viewers. Similarly, when another grandpa, Shin Gu, goes grocery shopping to buy instant rice and soju in preparation for the trip, a low-angle camera follows him around, in effect giving a vicarious look into a South Korean grocery store.

The cameras do not remain just simple devices to render a close look into the everyday life of South Koreans; all too soon they become rather abrasive means of surveillance. But the show's guests, just like the toddlers in *The Return of Superman*, play this to their advantage. During the first season where the guests travel to Taiwan, porter Yi Seo-jin gets to travel with Sunny, a temporary assistant to help him lead the tourist group. A member of the popular K-pop group Girls' Generation, Sunny is often mentioned in the show as Seo-jin's potential romantic interest. In fact, the show implies that they used Sunny as bait to make unsuspecting Seo-jin sign up. Before he commits to joining *Grandpas over Flowers* as a porter, a secret camera captures him being told by the production staff that he will be traveling with Sunny on a different reality show. Not knowing about the hidden camera, Seo-jin is elated that he will be signed on to a show with his longtime crush. Having taken pity on Seo-jin, the show finally invites Sunny as the one-day assistant in Taiwan. On the flight there, Seo-jin and Sunny are seated next to each other, but the production team mischievously places a camera and a microphone to record their interaction. As if getting revenge for the incident where his confession that he has a crush on Sunny was captured on camera, Seo-jin protests that he will turn the camera off this time. He even tells the flight attendant that the microphone and camera have to be turned off.[70] When the staff visits him suddenly, Seo-jin intensely stares at the camera secretly carried by a prankster staff member and turns it off.

As contrived as these scenes might be to induce lighthearted humor, they nevertheless present the truth about the nuisance of surveillance possibilities and the burdens of having to live with all-seeing eyes in a highly technologized world. South Korea's iteration of the #MeToo movement involved heavy criticism of many hidden cameras violating women's dignity and privacy. As the movement's representative slogan ("My life is not your pornography") emblematizes, South Korea's #MeToo movement cannot be separated from the sexual violence emerging from surveillance mechanisms. The scene featuring Seo-jin on a flight to Taiwan could be construed as a humorous reversal of the gender of supposed victims of hidden cameras, but it could also be read as a cautionary tale about how surveillance prevails in seemingly disparate societies like North Korea and South Korea.

The Gravity of Nonfictions

Reality shows are perched on the borderline of reality and nonreality. By means of an invasive staging of interpersonal dynamics and manipulative editing, they simultaneously present what life really is and what life is supposed to look like. Most South Korean and foreign viewers of *yeneung* know that the reality in such shows is imbricated with fictional elements, making a spectacle palatable for TV. However, North Korean viewers who secretly watch shows such as *The Return of Superman* and *Grandpas over Flowers* do not have the same sensibilities to tell documentarian truth apart from fiction, much like many of them take the reality within TV dramas literally as the societal realities of South Koreans.

Still, shows that promote themselves as nonfictional, such as news, documentaries, and radio talk shows, carry a different level of gravity for North Korean viewers. Resettlers themselves consider the veracity of media content to be important when considering the priority of media made available to North Koreans: according to a 2019 *BBC News Korea* survey, four out of ten resettlers believe that coverage about South Korea is the most pressing content that people in North Korea should watch.[71] For them, nonfictional news and documentaries carry more weight than the conspicuously fictional dramas and films.

An anonymous interviewee (male in his early thirties, neither from Pyongyang nor from a border region, who left North Korea in 2014) tells how he first watched South Korean cell phone commercials and dramas on TV when he was a high school student in North Korea. The commercials and dramas featured prosperous South Korean life, but due to their fictionality, he was reluctant to believe in what he saw. He thought that they were South Korean propaganda designed to persuade North Korean viewers of the superiority of the South. But when he watched news coverage of sporting events, such as the Doha Asian Games and the preparation for the Beijing Olympics, he started to believe in the content as these events were known to North Koreans as well.[72]

As interesting as this story is in terms of how North Korean viewers come to accept the realities of South Korean media content, what should be noted is the differentiation between fictional genres (drama) and nonfictional genres (news) and his embedded trust in the latter. Ahlam Lee points out that there is a perceivable trend where North Korean viewers' fascination begins with entertainment content and eventually expands to nonfictional coverage: "Many North Koreans were first addicted to listening to K-pop music that has lyrical melodies and words and differs greatly from North Korea's revolutionary songs. Subsequently, they became interested in South Korean news or radio programs that provide a wide range of information, including South Korean politics, social issues, and stories about North Korean defectors who have resettled in South Korea."[73]

Nowadays, as an increasing number of North Koreans request smugglers bring in the "documentary about [a North Korean spy] Gim Hyeon-hui's bombing of Korean Airlines or historical shows," they seem to be more open to radio as a source to quench their curiosity.[74] Just as the barriers to enjoying South Korean songs were lower than, say, that of watching South Korean TV dramas or films, radio is cheaper to acquire than laptops or cell phones.

But even for those who have means to access all media platforms, radio offers a different kind of coverage.

According to Kretchun and Kim, "North Korean elites generally turn first to reliable people and then to the radio as their main sources of credible information for conducting business."[75] Likewise, Choe Ju-yeon (female born in 1992 in Cheongjin who left North Korea in 2014), who enjoyed an affluent life in North Korea, recounts how she came into contact with crucial information about the fate of defectors by listening to South Korean radio:

> We owned a Sony radio in Cheongjin with a dial that was not fixed. When you scan channels, you hear many foreign languages, such as Japanese. Then, one day, I discovered a Korean-language channel: KBS Radio. It offered different kinds of programs than TV dramas. The announcers spoke quite naturally, and they told ordinary stories from everyday life, which were so interesting. Then, one day, a North Korean resettler appeared as a guest, and that resettler told unbelievable stories of how successfully they settled in South Korea, even having attended a South Korean college and now owning a house. I was shocked at first, but what I heard eventually helped me make a decision to leave North Korea. Until then, we in the North did not know what would happen to you once you entered South Korea—whether the South Korean authorities would kill us or not.[76]

Once again, radio as a particular media format enabling an authentic perspective on South Korean life prevails in this account. Media platforms themselves perform as mechanisms to calibrate varying degrees of veracity, which is remarkable in a place like North Korea, where these media, regardless of their format, are categorically forbidden. Discerning the truth and remaining confidential while accessing these media require nothing short of shrewd tactfulness. Whether we call it "reactive creativity," "antibehavior," or even "trickery," it signals resilience characteristic of today's North Korean millennials. Limited though their access to worldwide information may be, they savor it when they encounter it and create new paths forward to reach unknown destinations filled equally with risks and opportunities.

CONCLUSION
Millennial Media

Not at the speed of technology, but at the speed of dreams.

—ZAPATISTAS SONG[1]

This book has attempted to put our ears closer to the heartbeat of today's North Korea. We have seen unique variants of network connectivity and market creativity unfold in North Korea while also sensing considerable cracks in its conventional sociopolitical order. How does media technology mitigate these matters? How do the widespread forbidden media influence the nation's social transformation? Can swift changes in the cultural realm override and even overturn the political regime in a foundational way?

Much has changed in North Korea in the new millennium, especially since Kim Jong Un assumed the country's leadership in 2012. Beyond the dramatic headlines about nuclear tests, more quotidian practices of embracing forbidden media—often by using cell phones—have brought irreversible changes to the country. Although North Koreans cannot publicly participate in the sharing of foreign media, its increasing circulation has prompted us to explore how the pervasiveness of the forbidden materials affects the shifts and realignment of traditional social ties in this astringently controlled society. The encroachment of foreign media cannot be divorced from tidal shifts in technological changes and marketization, providing a litmus test on how subversive views can be forged even under exceptional circumstances.

To be sure, proliferating media technology cuts both ways in North Korea. It expedites the exchange of communication among North Koreans but has also become an effective tool for surveillance by the North Korean regime. Much of this book has been dedicated to reading the intricate dynamics between these two forces, with a particular emphasis on how North Korean millennials circumvent censorship according to their unique perception of cultural ownership and creative repurposing of foreign media. Departing from the West-centric notion of intellectual property as associated with strictly articulated authorship and copyrights, North Korean users tend to approach foreign-media content with a sense of communal ownership shared by their social milieu. Millennials in particular tend to regard foreign media as an open source and use it to discern trustworthy members of their social network. I hope this book has begun to unravel North Korean users' unique understanding of media ownership against the backdrop of North Korean copyright practices, which emphasize collective users rather than individual creators.

At the same time, I urge readers to see this process as part and parcel of a broader global trend in the circulation of digital information where "imitation, appropriation, and copying are crucial postmodern production practices and that practices of digital appropriation and pastiche have a direct impact on how we think about and value authorship and originality."[2] North Korean creativity—a seemingly paradoxical yet central concept in this book—spins a story tied to the modes of collective consumption in North Korea that symptomatically reflect the global tendencies of information sharing. Media users find creative ways to participate in the discursive modes of information circulation, quite akin to how younger media users around the globe prefer blockchain technology, which guarantees transparency to the centralized systems often managed by states and other powerful financial entities.

Cell phones enter this discussion as central forces; they are not only convenient tech gadgets but also potent symbols of connection to the world that transcend many layers of restrictions imposed by the state. Cell phones have come to stand as an embodiment of millennial aspirations, entrepreneurial desires, and exit strategies from the devastating deadlock of North Korean reality—whether by indulging in escape fantasies enabled by media consumption or by using cell phones to aid actual departure from North Korea. In a place where idiosyncratic thoughts and actions are met with grave consequences, cell phones and related media networks have come to stand as shorthands for creativity. In a way, the North Korean love for cell phones confirms why cell phones are loved universally around the globe. "We love our phones for the same reason we love most things: for their beauty and our possession of them," notes McCracken.[3] The temporary creative freedom associated with the sense of subversion and ownership of media consumed adds to the deep lure and beauty of the phones in North Korea.

Discussions of millennial North Korea and North Korean millennials cannot be complete without examining the bottom-up, everyday practices that overshadow the official state rhetoric. A close reading of South Korean media texts provides insight into how cell phones and media technologies surface as prominent themes, cultivating the cryptolect to forge antibehavior for the viewers. But as strongly as South Korean dramas present a counternarrative to the official state value system, equally strong is North Korean viewers' tendency to identify with the themes presented in South Korean materials, such as family bonding, friendship, and changing gender dynamics. In other words, what connects is as strong as what divides, and these dual forces are often encapsulated in the way cell phones are mobilized in South Korean narratives as a means to broker social relationships.

One unique aspect of the North Korean use of cell phones and other related media technologies concerns an intriguing convergence of online and offline modes of communication. Although cell phones are prime enablers of online communication, in the case of North Korea, the most critical information cannot be exchanged online. This type of exchange must rely on trustworthy person-to-person transmission—carefully, from hand to hand—which occurs via USB drives and SD cards loaded with information forbidden by the state. In this regard, millennial North Korea presents a special case where social networks do not—and should not—leave a digital footprint behind as users must dodge the state surveillance system and, by extension, the pervasive big-data-collection system. This is why a peculiar analogy can be drawn between the North Korean version of social networks and blockchain technology: the premise of the North Korean information transaction is built on the trust that enables person-to-person relationships, much like how blockchain technology creates a transparent and traceable human network, but in the case of North Korea, that transparency can only be shared by the inner members—never by monitors of online activities.

Although this book's primary focus has been on cell phones and interrelated media and communication practices of the new millennium, I would be remiss not to mention North Korea's other technological ambitions. Today, their media coverage touts the nation's soaring achievements in science and technology, such as how artificial intelligence is deployed for developing new medicine, how North Korea's DNASTAR program successfully analyzed the genome system devised by the US National Center for Biotechnology Information, and how the automated forestry-management system was generated using open-source software, just to name a few.[4] Although many of the state media's celebratory headlines conceal lingering contradictions—shaped by the state's unstoppable ambition in scientific progress while adhering to relentless oppression—they nevertheless reflect a nation that is taking steps forward into the future.

At the end of the day, we are left with a big question: Will the influx of new media and cell phones broker the arrival of civil society? Relatedly, will we witness North Korean Solzhenitsyns emerge to voice their dissent directly in the face of authority? Or to paraphrase by means of analogy, is an Arab Spring possible in North Korea? Although quite different in social circumstances and political history, the Arab Spring leaves us with layers of questions. Political scientist Deborah L. Wheeler, whose work focuses on the risks and benefits of digital resistances enabled by access to the internet and social media, eloquently asks, "Why, when the costs for disobedience can be so high, are Middle Eastern citizens in authoritarian contexts oppositional? . . . Middle Eastern citizens find the Internet useful in efforts to resist institutionalised power and social norms. Internet use reduces opportunity costs to participation and facilitates the concentration of agency."[5] Although North Koreans do not have full access to the worldwide internet and cannot be openly oppositional, their attitude toward and conception of cell phones and new technology seems entrenched in the subversion of social norms, if not a full-on open resistance.

To this point, Kim Yonho provides a glimmer of hope by noting how "historically, cell phones tend to strengthen individuality and social movements, provide an opportunity for dissent and eventually lead to political upheaval, such as the 2001 'text-message revolution' in the Philippines and the Arab Spring in the Middle East."[6] But millennial North Korea is neither the Philippines nor the Middle East, at least for now and in the near future. Analogous to the way North Korean citizens can accumulate private assets through market activities while having no legal system to protect them, they have means to accrue forbidden knowledge in private settings while having no social measures to protect themselves when caught. Against my hope to see an optimistic future, I have to agree with Joo that, at least for the foreseeable future, there is a lack of "a political centre with an alternative ideology," and hence "'revolution by mouth' is unlikely to develop into a major social revolution."[7]

Looking into the more distant future of our millennium, the extending fissures in the system brought about by the incommensurability between the surveillance state and the creativity of the people might force us to reconsider what I would call "malign historiography"—an assumption that a state— here, North Korea—is not capable of progress, and therefore the pathway to its transformation is foreclosed. This proleptic vision glides over the glaring gap between the state and the people and therefore overlooks the social substrata in flux. Perhaps the real crisis of today's North Korea will erupt from such a partial vision.

If we were to accept Antonio Gramsci's notion that "the crisis consists precisely in the fact that the old is dying and the new cannot be born," then North Korean millennials, as observed in this book, are far from crisis.[8] Kim Yonho is right that cell phones "made possible the sharing of information on the movement of people and products in real time between average citizens. At least in this respect, North Korea can no longer be seen as an underdeveloped and closed country where freedom of movement and expression are completely suppressed."[9] The new generation embroiled in new media and new technology has sprung up, gesturing toward gradual but foundational changes. The ever-spreading network of cell phones as a metric for gauging the fervid desire for change might be what defies the overdetermined conjecture of impending doomsday.

Lastly, never to be forgotten is the fact that the future of North Korea is foremost a human story. For many resettlers whose voices have shaped this book, the future of the nation they left behind is the future of their family members they left behind. O Eun-jeong (female born in North Hamgyeong Province in 1992, left North Korea in 2009) had to defect from North Korea without her younger sibling, to whom she was a parent figure. Six years after their separation, she published a collection of poems titled *Calling Out for Hometown* (Gohyang-eul bureuda) in South Korea, in which the poem "At Dusk Falls Rain" (Sae-byeok bi) appears. It reads,

> In the thick of the night
> When all are asleep,
> You come and go like a thief,
> Leaving only traces behind.
> Like you,
> I long to be a thief.
>
> Were I to knock on your window
> While the moon is asleep,
> Would this longing
> Dissipate?
> Disappear?[10]

The many faces of millennial North Korea have emerged in this book, at times with hope for change and at times with a sense of despair, but the country's significance for many resettlers is as a place where they long to return. For them, the tide of changes that have engulfed the nation is not just a subject of intellectual curiosity but a glimpse into the actual lives of their kin. Every tick of the clock and every beat of the heart buoy them back to their place of origin, flowing back and forth with the currents of time.

List of Resettler Interviews

Primary Interviews

Anonymous (male in his early twenties, left North Korea in 2016). Interview by author. Seoul, Korea, December 13, 2019.[1]

Anonymous (male in his early thirties, neither from Pyongyang nor from a border region, left North Korea in 2014). Interview by author. Seoul, Korea, December 17, 2019.

Anonymous (female born in Hoeryeong in 1971, left North Korea in 1998). Interview by author. Seoul, Korea, December 18, 2019.

Anonymous. Email interview by author. May 28, 2020.

Anonymous (female in her thirties, born in Pyongyang, left North Korea in 2008, settled in South Korea in 2013). Zoom interview by author. September 3, 2021.

Anonymous (female in her twenties, born in Hyesan, left North Korea in 2017). Interview by author. Seoul, Korea, July 22, 2022.

Anonymous (male in his early thirties, born in Pyongyang, left North Korea in 2017, soon arrived in South Korea). Interview by author. Seoul, Korea, July 28, 2022.

Anonymous (female in her midthirties, born in Yanggang Province, left North Korea in 2018, came to South Korea in 2019). Interview by author. Seoul, Korea, July 29, 2022.

Anonymous (male in his twenties, born in Yanggang Province, left North Korea in 2020, came to South Korea in 2021). Interview by author. Seoul, Korea, July 31, 2022.

Anonymous (female in her midthirties, born in Cheongjin, left North Korea in 2019, came to South Korea in 2020). Interview by author. Seoul, Korea, August 3, 2022.

Gim Hae-suk (female in her forties, born in South Pyeongan Province, left North Korea in 2018, came to South Korea in 2019). Interview by author. Seoul, Korea, July 27, 2022.

Go Na-hae (female born in Dancheon, South Hamgyeong Province, left North Korea in 2018, came to South Korea in 2019). Interview by author. Seoul, Korea, July 28, 2022.

Jeong Gwang-il (male born in the early 1960s, worked in Pyongyang, left North Korea in 2003). Interview by author. Seoul, Korea, December 14, 2019.

Na Min-hui (female born in 1991 in Pyongyang, left North Korea in 2014, came to South Korea in 2015). Interview by author. Seoul, Korea, July 14, 2022.

Park Eunhee (female in her twenties, born in Wonsan, left North Korea in 2012). Email interview by author. December 6, 2023.

Son Myung-hui (female in her midthirties, born in Dancheon, Hamgyeong Province, left North Korea first in 2007 and again in 2014). Interview by author. Seoul, Korea, December 18, 2019.

Secondary Source Interviews

An Hye-gyeong (female in her thirties, born in Cheongjin, left North Korea in 2006). [In Korean.] Interview by Baena TV. *Baenamu isahoe*, December 16, 2019. https://www.youtube.com/watch?v=3LrzoSH5k_I.

Anonymous (male in his late forties, born in Pyongyang, left North Korea in 2010). *A Quiet Opening: North Koreans in a Changing Media Environment*. Interview by Nat Kretchun and Jane Kim, 44. Washington, DC: InterMedia, 2012.

Anonymous (resettler). "South Korean Cultural Boom in North Korea" [Bukhan-e buneun hanryu yeolpung]. Interview by Gang Dong-wan. *Joongang ilbo*, November 29, 2014. https://news.joins.com/article/16558635.

Anonymous (female born in 1994 in Musan, left North Korea in 2015). "North Koreans Say that the Country Cannot Sustain Itself Without the Marketplace" [Buk jumindeul saenghwal jangmadang eopsineun an doraganda]. Interview by Gim Ji-hwan. *Gyeonghyang sinmun*, January 9, 2019. http://news.khan.co.kr/kh_news/khan_art_view.html?art_id=201901090600045.

Anonymous (male resettler in his twenties, left North Korea in 2011). "North Korean Defector Claims that the Drama Beautifies North Korea Since the Reality Is Much Grimmer" [Talbukmin, mihwa-ra-neun dan-eo-jo-cha gwa-hae, hyeonsil hweolssin deo yeol-ak]. Interview by Hangyeore TV. *Hangyeore TV*, December 19, 2020. https://www.youtube.com/watch?v=35NPx7BI6b8.

Bak Hyeon-jeong (female in her thirties, born in Hyesan, left North Korea in 2018). [In Korean.] Interview by Channel A. *On the Way to Meet You* [Ije mannaro gapnida], October 6, 2019. https://www.youtube.com/watch?v=o_3t5_C2MGo.

Bak Hyun-suk (female in her forties, born in Hyesan, left North Korea in 2013). "Baenamu Hakdang." Interview by Baena TV. *Baena TV*, May 20, 2019. https://www.youtube.com/watch?v=qdcUhoCTt4o.

Bak Na-ri (born in Hoeryeong in 1990, left North Korea in 2015). [In Korean.] Interview by Baena TV. *Tal tal tal*, December 19, 2016. https://www.youtube.com/watch?v=vXF21DSNIgU.

Bak Yeong-chan (male in his twenties, place of birth unknown, left North Korea in late 2010s). [In Korean.] Interview by Channel A. *On the Way to Meet You* [Ije mannaro gapnida], September 8, 2019. https://www.youtube.com/watch?v=lEUl5kCs3MM.

Bak Yu-seong (male born in Hoeryeong in 1990, left North Korea in 2007). "North Korean Man's Surprise Reaction to *Crash Landing on You*" [Sarang-ui bulsichak deuramareul bogo chunggyeok bat-eun bukhan namja-ui ban-eung-eun]. Interview by CLAB. *CLAB*, January 11, 2020. https://www.youtube.com/watch?v=DuDSj6qNpIM.

Choe Ju-yeon (female born in 1992 in Cheongjin, left North Korea in 2014). [In Korean.] Interview by Baena TV. *Tal tal tal*, December 15, 2020. https://www.youtube.com/watch?v=TaJ2ycTnvWM.

Choe Seong-guk (male born in the early 1980s in Pyongyang, came to South Korea in 2010). "Influenced by South Korean Dramas, North Korean Women's Ideal Male Types Have Changed" [Buk yeo-seong-deul, hanguk deurama bo-myeo nam-seong-sangdo dal-a-jyeot-jyo]. Interview by Yi Yun-ju. *Hankook ilbo*, June 29, 2018. https://www.hankookilbo.com/News/Read/201806281389742821.

Choe Yu-jin (female born in Hyesan in 1982, left North Korea in 2020). [In Korean.] Interview by Baena TV. *Tal tal tal*, November 25, 2020. https://www.youtube.com/watch?v=O9bPvQjQofM.

Gang Li-hyeok (male born in 1987 in Bukcheon, Jagang Province, left North Korea in 2013). [In Korean.] Interview by Baena TV. *Tal tal tal*, March 25, 2018. https://www.youtube.com/watch?v=26IjeOgCFsQ.

———. "Baenamu Hakdang." Interview by Baena TV. *Baena TV*, May 20, 2019. https://www.youtube.com/watch?v=qdcUhoCTt4o.

Gang Na-ra (female born in 1997 in Cheongjin, left North Korea in 2014). [In Korean.] Interview by Baena TV. *Tal tal tal*, December 1, 2017. https://www.youtube.com/watch?v=w4ZICkiYN5s.

———. "A North Korean Defector Reacts to *Crash Landing on You*." [In Korean.] Interview by Yeontong TV. *Yeontong TV*, January 5, 2020. https://www.youtube.com/watch?v=R8vuc9ed4rA.

Gim A-ra. [In Korean.] Interview by Channel A. *On the Way to Meet You* [Ije mannaro gapnida], January 12, 2020. https://www.youtube.com/watch?v=MEs8jxYEGYk.

Gim Ga-yeong (female born in Hyesan in her twenties, left North Korea in 2012). "There Is No *Parasite* in North Korea" [Buk-han-e *Gisaengchung*-eun eopda]. Interview by Gim Jin-guk. *Radio Free Asia*, February 17, 2020. https://www.rfa.org/korean/weekly_program/market_gen/fe-jk-02172020110255.html.

Gim Ha-na (female born in 1988 in Hyesan, left North Korea in 2014). [In Korean.] Interview by Baena TV. *Tal tal tal*, October 30, 2020. https://www.youtube.com/watch?v=M7-IdvTbIAo&list=WL&index=2.

Gim Ji-yeong (female in her early thirties, born in Hyesan, left North Korea in 2012). [In Korean.] Interview by Baena TV. *Tal tal tal*, February 20, 2017. https://www.youtube.com/watch?v=qrbOaeyFlfE.

Gim Jun-hyeok (male born in 1991 in Pyongyang, left North Korea in 2010). [In Korean.] Interview by Channel A. *On the Way to Meet You* [Ije mannaro gapnida], April 7, 2019. https://www.youtube.com/watch?v=CevxkFBmvAo.

Gim Ju-seong (male born in 1963 in Japan, went to North Korea in 1979 and left the country in 2008). [In Korean.] Interview by Baena TV. *Baenamu isahoe*, October 3, 2018. https://www.youtube.com/watch?v=m6wlxivdNUE&t=2362s.

Gim Tae-hui (female born in the early 1970s, settled in South Korea in 2007). "2011 New Year's Special Report: New Waves of Change in North Korea, Part 3, 'South Korean Dramas Are So Interesting'" [2011nyeon sinnyeon teukjip: Bukhan-e buneun byeonhwa-ui baram 3, "namhan deurama jae-mitseoyo"]. Interview by Yi Won-hui. *Radio Free Asia*, January 11, 2011. http://www.rfa.org/korean/temp/new_year_sp-01052011113720.html.

Gwak Mun-wan (male in his fifties, settled in South Korea in 2005). "Interview with the North Korean Defector Turned Assistant Writer of *Crash Landing on You*" [*Sarang-ui bulsichak* talbukja bojojakga inteobeu]. Interview by Gim Su-bin. *BBC News Korea*, February 16, 2020. https://www.bbc.com/korean/51519885.

Gweon Seol-gyeong (female born in Onseong, Northern Hamgyeong Province, in 1982, left North Korea in 2007). "Although North Korean Stations Edited Out Red Velvet, North Koreans Watch Their Performance on a Secretly Secured USB" [Buk bangsong ledeu belbet tong-pyeon-jip haetjiman jumin-deul USB mollae guhae-seo-bwa]. Interview by Ju Seong-ha and Jang Won-jae. *Donga ilbo*, April 10, 2018. http://www.donga.com/news/BestClick/article/all/20180410/89534017/1.

———. [In Korean.] Interview by Baena TV. *Baenamu isahoe*, September 20, 2018. https://www.youtube.com/watch?v=TQsv4k10jOU.

Han Song-i (female born in 1993 in Hyesan, left North Korea in 2013). "*Crash Landing on You* Has Landed Dramatically in North Korea" [*Sarang-ui bulsichak* bukhan gangta]. Interview by SsongiTube. *SsongiTube*, March 18, 2020. https://www.youtube.com/watch?v=JmDu50E8yGY.

———. [In Korean.] Interview by Baena TV. *Tal tal tal*, December 10, 2017. https://www.youtube.com/watch?v=ZFSrJpBSyU4/.

———. [In Korean.] Interview by Channel A. *On the Way to Meet You* [Ije mannaro gapnida], October 21, 2018. https://www.youtube.com/watch?v=kzdg7GKb9Wo.

Jeon Hyo-jin (female born in 1987 in Hyesan, left North Korea in 2013). "There Is No *Parasite* in North Korea" [Buk-han-e *Gisaengchung*-eun eopda]. Interview by Gim Jin-guk. *Radio Free Asia*, February 17, 2020. https://www.rfa.org/korean/weekly_program/market_gen/fe-jk-02172020110255.html.

———. "What Are the Most Popular South Korean Songs for North Korean Youth?" [Bukhan jeol-meun-i-deul-i gajang joahaneun hanguk gayoneun?]. Interview by Gim Seong-hun. *Jugan Chosun*, December 13, 2017. https://www.chosun.com/site/data/html_dir/2017/12/01/2017120102037.html.

Jeong Shi-u (male born in 1991 in Pyongyang, left North Korea in 2017). [In Korean.] Interview by Channel A. *On the Way to Meet You* [Ije mannaro gapnida], October 21, 2018. https://www.youtube.com/watch?v=hEyuofUtEU8.

Jeong Yu-na (female born in 1988 in Hoeryeong, left North Korea in 2008). [In Korean.] Interview by Channel A. *On the Way to Meet You* [Ije mannaro gapnida], October 21, 2018. https://www.youtube.com/watch?v=hEyuofUtEU8.

———. [In Korean.] Interview by Channel A. *On the Way to Meet You* [Ije mannaro gapnida], June 24, 2018. https://www.youtube.com/watch?v=I-nFPfRNOUU.

Jo Ye-na (female born in 1993 in Yanggang Province, left North Korea in 2012). [In Korean.] Interview by Baena TV. *Tal tal tal*, May 23, 2019. https://www.youtube.com/watch?v=UO6Li3bpvYY.

Ju Chan-yang (female born in 1991 in Cheongjin, left North Korea in 2010). [In Korean.] Interview by Channel A. *On the Way to Meet You* [Ije mann-aro gapnida], February 25, 2017. https://www.youtube.com/watch?v=IHIA5aBOmoM.

Li Eun-hui (born in the 1990s in Kim Jong-suk Province, left North Korea in 2015). [In Korean.] Interview by Baena TV. *Tal tal tal*, December 25, 2018. https://www.youtube.com/watch?v=xw1-ytdQYZ4&t=1489s.

Li Hyang-mi (female born in Cheongjin in 1992, left North Korea in 2013). [In Korean.] Interview by Baena TV. *Tal tal tal*, September 7, 2020. https://www.youtube.com/watch?v=WlAzaGiL244.

Li Hyeong-seok (male born in Pyongyang in 1984, left North Korea in 2002). [In Korean.] Interview by Baena TV. *Tal tal tal*, November 26, 2020. https://www.youtube.com/watch?v=aQHu4COR8kE.

Li Seo-eun (born in 1989 in Hyesan, left North Korea in 2010). [In Korean.] Interview by Baena TV. *Tal tal tal*, February 25, 2018. https://www.youtube.com/watch?v=Q_aVtc3XteY.

Li Seon-ju (female in her late twenties, born in Hoeryeong, left North Korea in 2004). [In Korean.] Interview by Baena TV. *Tal tal tal*, November 26, 2020. https://www.youtube.com/watch?v=aQHu4COR8kE.

Li Su-ryeon (female in her thirties born in Musan, left North Korea the first time around 2007). [In Korean.] Interview by Baena TV. *Tal tal tal*, November 20, 2020. https://www.youtube.com/watch?v=fOpJ5fBBI04.

Li Ung-gil (male born in 1981 in Cheongjin, first left North Korea in 2003, permanently left in 2006). [In Korean.] Interview by Baena TV. *Baenamu isahoe*, December 16, 2019. https://www.youtube.com/watch?v=3LrzoSH5k_I.

———. [In Korean.] Interview by Baena TV. *Tal tal tal*, December 18, 2018. https://www.youtube.com/watch?v=afjRARYTfeo.

———. *A Quiet Opening: North Koreans in a Changing Media Environment*. Interview by Nat Kretchun and Jane Kim, 16. Washington, DC: InterMedia, 2012.

Li Wi-ryeok (male born in 1985 in Gimchaek, left North Korea in 2010). [In Korean.] Interview by Baena TV. *Baenamu isahoe*, October 1, 2019. https://www.youtube.com/watch?v=3XFiCogSsmg.

———. [In Korean.] Interview by Channel A. *On the Way to Meet You* [Ije mannaro gapnida], June 24, 2018. https://www.youtube.com/watch?v=I-nFPfRNOUU.

Na Min-hui (female born in 1991 in Pyongyang, left North Korea in 2014, came to South Korea in 2015). [In Korean.] Interview by Baena TV. *Baenamu isahoe*, December 16, 2019. https://www.youtube.com/watch?v=3Lrz0SH5k_I.

———. [In Korean.] Interview by Baena TV. *Tal tal tal*, December 15, 2020. https://www.youtube.com/watch?v=TaJ2ycTnvWM.

———. [In Korean.] Interview by Channel A. *On the Way to Meet You* [Ije mannaro gabnida], June 24, 2018. https://www.youtube.com/watch?v=I-nFPfRNOUU.

———. [In Korean.] Interview by Channel A. *On the Way to Meet You* [Ije mannaro gapnida], October 6, 2019. https://www.youtube.com/watch?v=0_3t5_C2MGo.

O Cheong-seong (male born in Gae-song in 1992, left North Korea in 2017). [In Korean.] Interview by Baena TV. *Tal tal tal*, June 23, 2019. https://www.youtube.com/watch?v=Wz07OOnDinc&t=2599s.

Park Eunhee (female in her twenties, born in Wonsan, left North Korea in 2012). [In Korean.] Interview by Baena TV. *Tal tal tal*, November 20, 2018. https://www.youtube.com/watch?v=D27EMudOQ3w.

Ryu Hui-jin (female born in 1991 in Pyongyang, left North Korea in 2012, came to South Korea in 2015). [In Korean.] Interview by Channel A. *On the Way to Meet You* [Ije mannaro gabnida], October 13, 2019. https://www.youtube.com/watch?v=JoktqTO6nTI.

Seo Hyeon-gyeong (female born in Hyesan in 2002, left North Korea in 2016). [In Korean.] Interview by Baena TV. *Tal tal tal*, August 15, 2017. https://www.youtube.com/watch?v=9Ozh4pWCpbA.

Song Mi-na (female born in 1992 in Hyesan, left North Korea in 2013). [In Korean.] Interview by Baena TV. *Tal tal tal*, February 18, 2018. https://www.youtube.com/watch?v=Vhl9pBJj5Ao.

Sunny [pseud.] (born in Pan-gyo, Gangwon Province, in 1996, grew up in Hoeryeong, left North Korea in 2007). [In Korean.] Interview by Baena TV. *Tal tal tal*, November 14, 2016. https://www.youtube.com/watch?v=oHni-OkbmMc&app=desktop.

Thae Yong-ho [Tae Yeong-ho]. "North Korea's Path to Normal Statehood, Part 1" [Bukhan, jeongsang gukgaro ganeungil 1bu]. Interview by Jo Mi-yeong. *Unification Media Group*, April 1, 2019. https://www.youtube.com/watch?v=Kuw3eBG5MQg.

Yun Ji-o (female born in 1995 in Musan, left North Korea in 2015). [In Korean.] Interview by Baena TV. *Tal tal tal*, November 22, 2017. https://www .youtube.com/watch?v=71NvnthaGIM.

Yun Ji-u (female born in Musan in 1990, left North Korea in 2015). [In Korean.] Interview by Baena TV. *Tal tal tal*, September 1, 2020. https://www .youtube.com/watch?v=zoitLz4KjAc.

Notes

Preface and Acknowledgments

1. North Korea ICT Research Committee [Buk-han ICT yeon-gu wi-won-hoe], 2020 *Survey on North Korean ICT Trends: Focus on North Korean Media* [Buk-han ICT dong-hyang josa 2020: Buk-han maeche-reul jung-sim-eu-ro] (Seoul: Korea Institute of Science and Technology Information, 2021), 5.

Introduction

1. This slogan first appeared in North Korea in December 2009 when Kim Jong Il sent a handwritten directive to Kim Il Sung University, which was later prominently displayed at the institution. North Korean leaders' directives often become political slogans displayed throughout the country.

2. Li Ung-gil, who worked as a distributor of smuggled VCDs in the Ho-eryeong area in North Korea, witnessed the public execution of his accomplice in 2004. Li Ung-gil, [in Korean,] interview by Baena TV, *Tal tal tal*, December 18, 2018, https://www.youtube.com/watch?v=afjRARYTfeo.

3. In the late 1990s, North Korea experienced devastating famine, resulting in the death of an estimated 330,000 people. During this time, commonly known as the Arduous March, control by the central government weakened, resulting in economic migrants' unprecedented movement around and beyond the country in search of food. In 2002, the North Korean state announced that it would gradually halt the central food-rationing system, prompting the rapid

introduction of a marketplace economy. The millennial generation was born and raised during these critical times of socioeconomic transition.

4. In 2008, Koryolink began operating as a wireless-telecommunications provider, offering the first 3G mobile network in North Korea. Koryolink was founded as a joint venture between Egyptian Orascom Telecom Media and Technology Holding and the North Korean state-owned Korea Post and Telecommunications Corporation.

5. Gang Jin-gyu, "North Korea Develops 4G and 5G Simultaneously in Preparation for the Future" [Da-eum-sedae idongtongsin junbihaneun bukhan 4G, 5G, dongsi yeongu], *NK Economy*, August 12, 2022, http://www.nkeconomy .com/news/articleView.html?idxno=10707.

6. Gang Jin-gyu, email interview by author, December 27, 2019.

7. Voice of America, "Cell Phones in North Korea?," March 20, 2014, https:// www.youtube.com/watch?v=txUmNFQUBc8.

8. Nat Kretchun and Jane Kim, *A Quiet Opening: North Koreans in a Changing Media Environment* (Washington, DC: InterMedia, 2012), 53.

9. Gim Ha-na, [in Korean,] interview by Baena TV, *Tal tal tal*, October 30, 2020, https://www.youtube.com/watch?v=M7-IdvTbIAo&list=WL&index=2.

10. Bak Hyun-suk, "Baenamu Hakdang," interview by Baena TV, *Baena TV*, May 20, 2019, https://www.youtube.com/watch?v=qdcUhoCTt4o.

11. Kim Yonho, *Cell Phones in North Korea: Has North Korea Entered the Telecommunications Revolution?* (Washington, DC: US-Korea Institute; Voice of America, 2014), 8.

12. Anonymous, interview by author, Seoul, Korea, August 3, 2022.

13. North Korean officials often extort private citizens' wealth by demanding bribes. Bribery is so pervasive that it has become a major means for North Korean state employees—from lower-level police to major government officials—to absorb money from the private sector into the government.

14. Kretchun and Kim, *Quiet Opening*, 3.

15. For the merchant community and the younger generation in their twenties and thirties, "cell phones are seen as a necessary item." Bak Jun-hyeong and Yi Seok-yeong, "Phone Handset Prices Fall as Users Rise" [in Korean], *Daily NK*, May 20, 2011.

16. See, e.g., Kim Suk-Young, *Illusive Utopia: Theater, Film, and Everyday Performance in North Korea* (Ann Arbor: University of Michigan Press, 2010); Ken Gause, *Coercion, Control, Surveillance, and Punishment: An Examination of the North Korean Police State* (Washington, DC: Committee for Human Rights in North Korea, 2012); and Kim Yonho, *Cell Phones*.

17. For more detailed coverage on the diverse makeup of millennials in the United States, see Samantha Raphelson, "Amid the Stereotypes, Some Facts about Millennials," NPR, November 18, 2014, https://www.npr.org/2014/11/18/354196302/amid-the-stereotypes-some-facts-about-millennials; and William Frey, "Diversity Defines the Millennial Generation," Brookings Institution, June 26, 2016, https://www.brookings.edu/blog/the-avenue/2016/06/28/diversity-defines-the-millennial-generation/.

18. *Chollima* refers to a legendary winged horse known for its ability to travel swiftly.

19. Jeon Jae-u, "Perspectives on Generational Changes in the North Korean Power Elite and Policy Direction" [Bukhan paweo eliteu-ui sedae-byun-hwa-wa jeong-chaek-ui bang-hyang-seong jeon-mang], *Korean Defense Issues and Analyses* 1726 (August 2018): 5.

20. Ji Hye-yeon, "What Are the Characteristics of North Korean Generations Seen through Historical Stages?" [Yeok-sa-jeok-eu-ro bon bukhan sae-dae-ui teukjing-eun?], *South Korean Ministry of Unification Blog*, February 21, 2012, https://unikoreablog.tistory.com/1902.

21. Abigail De Kosnik et al., "Transcultural Fandom in the Age of Streaming Media" (panel, Transforming Hollywood: U.S. Streaming and International Co-productions, University of California, Los Angeles, CA, December 3, 2021), https://transforminghollywood.tft.ucla.edu/previous-years/transforming-hollywood-9-2021/.

22. O Ga-hyeon, *How to Deal with North Koreans* [Bukhan-saram-gwa geo-rae-ha-neun beop] (Seoul: Hangyeore, 2019), 27.

23. Yi Jae-won et al., "N Generation Kim Jong Un: New North Korea beyond Imagination" [in Korean], *Money Today*, May 1, 2018, http://news.mt.co.kr/mtview.php?no=2018043021204646432.

24. Gim Chang-pung, "Changes in North Korea" [in Korean], *Brunch Blog*, January 20, 2018, https://brunch.co.kr/@cpk78/71.

25. Na Min-hui, [in Korean,] interview by Channel A, *On the Way to Meet You* [Ije mannaro gabnida], June 24, 2018, https://www.youtube.com/watch?v=I-nFPfRNOUU.

26. Na Min-hui, interview, *On the Way to Meet You*, June 24, 2018.

27. Na Min-hui, interview, *On the Way to Meet You*, June 24, 2018.

28. Kretchun and Kim, *Quiet Opening*, 45.

29. Kretchun and Kim, *Quiet Opening*, 47.

30. In North Korea, *todae* is used in reference to one's political status based on class categorization. *Seongbun* similarly defines one's social status demarcated

by family origin and political orientation. Until marketization started to transform North Korea, where money now can buy convenience and even social privilege, *todae* and *seongbun* exerted formidable power over the fate of North Koreans. For more detailed accounts, see Gang Sun-gyeo, *My Hometown* [Naeui saldeon gohyangeun] (Seoul: Hangbok Eneoji, 2015); Kim Yong and Kim Suk-Young, *Long Road Home: Testimony of a North Korean Camp Survivor* (New York, NY: Columbia University Press, 2009).

31. Ryu Hui-jin, [in Korean,] interview by Channel A, *On the Way to Meet You* [Ije mannaro gabnida], October 13, 2019, https://www.youtube.com/watch?v=JoktqTO6nTI.

32. Gim Ha-na, interview.

33. Gim Seong-guk, "Our Country Placed Young People at the Core of the National and Party Strategic Plans and Established a Strong Nation of Young People" [Uri naraneun cheongnyeon jungsireul danggwa gukgaui jeonryak-jeok-roseon-eu-ro suriphago geonseolhan cheong-nyeon gang-guk], *Cheolhak, Saheo-jeongchihak Yeongu* 3 (2019): 33.

34. Li Seong-nam, "The Great Leader Paved the Everlasting Foundation for a Strong Nation of Youth" [Cheongnyeongangguk-ui mannyeongiteuleul maryeonhayeo-jusin widaehan ryeondoja], *Chollima* 8 (2018): 15.

35. Li Seol-ju, ed., *March Forward, Strong Nation of Young People* [Cheong-nyeon gangguk-i-yeo appeuro] (Pyongyang: Munhakyesulchulpansa, 2016). The editor's name is identical to that of Kim Jong Un's wife, but I could not verify if they are the same person.

36. O Jeong-ro, "My Country Is a Strong Nation of Young People" [Nae jogukeun cheongnyeon gangguk], *Joseon munhak* 1 (2016): 10.

37. Mun Seong-hwi, "North Korean Mobile Network Expands to Counties" [in Korean], *Radio Free Asia*, February 10, 2011, http://www.rfa.org/korean/in_focus/cell_phone-02102011113753.html.

38. Bak Gwang-cheol, "Bolstering the Nation with Strength in Science, Technology, and Talented People" [Gwahak-gisul-gang-guk, injaegang-guk geonseol-ui naraereul pyeolcheojusiryeo], *Chollima* 6 (2016): 32.

39. Kang Hyun-kyeong, "Has N. Korean Leader's Daughter Been Confirmed as Heir Apparent?," *Korea Times*, December 3, 2023, https://www.koreatimes.co.kr/www/nation/2023/12/103_364361.html.

40. See Alexandre Mansourov, "North Korea on the Cusp of Digital Transformation," Nautilus Institute, October 20, 2011, http://www.nautilus.org/wp-content/uploads/2011/12/DPRK_Digital_Transformation.pdf; Ellen

Nakashima, Gerry Shih, and John Hudson, "Leaked Documents Reveal Huawei's Secret Operations to Build North Korea's Wireless Network," *Washington Post*, July 22, 2019, https://www.washingtonpost.com/world/national-security/leaked-documents-reveal-huaweis-secret-operations-to-build-north-koreas-wireless-network/2019/07/22/583430fe-8d12-11e9-adf3-f70f78c156e8_story.html?utm_term=.fbc417a5aabc.

41. See Sunny Yoon, "South Korean Media Reception and Youth Culture in North Korea," in *South Korean Popular Culture and North Korea*, ed. Kim Youna (London: Routledge, 2019), 120–32.

42. O Ga-hyeon, *How to Deal*, 58.

43. An Hye-gyeong, [in Korean,] interview by Baena TV, *Baenamu isahoe*, December 16, 2019, https://www.youtube.com/watch?v=3LrzoSH5k_I.

44. Gim Hae-suk, interview by author, Seoul, Korea, July 27, 2022.

45. Go Na-hae, interview by author, Seoul, Korea, July 28, 2022.

46. Anonymous, interview by author, Seoul, Korea, July 22, 2022.

47. Ministry of Unification [Republic of Korea], *White Paper on Korean Unification* [Tong-il Baek-seo] (Seoul: Ministry of Unification, 2023), 121.

48. Throughout this book, I will use "resettlers" to refer to the diverse group of people who originated from North Korea but have left the country and settled elsewhere—predominantly, in South Korea—for political, economic, personal, and family reasons. I use this term to encompass various needs and address predicaments that are embedded in alternative terms, such as "defectors" and "refugees," and to emphasize their rooted agency.

49. The most prominent platform for in-depth interviews with North Korean resettlers is Baena TV, a YouTube channel specializing in the coverage of North Korean resettlers' stories from their own perspective. Cable TV shows—*On the Way to Meet You* (Ije mannaro gapnida) on Channel A being the most representative—provide some insight into the lives of North Korean millennials as well. However, due to the sensationalized nature of the cable shows in which certain stories are distorted and exaggerated to elicit higher ratings, I use Baena TV's interviews more extensively in this book.

50. Martyn Hammersley, "Ethnography: Problems and Prospects," *Ethnography and Education* 1, no. 1 (2006): 3–14, https://doi.org/10.1080/17457820500512697.

51. Kathleen Gallagher, *Hope in a Collapsing World: Youth, Theatre, and Listening as a Political Alternative* (Toronto: University of Toronto Press, 2022), 80, ProQuest Ebook Central.

52. Gallagher, *Hope*, 81.

Chapter 1

1. The video started appearing on YouTube on February 19, 2019.

2. Janet McCracken, "Why We Love Our Phones: A Case Study in the Aesthetics of Gadgets," in *Comparative Everyday Aesthetics: East-West Studies in Contemporary Living*, ed. Jeffrey Petts and Eva Kit Wah Man (Amsterdam: Amsterdam University Press, 2023), 210.

3. For a fuller account of human suffering during the time of the Arduous March, see Sandra Fahy, *Marching through Suffering: Loss and Survival in North Korea* (New York, NY: Columbia University Press, 2015). For an account of the North Korean famine according to the macroanalysis of political economy, see Stephan Haggard and Marcus Noland, *Famine in North Korea: Markets, Aid, and Reform* (New York, NY: Columbia University Press, 2007).

4. Daniel Gordon's documentary film *The State of Mind* features a meal scene where a family in Pyongyang talk about the hardships they endured, especially in terms of food shortage, during the Arduous March. *The State of Mind*, directed by Daniel Gordon (Sheffield, UK: VeryMuchSo Productions, 2004), DVD.

5. Li Wi-ryeok, [in Korean,] interview by Baena TV, *Baenamu isahoe*, October 1, 2019, https://www.youtube.com/watch?v=3XFiCogSsmg.

6. Jo Ye-na, [in Korean,] interview by Baena TV, *Tal tal tal*, May 23, 2019, https://www.youtube.com/watch?v=UO6Li3bpvYY.

7. Kim Yonho, *Cell Phones*, 36.

8. Mansourov, "North Korea," 2.

9. "The Future of Electrical Engineering" [Daeum sedae jeonja gonghak-eui jeonmang], *Jeonja jadonghwa* 3 (1998): 7.

10. The foreign journals regularly introduced included *Journal of Electronic Materials*, Электросвязь, 电子技术, 电子技术应用, 半导体技术, and 自动化技术.

11. For example, in 2001, *Joseon munhak*, North Korea's prime literary magazine, introduced the importance of virtual reality (VR), predicting that "although VR bears the greatest significance in military technology, in the future, VR will easily be applicable to everyday life such as the television format." "Application of Computer Virtual Reality Technology" [Kompiuteo gasang-hyeonsil-ui liyonggisul], *Joseon munhak* 4 (2001): 71.

12. *Anyone Can Learn Computers* [Nuguna bae-ulsu ittneun kompiuteo] (Pyongyang: Gyoyukdoseo-Chulpansa, 2002), 2.

13. "Computer Logic and Pedagogy" [Kompiuteo noliwa gyoyanggyegi], *Gyoyangwon* 4 (2017): 32.

14. "Conversation with the Dead Using Computers" [Kompiuteoro jukeun saramgwa daehwa], *Munhwaeohakseup* 2 (2002): 23.

15. Li Myeong-cheol, "Why Do I Love Computers?" [Naneun woe kompiuteo-reul sarang-haneunga?], *Cheongnyeon munhak* 8 (2001): 48.

16. Katerina Clark, *The Soviet Novel: History as Ritual* (Chicago: University of Chicago Press, 1981), 183.

17. North Korean ICT Research Committee [Buk-han ICT yeon-gu wi-won-hoe], 2022 *Survey on North Korean ICT Trends: Focus on North Korean Media* [Buk-han ICT dong-hyang josa 2022: Buk-han maeche-reul jung-sim-eu-ro] (Seoul: Korea Institute of Science and Technology Information, 2023), 29.

18. "Health Risks and Exercise Recommendations for Computer Users" [Kompiuteo sayongjadeului geongang-gwa undong], *Joseon nyeoseong* 7 (2011): 55.

19. "Computers and Water" [Kompiuteo-wa mul], *Joseon nyeoseong* 6 (2019): 55.

20. "Computer Keyboards and Bacteria" [Kompiuteo geonbangwa segyun], *Joseon nyeoseong* 12 (2011): 35.

21. "Why Should We Wash Our Face after Using the Computer?" [Kompiuteo jakeop-hu oe eolguleul ssiseoya haneuga?], *Joseon nyeoseong* 5 (2019): 55.

22. "Four Teas Beneficial for Computer Users" [Kompiuteo sayongjadeul-ui geongang-e joeun 4gaji cha], *Chollima* 5 (2012): 65.

23. For more detailed information on how the North Korean government touted the use of computers in everyday life, see Hwang Su-jeong, "Foreign-Language Education Based on a Computer Network" [Kompiuteo-mang-e ui-han oeguk-eo gyoyuk], *Chollima* 3 (2016): 83; Hwang Myung-cheol and Li Myung-cheol, "Computer-Aided Automatic Temperature Control of a Bread Oven" [Hansopyeon kompiuteo-reul liyounghan ppangro jadong-ondo-jangchi], *Sigryo gong-eop* 3 (2016): 25; Sin Myung-jin and Jeon Ji-hyeon, "Evaluating Piano Tunes by Using Computers" [Kompiuteo-e uihan piano-eum-ui eumjeong-pyeongga], *Gimchaek-gong-eop-jonghap-daehak-hakbo* 10 (2011): 115–16; Li Sun-hye and Gim Yeong-bok, "Realizing the Sound Effects of National Rhythm by Using Hansopyeon Computers" [Hansopyeon-kompiuteo-e uihan minjokjang-dan-eumhyang-hyogwa-silhyeon], *Gimchaek-gong-eop-jonghap-daehak-hakbo* 1 (2010): 66–68; Jeong Cheol-ho, "Problems of Computer Control in the Process of Beer Brewing" [Maekju-balhyo-gong-jeong-ui kompiuteo-jojong-eseo naseoneun munje], *Gimchaek-gong-eop-jonghap-daehak-hakbo* 9 (2014): 80–82.

24. Gim Ji-yeong, [in Korean,] interview by Baena TV, *Tal tal tal*, February 20, 2017, https://www.youtube.com/watch?v=qrbOaeyFlfE.

25. Son Myung-hui, interview by author, Seoul, Korea, December 18, 2019.

26. Ju Chan-yang, [in Korean,] interview by Channel A, *On the Way to Meet You* [Ije mannaro gapnida], February 25, 2017, https://www.youtube.com/watch?v=IHIA5aBOmoM.

27. Jeong Yu-na, [in Korean,] interview by Channel A, *On the Way to Meet You* [Ije mannaro gapnida], October 21, 2018, https://www.youtube.com/watch?v=hEyuofUtEU8.

28. Anonymous, interview by author, Seoul, Korea, December 13, 2019.

29. Kim Yonho, *Cell Phones*, 27.

30. Kim Yonho, *Cell Phones*, 11.

31. Yi Yeong-jong, [in Korean,] interview by Baena TV, *Tal tal tal*, December 18, 2018, https://www.youtube.com/@bnatv1004. The direct URL no longer exists as of April 4, 2024.

32. Kim Yonho, *Cell Phones*, 11.

33. Yi Yeong-jong, [in Korean,] interview by Baena TV, *Baenamu isahoe*, October 3, 2018, https://www.youtube.com/watch?v=m6wlxivdNUE&t=2362s.

34. Anonymous, interview, August 3, 2022.

35. Gim Ju-seong, [in Korean,] interview by Baena TV, *Baenamu isahoe*, October 3, 2018.

36. For a detailed account of the legacies of the Digital Korea campaign launched by then South Korean president Kim Dae-jung (Gim Dae-jung), see Yi Dae-hui, "Former President Kim Dae-jung Laid Ground for the Nation's Rise to IT Power" [Ai-ti gang-guk todae dakgeun Gim Dae-jung jeon daetongryeong], *Digital Times*, August 23, 2009, http://www.dt.co.kr/contents.html?article_no=2009082402012369697001.

37. Yi Yeong-jong, interview, *Baenamu isahoe*.

38. Kim Yonho, *Cell Phones*, 11.

39. Nakashima, Shih, and Hudson, "Leaked Documents."

40. Mansourov, "North Korea."

41. Kim Yonho, *Cell Phones*, 38.

42. Kim Yonho, *Cell Phones*, 39.

43. Kretchun and Kim, *Quiet Opening*, 16.

44. Anonymous, Zoom interview by author, September 3, 2021.

45. Li Ung-gil, interview, *Tal tal tal*. Kretchun and Kim's research reveals that "many of the qualitative interview respondents mentioned the important role that ethnic Chinese living in North Korea and ethnic Koreans living in China play in circulating prohibited goods, particularly DVDs." Kretchun and Kim, *Quiet Opening*, 16.

46. Li Ung-gil, interview, *Tal tal tal*.

47. Anonymous, *A Quiet Opening: North Koreans in a Changing Media Environment*, interview by Nat Kretchun and Jane Kim (Washington, DC: InterMedia, 2012), 44.

48. O Cheong-seong, [in Korean,] interview by Baena TV, *Tal tal tal*, June 23, 2019, https://www.youtube.com/watch?v=Wz07OOnDinc&t=2599s.

49. Go, interview.

50. Na Min-hui, interview by author, Seoul, Korea, July 14, 2022.

51. Kim Yonho, *Cell Phones*, 40.

52. Kim Yonho, *Cell Phones*, 19.

53. Jeong Yeon, "Kim Jong Un Gives Directives for New Economic Policy and Orders the Expansion of Self-Supporting Account System" [Gim Jeong-un, dokrip chaesanjae hwakdae sae gyeongje daechaek jisi], *SBS News*, November 27, 2014, https://news.sbs.co.kr/news/endPage .do?news_id=N1002707521.

54. According to an anonymous source, the Byeol network differs significantly from the Koryolink and Gangseong networks in that it was not created to serve paying network subscribers. As a special network service provider, Byeol was created and has been managed—most likely—by the State Security Bureau in order to limit internet service between North Korea and the outside world as well as to handle international phone calls made by North Koreans abroad. Anonymous, email interview by author, May 28, 2020.

55. The North Korean government started to allow foreigners' use of cell phones starting in 2013. Wideband, WCDMA-compatible mobile phones can be brought into the country, whereas satellite phones are prohibited. Foreign visitors can rent a local handset at the airport and purchase a local SIM card for use in North Korea. With a SIM card, they are able to call most foreign countries (but not South Korea), foreign embassies in Pyongyang, and international hotels in the North Korean capital. Purchase of a SIM card on a monthly plan provides 3G mobile internet access with an activation fee of seventy-five euros; ten euros per month provides fifty megabytes of data; and additional MB cost 0.15 euros. Renting a mobile internet USB modem allows internet access from a personal laptop with a connection fee of one hundred euros. Data costs 150 euros per month for two gigabytes, 400 euros per month for ten gigabytes.

56. Yi Yeong-jong, interview, *Baenamu isahoe*.

57. Anonymous, interview by author, Seoul, Korea, July 28, 2022.

58. "Using the Science, Technology, and Information Search Database 'Gwangmyeong' through a Computer Network" [Kompiuteo-mangeul tong-han gwahakgisul-jeongbo-geomsaek-chegye 'Gwangmyeong'eu liyong], *Jeonja jadonghwa* 4 (1998): 4.

59. Echo of Truth, "What's Up Pyongyang? Covid 19 Situation in DPRK," April 12, 2020, https://www.youtube.com/watch?v=_JEaZlIoEmM&t=3s.

60. Echo of Truth, "I Missed You, My School," June 4, 2020, https://www
.youtube.com/watch?v=-YKN5MXP6NQ.

61. Echo of Truth, "What's Up Pyongyang?"

62. SBS News, "Eun-a from Pyongyang Gets Deleted," January 8, 2021,
https://www.youtube.com/watch?v=BYJvIxMiyG8.

63. YTN, "North Korea Transmits Numbers Station via YouTube" [Buk
pyeongyang bangsong Yutubeu-ro annsubangsong], August 29, 2020, https://
www.youtube.com/watch?v=Ccl8QLMw-yY.

64. Gim Ju-seong, On the Way to Meet You [Ije mannaro gapnida], Channel
A, February 25, 2017, https://www.youtube.com/watch?v=IHIA5aBOmoM.

65. Choe Seong-guk, "Influenced by South Korean Dramas, North Korean
Women's Ideal Male Types Have Changed" [Buk yeo-seong-deul, hanguk deurama
bo-myeo nam-seong-sangdo dal-a-jyeot-jyo], interview by Yi Yun-ju, Hankook ilbo,
June 29, 2018, https://www.hankookilbo.com/News/Read/201806281389742821.

66. Gim Ju-seong, interview.

67. Li Seon-ju, [in Korean,] interview by Baena TV, Tal tal tal, November 26,
2020, https://www.youtube.com/watch?v=aQHu4COR8kE.

68. Anonymous, interview by author, Seoul, Korea, December 17, 2019.

69. Anonymous, interview by author, Seoul, Korea, July 29, 2022.

70. Yi Yeong-jong, interview, Baenamu isahoe.

71. Yi Yeong-jong, interview, Baenamu isahoe.

72. Kim Yonho, Cell Phones, 18.

73. "New Cell Phone Numbers Starting with 1913 in North Korea" [in
Korean], Radio Free Asia, July 27, 2012, quoted in Kim Yonho, Cell Phones, 21.

74. Unification Observatory, "Revealing North Korean Smartphone Pyongyang 2545" [in Korean], featuring Gang Jin-gyu, aired September 21, 2019, on
MBC TV, https://www.youtube.com/watch?v=rZ2fUax4K_8.

75. Gim Ji-eun and No Ji-won, "Latest North Korean Smartphone, Pyongyang 2423" [Bukhan choesin seumateupon Pyeongyang 2423], Hangyeore, March
11, 2019, http://www.hani.co.kr/arti/politics/defense/885344.html.

76. Gim Ji-eun and No, "Latest North Korean Smartphone."

77. For instance, Arirang is considered a better brand than Pyongyang,
whereas Jindalae 3 is similar to the iPhone in design.

78. North Korean ICT Research Committee, 2022 Survey, 36.

79. The calculation is based on the 2019 black-market exchange rate that
shows one US dollar to 8,000 North Korean won. Needless to say, it is impossible to survive on this income alone, and most North Koreans make supplemen-
tary income via marketplace trade.

80. Voice of America, "Cell Phones in North Korea?"

81. Kim Yonho, *Cell Phones*, 13–14.

82. Na Min-hui, [in Korean,] interview by Baena TV, *Tal tal tal*, December 15, 2020, https://www.youtube.com/watch?v=TaJ2ycTnvWM.

83. Anonymous, interview, July 28, 2022.

84. Na Min-hui, [in Korean,] interview by Channel A, *On the Way to Meet You* [Ije mannaro gapnida], October 6, 2019, https://www.youtube.com/watch?v=o_3t5_C2MGo.

85. Choe Ju-yeon, [in Korean,] interview by Baena TV, *Tal tal tal*, December 15, 2020, https://www.youtube.com/watch?v=TaJ2ycTnvWM.

86. Son, interview.

87. Anonymous, interview, December 17, 2019.

88. *Unification Observatory*, "Revealing North Korean Smartphone."

89. "E-commerce" [Jeonja sangeop], *Joseon nyeoseong* 10 (2018): 55.

90. North Korean ICT Research Committee, 2022 *Survey*, 17.

91. Kim Yonho, *Cell Phones*, 30.

92. Na Min-hui, interview by author.

93. Gang Na-ra, [in Korean,] interview by Baena TV, *Tal tal tal*, December 1, 2017, https://www.youtube.com/watch?v=w4ZICkiYN5s.

94. Na Min-hui, interview by author.

95. Gim Ju-seong, interview.

96. Kretchun and Kim, *Quiet Opening*, 52.

97. North Korean ICT Research Committee, 2022 *Survey*, 37.

98. Song Hong-geun, "Two Faces of the South Korean and US Presidents as Seen by the Escapee Jeong Gwang-il" [Talchulja Jeong Gwang-il-i-bon hanmi daetongryeong-ui du eolgul], *Shindonga*, April 2, 2019, http://shindonga.donga.com/3/home/13/1683245/1.

99. Jeong Gwang-il, interview by author, Seoul, Korea, December 14, 2019.

100. CBS News: The National, "Infiltrating North Korea, One USB Drive at a Time," February 23, 2018, https://www.youtube.com/watch?v=jKINA-ikgE4.

101. Jeong Gwang-il, interview.

102. Gang Li-hyeok, [in Korean,] interview by Baena TV, *Tal tal tal*, March 25, 2018, https://www.youtube.com/watch?v=26IjeOgCFsQ.

103. Song Mi-na, [in Korean,] interview by Baena TV, *Tal tal tal*, February 18, 2018, https://www.youtube.com/watch?v=Vhl9pBJj5Ao.

104. Gang Na-ra, interview, *Tal tal tal*.

105. Yun Ji-o, [in Korean,] interview by Baena TV, *Tal tal tal*, November 22, 2017, https://www.youtube.com/watch?v=71NvnthaGIM.

106. Kim Yonho, *Cell Phones*, 63.

107. Seo Jae-pyong, interview by Kim Yonho, July 2013, quoted in Kim Yonho, *Cell Phones*, 25.

108. Yi Yeong-jong, interview, *Baenamu isahoe*.

109. Son, interview.

110. Anonymous, interview, December 13, 2019. The interviewee is a male in his early twenties who left North Korea in 2016.

111. Kretchun and Kim, *Quiet Opening*, 54.

112. Kretchun and Kim, *Quiet Opening*, 54.

113. Kim Yonho, *Cell Phones*, 17.

114. O Cheong-seong, interview.

115. Seo Hyeon-gyeong, [in Korean,] interview by Baena TV, *Tal tal tal*, August 15, 2017, https://www.youtube.com/watch?v=9OZh4pWCpbA.

116. Anonymous, interview, December 13, 2019.

Chapter 2

1. A female born in Musan in 1990, Yun Ji-u first attempted to leave North Korea in 2011 but was caught in China and sent back to North Korea in 2015. In recounting her intricate plans to defect for the second time, she commented on the importance of being creative in order to survive. Yun Ji-u, [in Korean,] interview by Baena TV, *Tal tal tal*, September 1, 2020, https://www.youtube.com/watch?v=zoitLz4KjAc.

2. Anonymous, interview by author, Seoul, Korea, December 18, 2019.

3. Anonymous, interview, December 18, 2019.

4. Na Min-hui, interview, *Tal tal tal*.

5. Gim Ji-yeong, interview.

6. Choe Ju-yeon, interview.

7. Ralph Hassig and Kongdan Oh, *The Hidden People of North Korea: Everyday Life in the Hermit Kingdom* (Lanham, MD: Rowman and Littlefield, 2009), 193.

8. Anonymous, "North Koreans Say that the Country Cannot Sustain Itself without the Marketplace" [Buk jumindeul saenghwal jangmadang eopsineun an doraganda], interview by Gim Ji-hwan, *Gyeonghyang sinmun*, January 9, 2019, http://news.khan.co.kr/kh_news/khan_art_view.html?art_id=201901090600045.

9. Gang Na-ra, interview, *Tal tal tal*.

10. Li Eun-hui, [in Korean,] interview by Baena TV, *Tal tal tal*, December 25, 2018, https://www.youtube.com/watch?v=xw1-ytdQYZ4&t=1489s.

11. Anonymous, interview, December 17, 2019.

12. Sunny [pseud.], [in Korean,] interview by Baena TV, *Tal tal tal*, November 14, 2016, https://www.youtube.com/watch?v=oHni-OkbmMc&app=desktop.

13. Jo Ye-na, interview.

14. Bak Na-ri, [in Korean,] interview by Baena TV, *Tal tal tal*, December 19, 2016, https://www.youtube.com/watch?v=vXF21DSNIgU.

15. Bak Yeong-chan, [in Korean,] interview by Channel A, *On the Way to Meet You* [Ije mannaro gapnida], September 8, 2019, https://www.youtube.com/watch?v=lEUl5kCs3MM.

16. Anonymous, interview, July 28, 2022.

17. Kim Yonho, *Cell Phones*, 20.

18. McCracken, "Why We Love," 211.

19. Sandra Fahy, "Hallyu in the South, Hunger in the North: Alternative Imaginings of What Life Could Be," in *South Korean Popular Culture and North Korea*, ed. Kim Youna (London: Routledge, 2019), 111.

20. Park Eunhee, [in Korean,] interview by Baena TV, *Tal tal tal*, November 20, 2018, https://www.youtube.com/watch?v=D27EMudOQ3w.

21. The question ("Do you want to have *ramyeon* with me?") originally appeared in the 2001 South Korean film *One Fine Spring Day*, which popularized it as a cryptolect of seduction.

22. Na Min-hui, interview, *On the Way to Meet You*, June 24, 2018.

23. Anonymous, interview, December 17, 2019.

24. M. A. K. Halliday, "Anti-languages," *American Anthropologist* 78, no. 3 (September 1976): 570.

25. Martin Puchner, *The Language of Thieves* (New York, NY: W. W. Norton, 2020), 19.

26. Gim Hae-suk, interview.

27. Go, interview.

28. Anonymous, interview by author, Seoul, Korea, July 31, 2022.

29. Anonymous, interview, August 3, 2022.

30. Jeong Yu-na, [in Korean,] interview by Channel A, *On the Way to Meet You* [Ije mannaro gapnida], June 24, 2018, https://www.youtube.com/watch?v=I-nFPfRNOUU.

31. For more details on how North Korean children were encouraged to emulate Kim Il Sung's youth, see Kim Yong and Kim, *Long Road Home*, 32–36.

32. According to Park Eunhee, in addition to addressing women's participation in the marketplace, the original lyrics have been changed into so many other versions to address new realities of the marketplace economy. Park Eunhee, email interview by author, December 6, 2023.

33. Bak Hyeon-jeong, [in Korean,] interview by Channel A, *On the Way to Meet You* [Ije mannaro gapnida], October 6, 2019, https://www.youtube.com/watch?v=o_3t5_C2MGo.

34. Fahy, "Hallyu in the South," 110.

35. For further discussions of creative economy in the Western capitalist economies, see Richard Florida, *The Rise of the Creative Class: And How It's Transforming Work, Leisure and Everyday Life* (New York, NY: Basic Books, 2002); Andrew Ross, *Nice Work If You Can Get It: Life and Labor in Precarious Times* (New York, NY: New York University Press, 2010).

36. Performance studies scholar Shannon Steen addresses the question of creativity in an authoritarian society, such as China, with much focus on the considerable gap between Silicon Valley's conception of creative labor and the harsh realities of the manufacturers in Shenzhen, China. The discussion of creativity in North Korea presents a much more extreme case since North Korean millennials have no open interlocutor to spin the contrasting perceptions, as we see in the transpacific tech-labor dynamics between Silicon Valley and Shenzhen. Shannon Steen, *The Creativity Complex: Art, Tech, and the Seduction of an Idea* (Ann Arbor: University of Michigan Press, 2023), 149–74.

37. O Gang-seon, *The End of the Harvard Era and Educational Revolution* [Habadeu sidae-ui jongmalgwa hakseup hyeokmyeong] (Seoul: Cloud Nine, 2020), 131–44.

38. Michel de Certeau, *The Practice of Everyday Life* (Berkeley: University of California Press, 1984), 37.

39. Kim Yonho, *Cell Phones*, 18.

40. Kim Yonho, *Cell Phones*, 20.

41. Gim Ha-na, interview.

42. Joo Hyung-min, "Hidden Transcripts in Marketplaces: Politicized Discourses in the North Korean Shadow Economy," *Pacific Review* 27, no. 1 (January 2014): 51.

43. Joo, "Hidden Transcripts in Marketplaces," 50.

44. Li Wi-ryeok, [in Korean,] interview by Channel A, *On the Way to Meet You* [Ije mannaro gapnida], June 24, 2018, https://www.youtube.com/watch?v=I-nFPfRNOUU.

45. Li Ung-gil, interview, *Tal tal tal*.

46. Baek Jieun's book *North Korea's Hidden Revolution* also uses "hidden" in the title, which likewise misses out on the not-so-hidden nature of North Korea's countercultural practices. Baek Jieun, *North Korea's Hidden Revolution* (New Haven, CT: Yale University Press, 2016).

47. "The Most Popular South Korean Drama for North Koreans is *Autumn in My Heart*" [in Korean], *BBC News Korea*, July 2, 2019, https://www.bbc.com/korean/news-48835889.

48. Jeong Yu-na, interview, June 24, 2018.

49. José van Dijick, Thomas Poell, and Martijn de Waal, *The Platform Society: Public Values in a Connective World* (Oxford: Oxford University Press, 2018), 4.

50. For more information on Eric Schmidt's trip to North Korea, see Associated Press, "Google Exec Calls for Open Internet in North Korea," *CBC*, January 9, 2013, https://www.cbc.ca/news/technology/google-exec-calls-for-open-internet-in-north-korea-1.1380646; Eric Pilkington, "Eric Schmidt in North Korea: Google Chairman's Step into the Unknown," *The Guardian*, January 7, 2013, https://www.theguardian.com/technology/2013/jan/07/google-eric-schmidt-trip-pyongyang.

51. Shoshana Zuboff, The Age of Surveillance Capitalism: The Fight for a Human Future at the New Frontier of Power (New York, NY: Public Affairs, 2019), 8.

52. Joo, "Hidden Transcripts in Marketplaces," 61.

53. Anonymous, interview, December 17, 2019.

54. "Most Popular."

55. Go, interview.

56. Anonymous, interview, September 3, 2021.

57. Li Ung-gil, interview, *Tal tal tal*.

58. Gang Li-hyeok, "Baenamu Hakdang," interview by Baena TV, *Baena TV*, May 20, 2019, https://www.youtube.com/watch?v=qdcUhoCTt40.

59. Anonymous, interview, July 31, 2022.

60. Anonymous, interview, August 3, 2022.

61. Anonymous, interview, August 3, 2022.

62. Li Hyeong-seok, [in Korean,] interview by Baena TV, *Tal tal tal*, November 26, 2020, https://www.youtube.com/watch?v=aQHu4COR8kE.

63. Li Ung-gil, interview, *Tal tal tal*.

64. Li Ung-gil, interview, *Tal tal tal*.

65. Anonymous, interview, July 28, 2022.

66. Choe Yu-jin, [in Korean,] interview by Baena TV, *Tal tal tal*, November 25, 2020, https://www.youtube.com/watch?v=O9bPvQjQofM.

67. Kretchun and Kim, *Quiet Opening*, 14.

68. Ahlam Lee, "The Korean Wave: A Pull Factor for North Korean Migration," in *South Korean Popular Culture and North Korea*, ed. Kim Youna (London: Routledge, 2019), 96.

69. Jeong Gwang-il, interview.

70. O Cheong-seong, interview.

71. Jo Ye-na, interview.

72. Anonymous, interview, December 13, 2019.

73. Na Min-hui, [in Korean,] interview by Baena TV, *Baenamu isahoe*, December 16, 2019, https://www.youtube.com/watch?v=3LrzoSH5k_I.

74. Gang Na-ra, interview, *Tal tal tal*.

75. Na Min-hui, interview, *Baenamu isahoe*.

76. Kretchun and Kim, *Quiet Opening*, 32.

77. Bishnupriya Ghosh and Bhaskar Sarkar, "Media and Risk: An Introduction," in *The Routledge Companion to Media and Risk*, ed. Bishnupriya Ghosh and Bhaskar Sarkar (New York, NY: Routledge, 2020), 3.

78. Ghosh and Sarkar, "Media and Risk," 2.

79. Ghosh and Sarkar, "Media and Risk," 3.

80. Robert J. Shiller, *Narrative Economics: How Stories Go Viral and Drive Major Economic Events* (Princeton, NJ: Princeton University Press, 2019), 30 and 41.

81. Stanford Center for Professional Development, "How Does Blockchain Work?" Stanford Online, accessed November 2, 2023, https://online.stanford.edu/how-does-blockchain-work.

82. Stanford Center for Professional Development, "How Does Blockchain Work?"

83. Anonymous, "South Korean Cultural Boom in North Korea" [Bukhan-e buneun hanryu yeolpung], interview by Gang Dong-wan, *Joongang ilbo*, November 29, 2014, https://news.joins.com/article/16558635.

84. Shiller, *Narrative Economics*, 33 and 41.

85. David Golumbia, "Zealots of the Blockchain," *The Baffler* 38 (March 2018), https://thebaffler.com/salvos/zealots-of-the-blockchain-golumbia.

86. Shiller, *Narrative Economics*, 38.

87. The same ambiguity could be applied to understanding the authority figure in the blockchain community. As Golumbia elaborates, "Cults typically have leaders. But digital utopias fetishize 'leaderless' organizations, often without being able to explain, let alone provide evidence for, the superiority of leaderless groups. Here is where Bitcoin, and blockchain technology more generally, arrive at a fitting paradox: they both do and don't have a leader." Golumbia, "Zealots."

88. Nishani Frazier, "Black Blockchain: The Future of Black Studies and Blockchain," *American Studies* (*Lawrence*) 61, no. 2 (2022): 14, https://doi.org/10.1353/ams.2022.0010.

89. Frazier, "Black Blockchain," 14–15.

90. Tony D. Sampson, *Virality: Contagion Theory in the Age of Networks* (Minneapolis: University of Minnesota Press, 2012), 14.

91. Yonhap News Agency, *North Korea Handbook* (New York, NY: M. E. Sharpe, 2003), 122.

92. "Paying Copyright Fees to North Korean Central Television?" [Joseon Joongang TV jeojak-kwonryo jibul?], *JCTB News*, April 20, 2016, https://news .jtbc.co.kr/article/article.aspx?news_id=NB11218004.

93. Gye Gwang-il, "Intellectual Property Plays an Important Role in the Development of Society and Culture" [Sahoe-gyeongje-baljeon-eseo jungyohan yeokhal-eul noneun jijeok soyugwon], *Chollima* 1 (2019): 56.

94. "The Difference between Intellectual Property Rights and Property Rights" [Jijeok soyugwon-gwa soyugwon-eui cha-i], *Joseon nyeoseong* 10 (2019): 55.

95. Zhang Weiqi and Mickey Lee, "Black Markets, Red States: Media Piracy in China and the Korean Wave in North Korea," in *South Korean Popular Culture and North Korea*, ed. Kim Youna (London: Routledge, 2019), 83.

96. *Unification Observatory*, "Revealing North Korean Smartphone."

97. Zhang and Lee, "Black Markets, Red States," 88.

98. Heo In, "Intellectual Properties of South and North Koreas and Plans for Cooperation" [Nambukhan-ui jijjeok jae-san-kwon-gwa hyeop-ryeok bang-an], *Korea Institute of Intellectual Property In-Depth Report* 3 (2018): 6.

99. Choe Gyeong-su, *Study on North Korean Copyright Law and the Cooperation and Exchange between the Two Koreas in the Copyrights Area* [Bukhan jeojakbeop-mit nambukgan jeojakkweon bunya gyoryu hyeopryeok-e gwanhan yeongu] (Jinju: Korea Copyright Commission, 2015), 17.

100. The case of China could be seen as foreshadowing the case of North Korea. According to communication studies scholar Jessica Gisclair, "The number of Internet users has led to much attention toward China's inadequate protection of intellectual property rights (IPR). For example, China has been placed on the 'Priority Watch List' by the Bush administration's Office of the U.S. Trade Representative." Jessica Gisclair, "The Dissonance between Culture and Intellectual Property in China," *Southeast Review of Asian Studies* 30 (2008): 183.

101. These words of an eleven-year-old *kkotjebi* (vagabond) are cited in an interview with Li Hyeong-seok (male born in Pyongyang in 1984 who left North Korea in 2002), who had to become *kkotjebi* himself in order to survive during the times of the Arduous March. Li Hyeong-seok, interview.

102. Zhang and Lee, "Black Markets, Red States," 86.

103. Dànielle Nicole DeVoss, "English Studies and Intellectual Property: Copyright, Creativity, and the Commons," *Pedagogy* 10, no. 1 (2010): 206, Project MUSE. Emphasis original. DeVoss cites Lawrence Lessig, *The Future of Ideas: The Fate of the Commons in a Connected World* (New York, NY: Random House, 2001); Lawrence Lessig, *Free Culture: How Big Media Uses Technology and the Law to Lock Down Culture and Control Creativity* (New York, NY: Penguin, 2004); Lawrence Lessig, *Remix: Making Art and Commerce Thrive in the Hybrid Economy* (New York, NY: Penguin, 2008).

104. Anne-Marie Boisvert, "On Bricolage: Assembling Culture with Whatever Comes to Hand," trans. Timothy Barnard, *HorizonZero* 8 (2003), www.horizonzero.ca/textsite/remix.php?is=8&file=4&tlang=0, quoted in DeVoss, "English Studies," 206. Boisvert's article was available January 2, 2005, but the website is no longer working as of February 2024.

105. Lisa Samuels, "Relinquish Intellectual Property," *New Literary History* 33, no. 2 (2002): 359, Project MUSE, https://doi.org/10.1353/nlh.2002.0022.

106. Kembrew McLeod, *Freedom of Expression: Resistance and Representation in the Age of Intellectual Property* (Minneapolis: University of Minnesota Press, 2007), 3, quoted in DeVoss, "English Studies," 207.

107. Jeong Gwang-il, interview.

108. Anonymous, interview, August 3, 2022.

109. Anonymous, interview, August 3, 2022.

Chapter 3

1. See Kim Suk-Young, *Illusive Utopia*, 1–32.

2. Li Seo-eun, [in Korean,] interview by Baena TV, *Tal tal tal*, February 25, 2018, https://www.youtube.com/watch?v=Q_aVtc3XteY.

3. Song Mi-na, interview.

4. Li Eun-hui, interview.

5. Anonymous, interview, July 31, 2022.

6. Gang Na-ra, interview, *Tal tal tal*.

7. Anonymous, interview, September 3, 2021.

8. Anonymous, interview, July 28, 2022.

9. Go, interview.

10. Anonymous, interview, December 17, 2019.

11. Li Ung-gil, interview, *Tal tal tal*.

12. Anonymous, interview, August 3, 2022.

13. Li Ung-gil, [in Korean,] interview by Baena TV, *Baenamu isahoe*, December 16, 2019, https://www.youtube.com/watch?v=3Lrz0SH5k_I.

14. Anonymous, interview, August 3, 2022.

15. Anonymous, interview, July 28, 2022.

16. Bak Yu-seong, "North Korean Man's Surprise Reaction to *Crash Landing on You*" [*Sarang-ui bulsichak* deuramareul bogo chunggyeok bat-eun bukhan namja-ui ban-eung-eun], interview by CLAB, *CLAB*, January 11, 2020, https://www.youtube.com/watch?v=DuDSj6qNpIM.

17. "Most Popular."

18. Li Su-ryeon, [in Korean,] interview by Baena TV, *Tal tal tal*, November 20, 2020, https://www.youtube.com/watch?v=fOpJ5fBBI04.

19. Anonymous, interview, September 3, 2021.

20. Go, interview.

21. Anonymous, interview, July 31, 2022.

22. Anonymous, interview, August 3, 2022.

23. *Autumn in My Heart* [in Korean], 16 episodes, directed by Yun Seok-ho, written by O Su-hyeon, featuring Song Hae-gyi, Won Bin, and Song Seung-heon, aired from September 18, 2000, to November 7, 2000, on Korea Broadcasting System, here episode 4, aired on September 26, 2000.

24. Anonymous, interview, September 3, 2021.

25. Na Min-hui notes that in the *Anti-espionage Exhibition* in Pyongyang, there is a *Stairway to Heaven* VCD on display as a reminder to North Korean citizens of how South Korean drama can pollute the revolutionary society. Na Min-hui, interview, *Baenamu isahoe*.

26. In 1993, then Samsung Corporation CEO Li Geon-hui made a so-called Frankfurt Declaration, presenting a decisively innovative path for Samsung's future. Many believe that 1993 was the turning point that would ultimately lead the company to a decisive market triumph two decades later. See Kim Suk-Young, *K-pop Live: Fans, Idols, and Multimedia Performance* (Stanford, CA: Stanford University Press, 2018), 25–52.

27. Anonymous, interview, July 22, 2022.

28. Mun Seong-hwi, "North Korea Falls for Drama *Boys over Flowers*" [*Deurama Kkotboda namja-e bbajin bukhan*], *Radio Free Asia*, September 15, 2011, http://www.rfa.org/korean/in_focus/skdrama-09152011130127.html.

29. Li Hyang-mi, [in Korean,] interview by Baena TV, *Tal tal tal*, September 7, 2020, https://www.youtube.com/watch?v=WlAzaGiL244.

30. Na Min-hui, interview, *Baenamu isahoe*.

31. Anonymous, interview, July 28, 2022.

32. Anonymous, interview, September 3, 2021.

33. Anonymous, interview, July 28, 2022.

34. Gang Na-ra, interview, *Tal tal tal*.

35. Kim Suk-Young, "For the Eyes of North Koreans? Politics of Money and Class in *Boys over Flowers*," in *The Korean Wave: Korean Media Go Global*, ed. Kim Youna (London: Routledge, 2013), 94.

36. *Boys over Flowers* [in Korean], 25 episodes, directed by Jeon Gi-sang, written by Yun Ji-ryeon, featuring Gu Hye-seon and Lee Min-ho (Yi Min-ho), aired on January 1, 2009, to March 22, 2009, on Korea Broadcasting System, here episode 2, aired on January 6, 2009.

37. Kim Suk-Young, "For the Eyes," 104.

38. *Boys over Flowers*, episode 1, aired on January 5, 2009.

39. *Boys over Flowers*, episode 2.

40. *Boys over Flowers*, episode 18, aired on March 9, 2009.

41. *Boys over Flowers*, episode 9, aired on February 2, 2009.

42. Yi Won-hui, "2011 New Year's Special Report: New Waves of Change in North Korea, Part 3, 'South Korean Dramas Are So Interesting'" [2011nyeon sinnyeon teukjip: Bukhan-e buneun byeonhwa-ui baram 3, "namhan deurama jaemitseoyo"], *Radio Free Asia*, January 11, 2011, http://www.rfa.org/korean/temp/new_year_sp-01052011113720.html.

43. There is a plethora of media coverage referencing the similarities among the three versions of *Boys over Flowers* made by Taiwanese, Japanese, and Korean TV channels: e.g., see Gwon Gyeong-sung, "The Success of *Boys over Flowers* in Taiwan, Korea, and Japan Lies in the Original Manga" [Samguk, kkotnam seongong-eun wonjak manhwa-ui him], *Media Today*, September 14, 2009, http://www.mediatoday.co.kr/news/articleView.html?idxno=82841; Song Hye-min, "Chinese Portal Claims that the Best Version of *Boys over Flowers* Is South Korean" [Jung potal, *Kkotboda namja* hangukpani gajang usu], *Now News*, January 15, 2009, http://nownews.seoul.co.kr/news/newsView.php?id=20090115601015.

44. Song Gi-yong, "*My Love from Another Star* Sends Cultural Shockwaves through China" [*Byeolgeudae* hyeonsang jungguk-e keun muhwa chung-gyekjwo], *News Joins*, March 6, 2014, https://news.joins.com/article/14084618.

45. Bak Min-sik, "*My Love from Another Star* Brings the Same Profit as Exporting 20,000 Sonatas" [*Byeolgeudae* sonata imandae hyogwa], *Hankook ilbo*, November 11, 2016, https://www.hankookilbo.com/News/Read/201611111640352284.

46. Gwon Hae-yeong, "55.3 Million iPhones versus 95 Million Galaxies Sold During the Fourth Quarter Smartphone Sales Report" [4 bun-gi seumateupon panmae Aipon 5530mandae vs Gaelluksi 9500mandae], *Asia gyeongje*, January 21, 2014, https://news.naver.com/main/read.nhn?mode=LSD&mid=shm&sid1 =105&oid=277&aid=0003175454.

47. *My Love from Another Star* was mired in a plagiarism scandal relating to the main plot, which was eventually settled outside of court. According to Gang Gyeong-ok, the eternal love between a young woman and a man who lived for four hundred years without aging was the defining plot of her graphic novel *Seol-hui*, which the screenwriter Bak Ji-eun stole liberally from. See Jo Eun-byeol, "The Plagiarism Dispute about *My Love from Another Star* Is Headed for Court" [*Byeolgeudae* pyojeol nonran, gyeolguk beopjeong ganda], *No Cut News*, May 20, 2014, https://www.nocutnews.co.kr/news/4027662.

48. Anonymous, interview, July 31, 2022.

49. *My Love from Another Star* [in Korean], 21 episodes, directed by Jang Tae-yu and O Chung-hwan, written by Bak Ji-eun, featuring Jun Ji-hyun (Jeon Ji-hyeon) and Kim Soo-hyun (Gim Su-hyeon), aired from December 18, 2013, to February 27, 2014, on Seoul Broadcasting System, here episode 1, aired on December 18, 2013.

50. *My Love from Another Star*, episode 1.

51. Gang Na-ra, "A North Korean Defector Reacts to *Crash Landing on You*" [in Korean], interview by Yeontong TV, *Yeontong TV*, January 5, 2020, https:// www.youtube.com/watch?v=R8vuc9ed4rA.

52. Bak Yu-seong, interview.

53. Gim A-ra, [in Korean,] interview by Channel A, *On the Way to Meet You* [Ije mannaro gapnida], January 12, 2020, https://www.youtube.com/ watch?v=MEs8jxYEGYk.

54. Han Song-i, "*Crash Landing on You* Has Landed Dramatically in North Korea" [*Sarang-ui bulsichak* bukhan gangta], interview by Ssongi-Tube, *SsongiTube*, March 18, 2020, https://www.youtube.com/watch?v =JmDu50E8yGY.

55. Anonymous, interview, July 31, 2022.

56. *Crash Landing on You* [in Korean], 16 episodes, directed by Yi Jeong-hyeon, Gim Hui-won, and Gim Na-yeon, written by Bak Ji-eun, featuring Son Ye-jin and Hyun Bin (Hyeon Bin), aired from December 14, 2019, to February 16, 2020, on tvN, here episode 3, aired on December 21, 2019.

57. Gwak Mun-wan, "Interview with the North Korean Defector Turned Assistant Writer of *Crash Landing on You*" [*Sarang-ui bulsichak* talbukja

bojojakga inteobeu], interview by Gim Su-bin, *BBC News Korea*, February 16, 2020, https://www.bbc.com/korean/51519885.

58. Seo Gwang, "Smart House Appliances" [Jineung-hyeong gajeong-yong-pum], *World of Science* 1 (2015): 66.

59. *Crash Landing on You*, episode 2, aired on December 15, 2019.

60. SsongiTube, "*Crash Landing on You* Seen by a Resettler" [in Korean], December 20, 2019, https://www.youtube.com/watch?v=4Eqbq3QQozc.

61. *Crash Landing on You*, episode 12, aired on February 2, 2020.

62. Anonymous, interview, September 3, 2021.

63. Bak Yu-seong, interview.

64. The particular function of presetting text messages up to a year in advance has been noted by South Korean viewers as well. For instance, one South Korean blogger shares how she learned to do the same with her Samsung Galaxy phone after having watched the romantic scene in *Crash Landing on You*. Haengbok Suni, "How to Preprogram Messages Like *Crash Landing on You*'s Li Jeong-hyuk Using a Galaxy Phone" [*Sarang-ui bulsichak* Li Jeong-hyuk cheorom gaeleoksi yeyakmunja bo-nae-neun-beop], *Naver*, February 22, 2020, https://blog.naver.com/sochonn/221819947691.

65. The article appeared on Uriminzokkiri.com on March 4, 2020, but was no longer posted as of January 2021.

66. Anonymous, "North Korean Defector Claims that the Drama Beautifies North Korea Since the Reality Is Much Grimmer" [Talbukmin, mihwa-ra-neun dan-eo-jo-cha gwa-hae, hyeonsil hweolssin deo yeol-ak], interview by Hangyeore TV, *Hangyeore TV*, December 19, 2020, https://www.youtube.com/watch?v=35NPx7BI6b8.

67. *Crash Landing on You*, episode 2.

68. *Crash Landing on You*, episode 4, aired on December 22, 2019.

69. A. Lee, "Korean Wave," 98.

70. Yoon, "South Korean Media Reception," 104.

Chapter 4

1. Mun Seong-hwi, "South Korean Films Are Still Popular among Young North Koreans" [Buk jeol-meun-i-deul-e-ge hanguk yeonghwa in-gi yeo-jeon], *Radio Free Asia*, April 24, 2015, https://www.rfa.org/korean/in_focus/skmovie-04242015095018.html.

2. Kim Suk-Young, *Illusive Utopia*.

3. Na Min-hui, interview by author.

4. Former North Korean diplomat Thae Yong-ho, in a 2019 interview, notes that watching movies such as director Im Kwon-taek's *Taebaeksan-maek* while he worked in Denmark was shocking: "The film centers on the partisan struggle of the Korean Workers' Party in southern Jeolla Province. I was shocked to see that South Korean film could propagate communism like this. But the end of the film features a scene with a message that 'communism cannot prevail because it kills people indiscriminately.' This was the time when the Arduous March in the North was just beginning, and many people were being arrested in the political purge. The film that was based on 1950s Korea was illustrating the realities of North Korea then." Thae Yong-ho, "North Korea's Path to Normal Statehood, Part 1" [Bukhan, jeongsang gukgaro ganeungil 1bu], interview by Jo Mi-yeong, *Unification Media Group*, April 1, 2019, https://www.youtube.com/watch?v=Kuw3eBG5MQg.

5. Jang Seul-gi, "*Along with the Gods* Is Also Becoming Popular in North Korea" [Buk-e-seo-do yeonghwa *Singwa hamkke* in-gi], *Daily NK*, June 26, 2019, https://www.dailynk.com/北에서-영화-신과-함께-인기-사후-세계에-흥미/.

6. Li Ung-gil, interview, *Tal tal tal.*

7. Gim Hae-suk, interview.

8. Gim Ha-na, interview.

9. Anonymous, interview, September 3, 2021.

10. Jeong Gwang-il, e.g., seems to relegate action films mostly to male viewers when he says, "Young men like to watch action flicks." Baek, *North Korea's Hidden Revolution*, 165.

11. Gim Tae-hui, "2011 New Year's Special Report: New Waves of Change in North Korea, Part 3, 'South Korean Dramas Are So Interesting'" [2011nyeon sinnyeon teukjip: Bukhan-e buneun byeonhwa-ui baram 3, 'namhan deurama jaemitseoyo], interview by Yi Won-hui, *Radio Free Asia*, January 11, 2011, http://www.rfa.org/korean/temp/new_year_sp-01052011113720.html.

12. Yun Go-eun, "*My Wife Is a Gangster* Being Considered for North Korean Screening" [Jopok manura, bukhan sang-yeong chu-jin], *Joongnang ilbo*, December 3, 2001, https://news.joins.com/article/1842381.

13. *My Wife Is a Gangster*, directed by Jo Jin-gyu (Seoul: Bear Entertainment and Premier Entertainment, 2002), DVD.

14. Gim Ji-hye, "North Korean News Reports the Film *Parasite*'s Oscar Winning" [Buk sinmun, gi-saeng-chung oseuka-sang bodo], *Joongang ilbo*, February 21, 2020, https://news.joins.com/article/23712152.

15. Gim Bo-yeon, "*Parasite* Effect?" [*Gisaengchung* hyo-gwa?], *Chosun ilbo*, March 1, 2020, https://www.chosun.com/site/data/html_dir/2020/03/01/2020030100652.html.

16. Gim Ga-yeong, "There Is No *Parasite* in North Korea" [Buk-han-e *Gisaengchung*-eun eopda], interview by Gim Jin-guk, *Radio Free Asia*, February 17, 2020, https://www.rfa.org/korean/weekly_program/market_gen/fe-jk-02172020110255.html.

17. Jeon Hyo-jin, "There Is No *Parasite* in North Korea" [Buk-han-e *Gisaengchung*-eun eopda], interview by Gim Jin-guk, *Radio Free Asia*, February 17, 2020, https://www.rfa.org/korean/weekly_program/market_gen/fe-jk-02172020110255.html.

18. Brian X. Chen, "'*Parasite*' and South Korea's Income Gap: Call It Dirt Spoon Cinema," *New York Times*, October 18, 2019, https://www.nytimes.com/2019/10/18/movies/parasite-movie-south-korea.html.

19. Kim Kyung Hyun, *Hegemonic Mimicry: Korean Popular Culture of the 21st Century* (Durham, NC: Duke University Press, 2021), 181.

20. *Parasite*, directed by Bong Joon-ho (Seoul: Barunson E&A, 2019), DVD.

21. Zack Sharf, "Bong Joon-ho Reacts to Historic Palme D'or Win, Denies '*Parasite*' Mocks North Korea," *Indie Wire*, May 25, 2019, https://www.indiewire.com/2019/05/bong-joon-ho-reacts-palme-dor-win-denies-parasite-mocks-north-korea-1202144877/.

22. Na Won-jeong, "North Korean Humor and *Jjapaguri* in *Parasite*" [Gisaengchung jjapaguri jongbuk gaegeu], *News Joins*, June 1, 2019, https://news.joins.com/article/23485510.

23. Go, interview.

24. Mi So-hae, "Bong Joon-ho Who Turned the Audience into Parasites" [in Korean], Brunch Blog, June 4, 2019, https://brunch.co.kr/@naomi-chun/29.

25. Artist and scholar Steve Mann replaced the "sur-" with "sous-" in order to provide a counternarrative to the conventional mechanism of surveillance. Steve Mann, Jonathan Nolan, and Barry Wellman, "Sousveillance: Inventing and Using Wearable Computing Devices for Data Collection in Surveillance Environments," *Surveillance and Society* 1, no. 3 (2003): 332–33. According to performance studies scholar Elise Morrison, Mann's term encapsulates the reversal of "the gaze of dominant, disciplinary surveillance," arguing for the "abolition of hierarchy in surveillance culture, stating his ideal as a society in which everyone would watch everyone else through instruments of surveillance that would be distinguished at

all levels of society." Elise Morrison, *Discipline and Desire: Surveillance Technologies in Performance* (Ann Arbor: University of Michigan Press, 2016), 112.

26. Anonymous, interview, July 31, 2022.

27. Han Song-i, [in Korean,] interview by Channel A, *On the Way to Meet You* [Ije mannaro gapnida], October 21, 2018, https://www.youtube.com/watch?v=kzdg7GKb9Wo.

28. Gang Na-ra, interview, *Tal tal tal.*

29. Choe Yu-jin, interview.

30. Jeong Shi-u, [in Korean,] interview by Channel A, *On the Way to Meet You* [Ije mannaro gapnida], October 21, 2018, https://www.youtube.com/watch?v=hEyuofUtEU8.

31. Song Hong-geun, "Jeong Si-u, Capitalist Youth from Pyongyang" [Pyeongyaang-e-seo on jabon-ju-ui cheong-nyeon Jeong Si-u], *Shindonga*, January 24, 2019, https://shindonga.donga.com/3/all/13/1613907/1.

32. Anonymous, interview, July 29, 2022.

33. Anonymous, interview, September 3, 2021.

34. Anonymous, interview, September 3, 2021.

35. Gim Jun-hyeok, [in Korean,] interview by Channel A, *On the Way to Meet You* [Ije mannaro gapnida], April 7, 2019, https://www.youtube.com/watch?v=CevxkFBmvA0.

36. O Cheong-seong, interview.

37. Choe Ju-yeon, interview.

38. Gim Ha-na, interview.

39. Li Eun-hui, interview.

40. Anonymous, interview, September 3, 2021.

41. Ju Seong-ha and Jang Won-jae, "Although North Korean Stations Edited Out Red Velvet, North Koreans Watch Their Performance on a Secretly Secured USB" [Buk bangsong ledeu belbet tong-pyeon-jip haet-jiman jumin-deul USB mollae guhae-seo-bwa], *Donga ilbo*, April 10, 2018, http://www.donga.com/news/BestClick/article/all/20180410/89534017/1.

42. Bak Jong-a, [in Korean,] interview by Channel A, *On the Way to Meet You* [Ije mannaro gapnida], October 21, 2018, https://www.youtube.com/watch?v=hEyuofUtEU8.

43. Han Song-i, [in Korean,] interview by Baena TV, *Tal tal tal*, December 10, 2017, https://www.youtube.com/watch?v=ZFSrJpBSyU4/

44. Jeong Si-u, interview by Channel A, *On the Way to Meet You* [Ije mannaro gapnida], October 21, 2018, https://www.youtube.com/watch?v=hEyuofUtEU8.

45. Anonymous, interview, July 28, 2022.

46. Gweon Seol-gyeong, [in Korean,] interview by Baena TV, *Baenamu isahoe*, September 20, 2018, https://www.youtube.com/watch?v=TQsv4k1ojOU.

47. Ju Seong-ha and Jang, "Although North Korean Stations."

48. Baek Ji-young, "Don't Forget" [in Korean], MP3 audio, YouTube Music, 2009, https://music.youtube.com/watch?v=tQ3CMaHEmdE.

49. Han Sang-mi, "Top 3 South Korean Pop Songs That Are Popular in North Korea" [Bukhan-e-seo ingi-it-neun hanguk gayo TOP3], *BBC News Korea*, April 9, 2018, https://www.bbc.com/korean/news-43696293.

50. Gim Gwang-seok, "A Letter from a Private" [in Korean], MP3 audio, YouTube Music, 1993, https://music.youtube.com/watch?v=CYtv_k3fZyU.

51. Mun Seong-hwi, "Even the National Security Agency Cannot Stop the Popularity of the Song 'A Letter from a Private'" [Bowuibu-do mot-mak-eun sang-deung-byeong-ui pyeonji], *Radio Free Asia*, April 12, 2016, https://www.rfa.org/korean/in_focus/nk_nuclear_talks/draft-04122016095227.html.

52. An Jae-uk, "Friend" [in Korean], MP3 audio, YouTube Music, 2003, https://music.youtube.com/watch?v=xYmB1jvvvYk.

53. Choe Ju-yeon, interview.

54. Jeon Hyo-jin, "What Are the Most Popular South Korean Songs for North Korean Youth?" [Bukhan jeol-meun-i-deul-i gajang joahaneun hanguk gayoneun?], interview by Gim Seong-hun, *Jugan Chosun*, December 13, 2017, https://www.chosun.com/site/data/html_dir/2017/12/01/2017120102037.html.

55. The initial stage of South Korean variety shows is much indebted to the styles and formats of its Japanese counterparts. See Lee Dong-Hoo, "A Local Mode of Programme Adaptation: South Korea in the Global Television Format Business," in *Television across Asia: Television Industries, Programme Formats and Globalization*, ed. Albert Moran and Michael Keane (London: Routledge, 2004), 38.

56. Grace Jung, "Crying Laughing: Masculinity, Queerness, and Nationalism in South Korean Variety TV" (PhD diss., UCLA, 2021), 22.

57. Jung, "Crying Laughing," 46.

58. Gweon Seol-gyeong, "Although North Korean Stations Edited Out Red Velvet, North Koreans Watch Their Performance on a Secretly Secured USB" [Buk bangsong ledeu belbet tong-pyeon-jip haet-jiman jumin-deul USB mollae guhae-seo-bwa], interview by Ju Seong-ha and Jang, *Donga ilbo*, April 10, 2018, http://www.donga.com/news/BestClick/article/all/20180410/89534017/1.

59. KBS Entertainment, "The Return of Superman" [in Korean], November 15, 2020, https://www.youtube.com/watch?v=tynxD2pQdNU.

60. KBS Entertainment, "The Return of Superman" [in Korean], November 29, 2020, https://www.youtube.com/watch?v=AjJwVRGFwUo.

61. KBS Entertainment, "The Return of Superman" [in Korean], October 11, 2020, https://www.youtube.com/watch?v=oA7-pQlBuuY.

62. For more details on the aging population in South Korea, see Eun Ki-Soo, "Changing Roles of the Family and State for Elderly Care: A Confucian Perspective," in *Global Aging and Challenges to Families*, ed. Vern Bengston (London: Routledge, 2003), 253–71.

63. Jeong Gwang-il, interview.

64. tvN, "Grandpas over Flowers: Europe and Taiwan" [in Korean], August 24, 2020, YouTube video, https://www.youtube.com/watch?v=3Xphzr5vQgQ.

65. tvN, "Grandpas over Flowers," August 24, 2020.

66. tvN, "Grandpas over Flowers: Greece" [in Korean], April 24, 2015, YouTube video, https://www.youtube.com/watch?v=KyUXICyaCbI.

67. tvN, "Grandpas over Flowers Returns: Craving Korean Pork Belly" [in Korean], August 24, 2018, YouTube video, https://www.youtube.com/watch?v=hPDevrN20-k.

68. tvN, "Grandpas over Flowers: Seventy-Two-Year-Old Mak-nae Is the Busiest without Seo-jin" [in Korean], June 29, 2018, YouTube video, https://www.youtube.com/watch?v=XJOyKKStBRw.

69. tvN, "Grandpas over Flowers: Li Seo-jin, a Porter with a Six-Year Experience" [in Korean], June 29, 2018, YouTube video, https://www.youtube.com/watch?v=3dEgjcZ1uWY.

70. eNEWS24, "Grandpas over Flowers: Li Seo-jin Goes on a Date with Sunny" [in Korean], June 28, 2018, YouTube video, https://www.youtube.com/watch?v=Ae-9CsyQChI.

71. "Most Popular."

72. Anonymous, interview, December 17, 2019.

73. A. Lee, "Korean Wave," 99.

74. Jang Won-jae, "Due to COVID-19, North Korean Students Are Watching More Dramas" [Korona 19 hyu-gyo-ro hak-saeng-deul sa-i-e-seo hanryu deurama si-cheong geup-jeung], *Wolgan Joseon*, July 2020, https://monthly.chosun.com/client/news/viw.asp?ctcd=H&nNewsNumb=202007100049.

75. Kretchun and Kim, *Quiet Opening*, 50.

76. Choe Ju-yeon, interview.

Conclusion

1. Quoted in Ricardo Dominguez, "Notes on Dissent and Risk," in *The Routledge Companion to Media and Risk*, ed. Bishnupriya Ghosh and Bhaskar Sarkar (New York, NY: Routledge, 2020), 471.

2. DeVoss, "English Studies," 208.

3. McCracken, "Why We Love," 202.

4. For more headlines covering North Korea's recent achievements in cutting-edge science and technology, see *NK Economy* (website), accessed February 1, 2024, http://www.nkeconomy.com.

5. Deborah L. Wheeler, *Digital Resistance in the Middle East: New Media Activism in Everyday Life* (Edinburgh: Edinburgh University Press, 2017), 2.

6. Kim Yonho, *Cell Phones*, 8.

7. Joo, "Hidden Transcripts in Marketplaces," 68.

8. Antonio Gramsci, *Selections from the Prison Notebooks* (London: Lawrence and Wishart, 1971), 276.

9. Kim Yonho, "North Korea's Mobile Telecommunications and Private Transportation Services in the Kim Jong-un Era," Committee for Human Rights in North Korea, January 10, 2019, http://www.hrnkinsider.org/2019/01/north-koreas-mobile-telecommunications.html.

10. Bada Sonyeo, *Calling Out for Hometown* [Gohyang-eul bureuda] (Seoul: Jak-eun tongil, 2015), 32.

Appendix

1. Anonymous interviews are sorted by date of interview as these dates are used to distinguish them in the shortened citations in the notes.

An Jae-uk. "Friend." [In Korean.] MP3 audio, YouTube Music, 2003. https://
music.youtube.com/watch?v=xYmB1jvvvYk.

Anyone Can Learn Computers [Nuguna bae-ulsu ittneun kompiuteo]. Pyongyang: Gyoyukdoseo-Chulpansa, 2002.

"Application of Computer Virtual Reality Technology" [Kompiuteo gasang-hyeonsil-ui liyonggisul]. *Joseon munhak* 4 (2001): 71.

Associated Press. "Google Exec Calls for Open Internet in North
Korea." *CBC*, January 9, 2013. https://www.cbc.ca/news/technology/
google-exec-calls-for-open-internet-in-north-korea-1.1380646.

Autumn in My Heart. [In Korean.] 16 episodes. Directed by Yun Seok-ho. Written by O Su-hyeon. Featuring Song Hae-gyi, Won Bin, and Song Seung-
heon. Aired from September 18, 2000, to November 7, 2000, on Korea
Broadcasting System.

Bada Sonyeo. *Calling Out for Hometown* [Gohyang-eul bureuda]. Seoul: Jak-eun
tongil, 2015.

Baek, Jieun. *North Korea's Hidden Revolution.* New Haven, CT: Yale University
Press, 2016.

Baek Ji-young. "Don't Forget." [In Korean.] MP3 audio, YouTube Music, 2009.
https://music.youtube.com/watch?v=tQ3CMaHEmdE.

Bak Gwang-cheol. "Bolstering the Nation with Strength in Science, Technology, and Talented People" [Gwahak-gisul-gang-guk, injaegang-guk geonseol-ui naraereul pyeolcheojusiryeo]. *Chollima* 6 (2016): 32–33.

Bak Jong-a. [In Korean.] Interview by Channel A. *On the Way to Meet You* [Ije mannaro gapnida], October 21, 2018. https://www.youtube.com/watch?v=hEyuofUtEU8.

Bak Jun-hyeong and Yi Seok-yeong. "Phone Handset Prices Fall as Users Rise." [In Korean.] *Daily NK*, May 20, 2011.

Bak Min-sik. "*My Love from Another Star* Brings the Same Profit as Exporting 20,000 Sonatas" [Byeolgeudae sonata imandae hyogwa]. *Hankook ilbo*, November 11, 2016. https://www.hankookilbo.com/News/Read/201611111640352284.

Boisvert, Anne-Marie. "On Bricolage: Assembling Culture with Whatever Comes to Hand." Translated by Timothy Barnard. *HorizonZero* 8 (2003). www.horizonzero.ca/textsite/remix.php?is=8&file=4&tlang=0.

Bong Joon-ho, dir. *Parasite*. Seoul: Barunson E&A, 2019. DVD.

Boys over Flowers. [In Korean.] 25 episodes. Directed by Jeon Gi-sang. Written by Yun Ji-ryeon. Featuring Gu Hye-seon and Lee Min-ho (Yi Min-ho). Aired from January 1, 2009, to March 22, 2009, on Korea Broadcasting System.

CBS News: The National. "Infiltrating North Korea, One USB Drive at a Time." February 23, 2018. https://www.youtube.com/watch?v=jKINA-ikgE4.

Chen, Brian X. "'*Parasite*' and South Korea's Income Gap: Call It Dirt Spoon Cinema." *New York Times*, October 18, 2019. https://www.nytimes.com/2019/10/18/movies/parasite-movie-south-korea.html.

Choe Gyeong-su. *Study on North Korean Copyright Law and the Cooperation and Exchange between the Two Koreas in the Copyrights Area* [Bukhan jeojakbeop-mit nambukgan jeojakkweon bunya gyoryu hyeopryeok-e gwanhan yeongu]. Jinju: Korea Copyright Commission, 2015.

Clark, Katerina. *The Soviet Novel: History as Ritual*. Chicago: University of Chicago Press, 1981.

"Computer Keyboards and Bacteria" [Kompiuteo geonbangwa segyun]. *Joseon nyeoseong* 12 (2011): 35.

"Computer Logic and Pedagogy" [Kompiuteo noliwa gyoyanggyegi]. *Gyoyangwon* 4 (2017): 32.

"Computers and Water" [Kompiuteo-wa mul]. *Joseon nyeoseong* 6 (2019): 55.

"Conversation with the Dead Using Computers" [Kompiuteoro jukeun saramgwa daehwa]. *Munhwaeohakseup* 2 (2002): 23.

Crash Landing on You. [In Korean.] 16 episodes. Directed by Yi Jeong-hyeon, Gim Hui-won, and Gim Na-yeon. Written by Bak Ji-eun. Featuring Son

Ye-jin and Hyun Bin (Hyeon Bin). Aired from December 14, 2019, to February 16, 2020, on tvN.

de Certeau, Michel. *The Practice of Everyday Life*. Berkeley: University of California Press, 1984.

De Kosnik, Abigail, Susan Kresnicka, Hye Jin Lee, and Aswin Punathambekar. "Transcultural Fandom in the Age of Streaming Media." Panel at Transforming Hollywood: U.S. Streaming and International Co-productions, University of California, Los Angeles, CA, December 3, 2021. https://transforminghollywood.tft.ucla.edu/previous-years/transforming-hollywood-9-2021/.

DeVoss, Dànielle Nicole. "English Studies and Intellectual Property: Copyright, Creativity, and the Commons." *Pedagogy* 10, no. 1 (2010): 201–15. Project MUSE.

"The Difference between Intellectual Property Rights and Property Rights" [Jijeok soyugwon-gwa soyugwon-eui cha-i]. *Joseon nyeoseong* 10 (2019): 55.

Dominguez, Ricardo. "Notes on Dissent and Risk." In *The Routledge Companion to Media and Risk*, edited by Bishnupriya Ghosh and Bhaskar Sarkar, 468–71. New York, NY: Routledge, 2020.

Echo of Truth. "I Missed You, My School." June 4, 2020. https://www.youtube.com/watch?v=-YKN5MXP6NQ.

Echo of Truth. "What's Up Pyongyang? Covid 19 Situation in DPRK." April 12, 2020. https://www.youtube.com/watch?v=_JEaZlIoEmM&t=3s.

"E-commerce" [Jeonja sangeop]. *Joseon nyeoseong* 10 (2018): 55.

eNEWS24. "Grandpas over Flowers: Li Seo-jin Goes on a Date with Sunny." [In Korean.] June 28, 2018. YouTube video. https://www.youtube.com/watch?v=Ae-9CsyQChI.

Eun, Ki-Soo [Eun Gi-su]. "Changing Roles of the Family and State for Elderly Care: A Confucian Perspective." In *Global Aging and Challenges to Families*, edited by Vern Bengston, 253–71. London: Routledge, 2003.

Fahy, Sandra. "Hallyu in the South, Hunger in the North: Alternative Imaginings of What Life Could Be." In *South Korean Popular Culture and North Korea*, edited by Kim Youna, 109–19. London: Routledge, 2019.

———. *Marching through Suffering: Loss and Survival in North Korea*. New York, NY: Columbia University Press, 2015.

Florida, Richard. *The Rise of the Creative Class: And How It's Transforming Work, Leisure and Everyday Life*. New York, NY: Basic Books, 2022.

"Four Teas Beneficial for Computer Users" [Kompiuteo sayongjadeul-ui geongang-e joeun 4gaji cha]. *Chollima* 5 (2012): 65.

Frazier, Nishani. "Black Blockchain: The Future of Black Studies and Block-chain." *American Studies (Lawrence)* 61, no. 2 (2022): 13–19. https://doi .org/10.1353/ams.2022.0010.

Frey, William. "Diversity Defines the Millennial Generation." Brookings Institution, June 26, 2016. https://www.brookings.edu/blog/ the-avenue/2016/06/28/diversity-defines-the-millennial-generation/.

"The Future of Electrical Engineering" [Daeum sedae jeonja gonghak-eui jeon-mang]. *Jeonja jadonghwa* 3 (1998): 7–8.

Gallagher, Kathleen. *Hope in a Collapsing World: Youth, Theatre, and Listening as a Political Alternative.* Toronto: University of Toronto Press, 2022. Pro-Quest Ebook Central.

Gang Jin-gyu. Email interview by author. December 27, 2019.

———. "North Korea Develops 4G and 5G Simultaneously in Preparation for the Future" [Da-eum-sedae idongtongsin junbihaneun bukhan 4G, 5G, dongsi yeongu]. *NK Economy,* August 12, 2022. http://www.nkeconomy .com/news/articleView.html?idxno=10707.

Gang Sun-gyeo. *My Hometown* [Naeui saldeon gohyangeun]. Seoul: Hangbok Eneoji, 2015.

Gause, Ken. *Coercion, Control, Surveillance, and Punishment: An Examination of the North Korean Police State.* Washington, DC: Committee for Human Rights in North Korea, 2012.

Ghosh, Bishnupriya, and Bhaskar Sarkar. "Media and Risk: An Introduction." In *The Routledge Companion to Media and Risk,* edited by Bishnupriya Ghosh and Bhaskar Sarkar, 1–24. New York, NY: Routledge, 2020.

Gim Bo-yeon. *"Parasite* Effect?" [*Gisaengchung* hyo-gwa?]. *Chosun ilbo,* March 1, 2020. https://www.chosun.com/site/data/html_dir/2020/03/ 01/2020030100652.html.

Gim Chang-pung. "Changes in North Korea." [In Korean.] *Brunch Blog,* January 20, 2018. https://brunch.co.kr/@cpk78/71.

Gim Gwang-seok. "A Letter from a Private." [In Korean.] MP3 audio, YouTube Music, 1993. https://music.youtube.com/watch?v=CYtv_k3fZyU.

Gim Ji-eun and No Ji-won. "Latest North Korean Smartphone, Pyongyang 2423" [Bukhan choesin seumateupon Pyeongyang 2423]. *Hangyeore,* March 11, 2019. http://www.hani.co.kr/arti/politics/defense/885344.html.

Gim Ji-hwan. "North Koreans Say that the Country Cannot Sustain Itself without the Marketplace" [Buk jumindeul saenghwal jangmadang eopsineun an dolaganda]. *Gyeonghyang sinmun,* January 9, 2019. http://news.khan.co.kr/ kh_news/khan_art_view.html?art_id=201901090600045.

Gim Ji-hye. "North Korean News Reports the Film *Parasite*'s Oscar Winning" [Buk sinmun, gi-saeng-chung oseuka-sang bodo]. *Joongang ilbo*, February 21, 2020. https://news.joins.com/article/23712152.

Gim Ju-seong. *On the Way to Meet You* [Ije mannaro gapnida]. Channel A, February 25, 2017. https://www.youtube.com/watch?v=IHIA5aBOmoM.

Gim Seong-guk. "Our Country Placed Young People at the Core of the National and Party Strategic Plans and Established a Strong Nation of Young People" [Uri naraneun cheongnyeon jungsireul danggwa gukgaui jeonryak-jeok-roseon-eu-ro suriphago geonseolhan cheong-nyeon gang-guk]. *Cheolhak, Saheo-jeongchihak Yeongu* 3 (2019): 33–35.

Gisclair, Jessica. "The Dissonance between Culture and Intellectual Property in China." *Southeast Review of Asian Studies* 30 (2008): 182–87.

Golumbia, David. "Zealots of the Blockchain." *The Baffler* 38 (March 2018). https://thebaffler.com/salvos/zealots-of-the-blockchain-golumbia.

Gordon, Daniel, dir. *The State of Mind*. Sheffield, UK: VeryMuchSo Productions, 2004. DVD.

Gramsci, Antonio. *Selections from the Prison Notebooks*. London: Lawrence and Wishart, 1971.

Gwon Gyeong-sung. "The Success of *Boys over Flowers* in Taiwan, Korea, and Japan Lies in the Original Manga" [Samguk, *Kkotnam* seongong-eun wonjak manhwa-ui him]. *Media Today*, September 14, 2009. http://www.mediatoday.co.kr/news/articleView.html?idxno=82841.

Gwon Hae-yeong. "55.3 Million iPhones versus 95 Million Galaxies Sold During the Fourth Quarter Smartphone Sales Report" [4 bun-gi seumateupon panmae Aipon 5530mandae vs Gaelluksi 9500mandae]. *Asia gyeongje*, January 21, 2014. https://news.naver.com/main/read.nhn?mode=LSD&mid=shm&sid1=105&oid=277&aid=0003175454.

Gye Gwang-il. "Intellectual Property Plays an Important Role in the Development of Society and Culture" [Sahoe-gyeongje-baljeon-eseo jungyohan yeokhal-eul noneun jijeok soyugwon]. *Chollima* 1 (2019): 56.

Haengbok Suni. "How to Preprogram Messages Like *Crash Landing on You*'s Li Jeong-hyuk Using a Galaxy Phone" [*Sarang-ui bulsichak* Li Jeong-hyuk cheorom gaeleoksi yeyakmunja bo-nae-neun-beop]. *Naver*, February 22, 2020. https://blog.naver.com/sochonn/221819947691.

Haggard, Stephan, and Marcus Noland. *Famine in North Korea: Markets, Aid, and Reform*. New York, NY: Columbia University Press, 2007.

Halliday, M. A. K. "Anti-languages." *American Anthropologist* 78, no. 3 (September 1976): 570–84.

Hammersley, Martyn. "Ethnography: Problems and Prospects." *Ethnography and Education* 1, no. 1 (2006): 3–14. https://doi.org/10.1080/17457820500512697.

Han Sang-mi. "Top 3 South Korean Pop Songs That Are Popular in North Korea" [Bukhan-e-seo ingi-it-neun hanguk gayo TOP3]. *BBC News Korea*, April 9, 2018. https://www.bbc.com/korean/news-43696293

Hassig, Ralph, and Kongdan Oh. *The Hidden People of North Korea: Everyday Life in the Hermit Kingdom*. Lanham, MD: Rowman and Littlefield, 2009.

"Health Risks and Exercise Recommendations for Computer Users" [Kompiuteo sayongjadeului geongang-gwa undong]. *Joseon nyeoseong* 7 (2011): 55.

Heo In. "Intellectual Properties of South and North Koreas and Plans for Cooperation" [Nambukhan-ui jijjeok jae-san-kwon-gwa hyeop-ryeok bang-an]. *Korea Institute of Intellectual Property In-Depth Report* 3 (2018): 1–12.

Hwang Myung-cheol and Li Myung-cheol. "Computer-Aided Automatic Temperature Control of a Bread Oven" [Hansopyeon kompiuteo-reul liyoung-han ppangro jadong-ondo-jangchi]. *Sigryo gong-eop* 3 (2016): 25.

Hwang Su-jeong. "Foreign-Language Education Based on a Computer Network" [Kompiuteo-mang-e ui-han oeguk-eo gyoyuk]. *Chollima* 3 (2016): 83.

Jang Seul-gi. "*Along with the Gods* Is Also Becoming Popular in North Korea" [Buk-e-seo-do yeonghwa *Singwa hamkke* in-gi]. *Daily NK*, June 26, 2019. https://www.dailynk.com/北에서-영화-신과-함께-인기-사후-세계에-흥미/.

Jang Won-jae. "Due to COVID-19, North Korean Students Are Watching More Dramas" [Korona 19 hyu-gyo-ro hak-saeng-deul sa-i-e-seo hanryu deurama si-cheong geup-jeung]. *Wolgan Joseon*, July 2020. https://monthly.chosun.com/client/news/viw.asp?ctcd=H&nNewsNumb=202007100049.

Jeon Jae-u. "Perspectives on Generational Changes in the North Korean Power Elite and Policy Direction" [Bukhan paweo eliteu-ui sedae-byun-hwa-wa jeong-chaek-ui bang-hyang-seong jeon-mang]. *Korean Defense Issues and Analyses* 1726 (August 2018): 1–14.

Jeong Cheol-ho. "Problems of Computer Control in the Process of Beer Brewing" [Maekju-balhyo-gong-jeong-ui kompiuteo-jojong-eseo naseoneun munje]. *Gimchaek-gong-eop-jonghap-daehak-hakbo* 9 (2014): 80–82.

Jeong Yeon. "Kim Jong Un Gives Directives for New Economic Policy and Orders the Expansion of Self-Supporting Account System" [Gim Jeong-un, dokrip chaesanjae hwakdae sae gyeongje daechaek jisi]. *SBS News*, November 27, 2014. https://news.sbs.co.kr/news/endPage.do?news_id=N1002707521.

Ji Hye-yeon. "What Are the Characteristics of North Korean Generations Seen through Historical Stages?" [Yeok-sa-jeok-eu-ro bon bukhan sae-dae-ui teukjing-eun?]. *South Korean Ministry of Unification Blog*, February 21, 2012. https://unikoreablog.tistory.com/1902.

Jin, Dal Yong. *New Korean Wave: Transnational Cultural Power in the Age of Social Media*. Chicago: University of Illinois Press, 2016.

Jo Eun-byeol. "The Plagiarism Dispute about *My Love from Another Star* Is Headed for Court" [Byeolgeudae pyojeol nonran, gyeolguk beopjeong ganda]. *No Cut News*, May 20, 2014. https://www.nocutnews.co.kr/news/4027662.

Jo Jin-gyu, dir. *My Wife Is a Gangster*. Seoul: Bear Entertainment and Premier Entertainment, 2002. DVD.

Joo, Hyung-min. "Hidden Transcripts in Marketplaces: Politicized Discourses in the North Korean Shadow Economy." *Pacific Review* 27, no. 1 (January 2014): 49–71.

Ju Seong-ha and Jang Won-jae. "Although North Korean Stations Edited Out Red Velvet, North Koreans Watch Their Performance on a Secretly Secured USB" [Buk bangsong ledeu belbet tong-pyeon-jip haet-jiman jumin-deul USB mollae guhae-seo-bwa]. *Donga ilbo*, April 10, 2018. http://www.donga.com/news/BestClick/article/all/20180410/89534017/1.

Jung, Grace. "Crying Laughing: Masculinity, Queerness, and Nationalism in South Korean Variety TV." PhD diss., University of California, Los Angeles, 2021.

Kang Hyun-kyeong. "Has N. Korean Leader's Daughter Been Confirmed as Heir Apparent?" *Korea Times*, December 3, 2023. https://www.koreatimes.co.kr/www/nation/2023/12/103_364361.html.

KBS Entertainment. "The Return of Superman." [In Korean.] October 11, 2020. https://www.youtube.com/watch?v=0A7-pQlBuuY.

KBS Entertainment. "The Return of Superman." [In Korean.] November 15, 2020. https://www.youtube.com/watch?v=tynxD2pQdNU.

KBS Entertainment. "The Return of Superman." [In Korean.] November 29, 2020. https://www.youtube.com/watch?v=AjJwVRGFwUo.

Kim, Kyung Hyun [Gim Gyeong-hyeon]. *Hegemonic Mimicry: Korean Popular Culture of the 21st Century*. Durham, NC: Duke University Press, 2021.

Kim, Suk-Young [Gim Suk-yeong]. "For the Eyes of North Koreans? Politics of Money and Class in *Boys over Flowers*." In *The Korean Wave: Korean Media Go Global*, edited by Kim Youna, 93–105. London: Routledge, 2013.

———. *Illusive Utopia: Theater, Film, and Everyday Performance in North Korea*. Ann Arbor: University of Michigan Press, 2010.

———. *K-pop Live: Fans, Idols, and Multimedia Performance*. Stanford, CA: Stanford University Press, 2018.

Kim Yong and Kim Suk-Young. *Long Road Home: Testimony of a North Korean Camp Survivor.* New York, NY: Columbia University Press, 2009.

Kim Yonho [Gim Yeon-ho]. *Cell Phones in North Korea: Has North Korea Entered the Telecommunications Revolution?* Washington, DC: US-Korea Institute; Voice of America, 2014.

———. "North Korea's Mobile Telecommunications and Private Transportation Services in the Kim Jong-un Era." Committee for Human Rights in North Korea, January 10, 2019. http://www.hrnkinsider.org/2019/01/north-koreas-mobile-telecommunications.html.

Kretchun, Nat, and Jane Kim. *A Quiet Opening: North Koreans in a Changing Media Environment.* Washington, DC: InterMedia, 2012.

Lee, Ahlam. "The Korean Wave: A Pull Factor for North Korean Migration." In *South Korean Popular Culture and North Korea*, edited by Kim Youna, 96–108. London: Routledge, 2019.

Lee, Dong-Hoo [Li Dong-hu]. "A Local Mode of Programme Adaptation: South Korea in the Global Television Format Business." In *Television across Asia: Television Industries, Programme Formats and Globalization*, edited by Albert Moran and Michael Keane, 36–53. London: Routledge, 2004.

Lessig, Lawrence. *Free Culture: How Big Media Uses Technology and the Law to Lock Down Culture and Control Creativity.* New York, NY: Penguin, 2004.

———. *The Future of Ideas: The Fate of the Commons in a Connected World.* New York, NY: Random House, 2001.

———. *Remix: Making Art and Commerce Thrive in the Hybrid Economy.* New York, NY: Penguin, 2008.

Li Myeong-cheol. "Why Do I Love Computers?" [Naneun woe kompiuteo-reul sarang-haneunga?]. *Cheongnyeon munhak* 8 (2001): 48.

Li Seong-nam. "The Great Leader Paved the Everlasting Foundation for a Strong Nation of Youth" [Cheongnyeongangguk-ui mannyeongiteuleul maryeonhayeo-jusin widaehan ryeondoja]. *Chollima* 8 (2018): 15–16.

Li Seol-ju, ed. *March Forward, Strong Nation of Young People* [Cheongnyeon gangguk-i-yeo appeuro]. Pyongyang: Munhakyesulchulpansa, 2016.

Li Sun-hye and Gim Yeong-bok. "Realizing the Sound Effects of National Rhythm by Using Hansopyeon Computers" [Hansopyeon-kompiuteo-e uihan minjokjangdan-eumhyang-hyogwa-silhyeon]. *Gimchaek-gong-eop-jonghap-daehak-hakbo* 1 (2010): 66–68.

Mann, Steve, Jonathan Nolan, and Barry Wellman. "Sousveillance: Inventing and Using Wearable Computing Devices for Data Collection in Surveillance Environments." *Surveillance and Society* 1, no. 3 (2003): 331–55.

Mansourov, Alexandre. "North Korea on the Cusp of Digital Transformation." Nautilus Institute, October 20, 2011. http://www.nautilus.org/wp-content/uploads/2011/12/DPRK_Digital_Transformation.pdf.

McCracken, Janet. "Why We Love Our Phones: A Case Study in the Aesthetics of Gadgets." In *Comparative Everyday Aesthetics: East-West Studies in Contemporary Living*, edited by Jeffrey Petts and Eva Kit Wah Man, 201–20. Amsterdam: Amsterdam University Press, 2023.

McLeod, Kembrew. *Freedom of Expression: Resistance and Representation in the Age of Intellectual Property*. Minneapolis: University of Minnesota, 2007.

Mi So-hae. "Bong Joon-ho Who Turned the Audience into Parasites." [In Korean.] *Brunch Blog*, June 4, 2019. https://brunch.co.kr/@naomi-chun/29.

Miller, Toby, and Marwan Kraidy. *Global Media Studies*. Cambridge: Polity Press, 2016.

Ministry of Unification [Republic of Korea]. *White Paper on Korean Unification* [Tong-il baek-seo]. Seoul: Ministry of Unification, 2023.

Morrison, Elise. *Discipline and Desire: Surveillance Technologies in Performance*. Ann Arbor: University of Michigan Press, 2016.

"The Most Popular South Korean Drama for North Koreans Is *Autumn in My Heart*." [In Korean.] *BBC News Korea*, July 2, 2019. https://www.bbc.com/korean/news-48835889.

Mun Seong-hwi. "Even the National Security Agency Cannot Stop the Popularity of the Song 'A Letter from a Private'" [Bowuibu-do mot-mak-eun sang-deung-byeong-ui pyeonji]. *Radio Free Asia*, April 12, 2016. https://www.rfa.org/korean/in_focus/nk_nuclear_talks/draft-04122016095227.html.

———. "North Korea Falls for Drama *Boys over Flowers*" [Deurama *Kkotboda namja*-e bbajin bukhan]. *Radio Free Asia*, September 15, 2011. http://www.rfa.org/korean/in_focus/skdrama-09152011130127.html.

———. "North Korean Mobile Network Expands to Counties." [In Korean.] *Radio Free Asia*, February 10, 2011. http://www.rfa.org/korean/in_focus/cell_phone-02102011113753.html.

———. "South Korean Films Are Still Popular Among Young North Koreans" [Buk jeol-meun-i-deul-e-ge hanguk yeonghwa in-gi yeo-jeon]. *Radio Free Asia*, April 24, 2015. https://www.rfa.org/korean/in_focus/skmovie-04242015095018.html.

My Love from Another Star. [In Korean.] 21 episodes. Directed by Jang Tae-yu and O Chung-hwan. Written by Bak Ji-eun. Featuring Jun Ji-hyun (Jeon Ji-hyeon) and Kim Soo-hyun (Gim Su-hyeon). Aired from December 18, 2013, to February 27, 2014, on Seoul Broadcasting System.

Na Won-jeong. "North Korean Humor and *Jjapaguri* in *Parasite*" [*Gisaengchung jjapaguri jongbuk gaegeu*]. *News Joins*, June 1, 2019. https://news.joins.com/article/23485510.

Nakashima, Ellen, Gerry Shih, and John Hudson. "Leaked Documents Reveal Huawei's Secret Operations to Build North Korea's Wireless Network." *Washington Post*, July 22, 2019. https://www.washingtonpost.com/world/national-security/leaked-documents-reveal-huaweis-secret-operations-to-build-north-koreas-wireless-network/2019/07/22/583430fe-8d12-11e9-adf3-f70f78c156e8_story.html?utm_term=.fbc417a5aabc.

North Korea ICT Research Committee [Buk-han ICT yeon-gu wi-won-hoe]. *2020 Survey on North Korean ICT Trends: Focus on North Korean Media* [Buk-han ICT dong-hyang josa 2020: buk-han maeche-reul jung-sim-eu-ro]. Seoul: Korea Institute of Science and Technology Information, 2021.

North Korean ICT Research Committee [Buk-han ICT yeon-gu wi-won-hoe]. *2022 Survey on North Korean ICT Trends: Focus on North Korean Media* [Buk-han ICT dong-hyang josa 2022: Buk-han maeche-reul jung-sim-eu-ro]. Seoul: Korea Institute of Science and Technology Information, 2023.

O Ga-hyeon. *How to Deal with North Koreans* [Bukhan-saram-gwa geo-rae-ha-neun beop]. Seoul: Hangyeore, 2019.

O Gang-seon. *The End of the Harvard Era and Educational Revolution* [Habadeu sidae-ui jongmalgwa hakseup hyeokmyeong]. Seoul: Cloud Nine, 2020.

O Jeong-ro. "My Country Is a Strong Nation of Young People" [Nae jogukeun cheongnyeon gangguk]. *Joseon munhak* 1 (2016): 10.

"Paying Copyright Fees to North Korean Central Television?" [Joseon Joon-gang TV jeojak-kwonryo jibul?]. *JCTB News*, April 20, 2016. https://news.jtbc.co.kr/article/article.aspx?news_id=NB11218004.

Pilkington, Eric. "Eric Schmidt in North Korea: Google Chairman's Step into the Unknown." *The Guardian*, January 7, 2013. https://www.theguardian.com/technology/2013/jan/07/google-eric-schmidt-trip-pyongyang.

Puchner, Martin. *The Language of Thieves*. New York, NY: W. W. Norton, 2020.

Raphelson, Samantha. "Amid the Stereotypes, Some Facts about Millennials." NPR, November 18, 2014. https://www.npr.org/2014/11/18/354196302/amid-the-stereotypes-some-facts-about-millennials.

Ross, Andrew. *Nice Work If You Can Get It: Life and Labor in Precarious Times*. New York, NY: New York University Press, 2010.

Sampson, Tony D. *Virality: Contagion Theory in the Age of Networks*. Minneapolis: University of Minnesota Press, 2012.

Samuels, Lisa. "Relinquish Intellectual Property." *New Literary History* 33, no. 2 (2002): 357–74.

Seo Gwang. "Smart House Appliances" [Jineung-hyeong gajeong-yongpum]. *World of Science* 1 (2015): 66.

Sharf, Zack. "Bong Joon-ho Reacts to Historic Palme D'or Win, Denies 'Parasite' Mocks North Korea." *Indie Wire*, May 25, 2019. https://www.indiewire .com/2019/05/bong-joon-ho-reacts-palme-dor-win-denies-parasite-mocks -north-korea-1202144877/.

Shiller, Robert J. *Narrative Economics: How Stories Go Viral and Drive Major Economic Events.* Princeton, NJ: Princeton University Press, 2019.

Sin Myung-jin and Jeon Ji-hyeon. "Evaluating Piano Tunes by Using Computers" [Kompiuteo-e uihan piano-eum-ui eumjeong-pyeongga]. *Gimchaek-gong-eop-jonghap-daehak-hakbo* 10 (2011): 115–16.

Song Gi-yong. "*My Love from Another Star* Sends Cultural Shockwaves through China" [Byeolgeudae hyeonsang jungguk-e keun muhwa chung-gyek-jwo]. *News Joins*, March 6, 2014. https://news.joins.com/article/14084618.

Song Hong-geun. "Jeong Si-u, Capitalist Youth from Pyongyang" [Pyeong-yaang-e-seo on jabon-ju-ui cheong-nyeon Jeong Si-u]. *Shindonga*, January 24, 2019. https://shindonga.donga.com/3/all/13/1613907/1.

———. "Two Faces of the South Korean and US Presidents as Seen by the Escapee Jeong Gwang-il" [Talchulja Jeong Gwang-il-i-bon hanmi daetongryeong-ui du eolgul]. *Shindonga*, April 2, 2019. http://shindonga.donga.com/3/ home/13/1683245/1.

Song Hye-min. "Chinese Portal Claims that the Best Version of *Boys over Flowers* is South Korean" [Jung potal, *Kkotboda namja* hangukpani gajang usu]. *Now News*, January 15, 2009. http://nownews.seoul.co.kr/news/newsView .php?id=2009011560I015.

SsongiTube. "*Crash Landing on You* Seen by a Resettler." [In Korean.] December 20, 2019. https://www.youtube.com/watch?v=4Eqbq3QQozc.

Stanford Center for Professional Development. "How Does Blockchain Work?" *Stanford Online.* Accessed on November 2, 2023. https://online.stanford .edu/how-does-blockchain-work.

Steen, Shannon. *The Creativity Complex: Art, Tech, and the Seduction of an Idea.* Ann Arbor: University of Michigan Press, 2023.

tvN. "Grandpas over Flowers: Europe and Taiwan." [In Korean.] August 24, 2020. YouTube video. https://www.youtube.com/watch?v=3Xphzr5vQgQ.

———. "Grandpas over Flowers: Greece." [In Korean.] April 24, 2015. YouTube video. https://www.youtube.com/watch?v=KyUXICyaCbI.

———. "Grandpas over Flowers: Li Seo-jin, a Porter with a Six-Year Experience." [In Korean.] June 29, 2018. YouTube video. https://www.youtube.com/watch?v=3dEgjcZ1uWY.

———. "Grandpas over Flowers Returns: Craving Korean Pork Belly." [In Korean.] August 24, 2018. YouTube video. https://www.youtube.com/watch?v=hPDevrN20-k.

———. "Grandpas over Flowers: Seventy-Two-Year-Old Mak-nae Is the Busiest without Seo-jin." [In Korean.] June 29, 2018. YouTube video. https://www.youtube.com/watch?v=XJOyKKStBRw.

Unification Observatory. "Revealing North Korean Smartphone Pyongyang 2545." [In Korean.] Featuring Gang Jin-gyu. Aired September 21, 2019, on MBC TV. https://www.youtube.com/watch?v=rZ2fUax4K_8.

"Using the Science, Technology, and Information Search Database 'Gwangmyeong' through a Computer Network" [Kompiuteo-mangeul tonghan gwahakgisul-jeongbo-geomsaek-chegye 'Gwangmyeong'eu liyong]. *Jeonja jadonghwa* 4 (1998): 4.

van Dijick, José, Thomas Poell, and Martijn de Waal. *The Platform Society: Public Values in a Connective World.* Oxford: Oxford University Press, 2018.

Voice of America. "Cell Phones in North Korea?" March 20, 2014. https://www.youtube.com/watch?v=txUmNFQUBc8.

Wheeler, Deborah L. *Digital Resistance in the Middle East: New Media Activism in Everyday Life.* Edinburgh: Edinburgh University Press, 2017.

"Why Should We Wash Our Face after Using the Computer?" [Kompiuteo jakeop-hu oe eolguleul ssiseoya haneuga?]. *Joseon nyeoseong* 5 (2019): 55.

Yi Dae-hui. "Former President Kim Dae-jung Laid Ground for the Nation's Rise to IT Power" [Ai-ti gang-guk todae dakgeun Gim Dae-jung jeon daetongryeong]. *Digital Times*, August 23, 2009. http://www.dt.co.kr/contents.html?article_no=2009082402012369697001.

Yi Jae-won, Jeong Jin-u, Bak So-yeon, and Jo Jun-yeong. "N Generation Kim Jong Un: New North Korea beyond Imagination." [In Korean.] *Money Today*, May 1, 2018. http://news.mt.co.kr/mtview.php?no=2018043021204646432.

Yi Won-hui. "2011 New Year's Special Report: New Waves of Change in North Korea, Part 3, 'South Korean Dramas Are So Interesting'" [2011nyeon sinnyeon teukjip: Bukhan-e buneun byeonhwa-ui baram 3, "namhan deurama jaemitseoyo"]. *Radio Free Asia*, January 11, 2011. http://www.rfa.org/korean/temp/new_year_sp-01052011113720.html.

Yi Yeong-jong. [In Korean.] Interview by Baena TV. *Baenamu isahoe*, October 3, 2018. https://www.youtube.com/watch?v=m6wlxivdNUE&t=2362s.

———. [In Korean.] Interview by Baena TV. *Tal tal tal*, December 18, 2018. https://www.youtube.com/@bnatv1004.

Yonhap News Agency. *North Korea Handbook*. New York, NY: M. E. Sharpe, 2003.

Yoon, Sunny. "South Korean Media Reception and Youth Culture in North Korea." In *South Korean Popular Culture and North Korea*, edited by Kim Youna, 120–32. London: Routledge, 2019.

YTN. "North Korea Transmits Numbers Station via YouTube" [Buk pyeong-yang bangsong Yutubeu-ro annsubangsong]. August 29, 2020. https://www.youtube.com/watch?v=Ccl8QLMw-yY.

Yun Go-eun. "*My Wife Is a Gangster* Being Considered for North Korean Screening" [*Jopok manura*, bukhan sang-yeong chu-jin]. *Joongnang ilbo*, December 3, 2001. https://news.joins.com/article/1842381.

Zhang, Weiqi, and Mickey Lee. "Black Markets, Red States: Media Piracy in China and the Korean Wave in North Korea." In *South Korean Popular Culture and North Korea*, edited by Kim Youna, 83–95. London: Routledge, 2019.

Zuboff, Shoshana. *The Age of Surveillance Capitalism: The Fight for a Human Future at the New Frontier of Power*. New York, NY: Public Affairs, 2019.

Index

Page numbers in italics denote figures, and endnotes are indicated by "n" followed by the endnote number.

phone production, 46–47; film,
TV, and game consumption, 38,
43–45, 51–52, 100; government
investment in, 12–13, 23–24,
33–34; growth in Pyongyang,
15; international communication,
55–58; media ownership, 89–96,
177; music consumption, 155–57;
paradoxical role of, 88, 104,
126–27, 132–36, 150–54, 177;
resettler-activism, 53–54, 53–55; in
state-led propaganda, 22–23; state
mobilization of YouTube, 41–42,
41–43. *See also* cell phones;
music, film, and variety TV;
television dramas
media piracy, 89–96
#MeToo movement, 173
microgenerations, 8–9
microsocieties, 69
millennials, characterized, 7–10
Missile Industry Day (Misail gong-
eob-jeol), 13
MMS (multimedia messaging
service), 39
mobility, 104, 124, 125, 169, 171
modernization, 86, 148
Morrison, Elise, 214n25
Mo Yan, 123
music, film, and variety TV: appeal
of South Korean film, 140–42;
appeal of South Korean music,
154–55; cathartic identification
with violence, 142–46; cell phones
as weapons, 147–54; illicit music
consumption, 155–57; music in
state propaganda, 11–12; news and
documentaries, 173–75; popular

music genres, 160–64; subversive
political meanings, 157–60; variety
shows, 164–73
My Love from Another Star (television
series), 102, 103, 123–28, 211n47
My Wife Is a Gangster (2001),
142–43, 144–46, 147

Nakashima, Ellen, 37
Na Min-hui, 9, 39, 48, 51, 52, 61, 68,
85, 117, 141
National Science Academy, 43
neologisms, 6, 68–73
N Generation, 9
Nokia, 46
Northeast Asia Telephone and
Telecommunications
(NEAT&T), 34
North Korea: author's approach,
1–2, 14–20, 183–90, 195n48; in
Crash Landing on You, 128–32;
generation-naming conventions,
7–8; North Korean millennials
and, 7–14; in *Parasite*, 150–52;
possible futures, 179–81; scientific
progress, 179; tech savviness and
sociocultural shifts, 2–7, 3. *See also*
media and technology; music, film,
and variety TV; North Korean
millennials; television dramas
North Korean millennials: antilanguage
and antibehavior, 68–73, 98, 102,
107, 117, 175; appeal of forbidden
media, 85; characterizing millennials,
7–10, 20; creative economy,
73–74; creative trickery, 74–76;
digital content ownership, 89–96,
177; as diverse and multifaceted,

Printed and bound by CPI Group (UK) Ltd, Croydon, CR0 4YY

20/05/2025

14673433-0001